The Films *of* Elizabeth Taylor

Photo: Gary Bernstein

The Films of Elizabeth Taylor

by
JERRY VERMILYE
and MARK RICCI

A Citadel Press Book
Published by Carol Publishing Group

Carol Publishing Group Edition - 1993

A Citadel Press Book
Published by Carol Publishing Group
Citadel Press is a registered trademark of
Carol Communications, Inc.

Editorial Offices:
600 Madison Avenue
New York, NY 10022

Sales & Distribution Offices:
120 Enterprise Avenue
Secaucus, NJ 07094

In Canada: Canadian Manda Group
P.O. Box 920, Station U
Toronto, Ontario, M8Z 5P9, Canada

Queries regarding rights and permissions should be addressed
to: Carol Publishing Group
600 Madison Avenue, New York, NY 10022

Manufactured in the United States of America
ISBN 0-8065-1151-6

Carol Publishing Group books are available at special
discounts for bulk purchases, for sales promotions, fund
raising, or educational purposes. Special editions can also be
created to specifications. For details contact: Special Sales
Department, Carol Publishing Group,
120 Enterprise Ave., Secaucus, NJ 07094

12 11 10 9 8 7 6 5 4 3

Library of Congress Cataloging-in-Publication Data

Vermilye, Jerry.
    The films of Elizabeth Taylor.
       1. Taylor, Elizabeth Rosemond, 1932-   I. Ricci,
Mark, Joint author. II. Title
PN2287.T18V4   791.43'028'0924   75-42427

for

Louise *and* Alfred Boone

As Fran Walker

Acknowledgments

This volume would not have been possible without the invaluable aid of the following individuals, organizations and publications:

ABC-TV; Altura Films International; The Associated Press; Avco-Embassy Pictures; Gary Bernstein; *Boxoffice;* The British Film Institute; Laurie Britton; Jim Butler; CBS-TV; Central Press Photos, Ltd.; Chen Sam & Associates (Nina Bertoncini); *The Christian Science Monitor; Cinema;* Cinerama Releasing Organization; Columbia Pictures Corp; Judith Crist; *Cue;* Henry Fera; *The Film Daily; Film Quarterly; Films and Filming; Holiday; The Hollywood Reporter;* Home Box Office; *The Independent Film Journal; Life;* Bill Lloyd; *The London Observer; Look;* Leonard Maltin; Ron Martinetti; Doug McClelland; The Memory Shop; Metro-Goldwyn-Mayer, Inc.; *Modern Screen; Monthly Film Bulletin; Motion Picture Herald;* NBC-TV; *The Nation; The New Leader; The New Republic; New York Daily News; New York Herald Tribune; New York Journal-American; New York Post; The New York Sun; The New York Times; The New York World Journal Tribune; The New York World-Telegram; The New Yorker; Newsweek;* Paramount Pictures Corp.; Clem Perry; *Pic;* Rizzoli Film S.p.A. (Walter Bedogni, Ralph Alexander); *Saturday Review; Sight and Sound;* Jim Tamulis; The Theatre Film Collection of the New York Public Library at Lincoln Center; *Time;* Allan Turner; 20th Century-Fox Film Corp.; United Press International; Universal Pictures Corp.; Lou Valentino; *Variety; The Village Voice;* David L. Wolper Productions; Warner Bros., Inc.; Christopher Young.

As Cleopatra

Contents

As Amy March

As Helen of Troy

As Flora "Sissy" Goforth

As Melinda Greyton

As Leslie Lynnton Benedict

As Angela Vickers

The Star

As Cynthia Bishop

Elizabeth, age two, contemplates the camera on an English beach.

The Star

Elizabeth Taylor. Her name has long been a household word. She is one of the great beauties of our time, which makes her any photographer's dream. But more often than not, it's been her devil-may-care, unorthodox lifestyle that's captured the attention of a public, if not disapproving of her behavior, only too ready to purchase the next periodical featuring her on its cover or offering to reveal hidden secrets about her private life.

As a child in the Hollywood limelight, she was already in many ways a woman. At twelve, her voluptuous figure yet unformed, she faced movie cameras with the cool assurance of a pro and the uncanny facial beauty of an adult. Casting such an unusual-looking child was not always easy, but Elizabeth Taylor was fortunate enough to be under contract, throughout the years of her physical and thespian development (1943-1960), to that king of Hollywood studios, Metro-Goldwyn-Mayer. It was a luxurious hothouse environment that nurtured her metamorphosis from beautiful child to stunning adolescent to full-blown actress in a series of films which, while

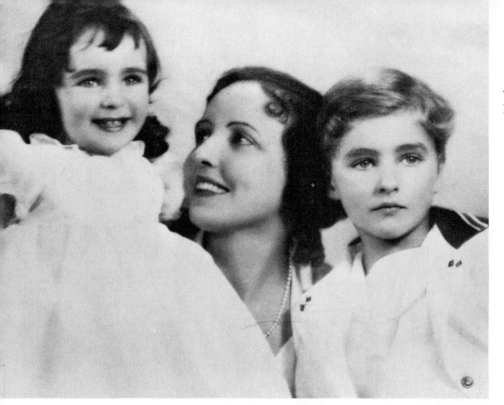

With her mother and brother
Howard.

largely undeserving of time-capsule preservation, were nevertheless shrewdly devised stepping-stones to a career that might not otherwise have developed.

Elizabeth's persistent mother set her on the performing trail. Studio executives cannily exploited her natural attractions and kept her there. To date, the thirty-three years of the actress's career have been sparked with rumors of retirement, of forsaking her career for a life of luxurious relaxation, commuting between her many homes far-flung about the western world. Her gradual development as a movie queen of skill as well as beauty helped keep her there. So did her need for the means with which to maintain her lifestyle. And with the realization that she *did* have some talents as a performer, Elizabeth Taylor came to enjoy acting, no longer as a mere showcase for pretty clothes against Technicolored backgrounds.

With brother Howard and part of their private menagerie.

Between scenes of *A Place in the Sun,* seated between her screen mother Frieda Inescort (left) and her real mother, Sara Taylor.

She doesn't like to be called "Liz," and claims this stems from childhood, when her brother Howard would get her goat with merciless teasing, calling her "Lizzy the Lizard" or "Lizzy the Cow."

Elizabeth does not consider herself to be a great beauty (she readily cites Ava Gardner as an example of *that*) and has said, "I don't have a complex about my looks, but I'm too short of leg, too big in the arms, one too many chins, big feet, big hands, too fat. My best feature is my gray hairs."

Her interviews reveal a candid woman with few delusions about herself. Her past record of marriages, divorces, romances, and illnesses needs little repetition in these pages. Her well-recorded life has been an open book, the pages of which few have left unturned. Many have envied her, more have condemned her, yet she endures. Eliz-

With Irene Dunne, William Powell and director Michael Curtiz at the party Warners gave to celebrate the completion of *Life With Father* in July 1947.

With her first husband, "Nicky" Hilton.

abeth Taylor, the beauty and the actress, prevails because she is so much larger than life, not only in the literal on-screen sense, but also in the details of the fabulous comedy-drama that she lives, whether as the last of the great movie queens, concerned mother of problem children, youthful grandmother, wife to five husbands, and first star to receive the once-scandalous sum of a million dollars for performing in a film.

No other actress of our time has graced so many magazine covers or consumed so much space in newspapers and journals as has Elizabeth Taylor. If Marilyn Monroe, twelve years after her death, remains Hollywood's supreme blonde sex goddess, then Elizabeth Taylor is her brunette counterpart. Years away from belonging to that once-great California colony of movie make-believe, Elizabeth now makes most of her films on the Continent, whether for tax or personal reasons. Yet she's firmly of Hollywood vintage and Hollywood trademark.

She's one of the rare film beauties to let herself age naturally, with little care spent on the preservation of face and form. Indeed, the cam-

Sharing a chocolate milkshake with Spencer Tracy between scenes of *Father of the Bride*.

With second husband, Michael Wilding, and their first-born, Michael Howard Wilding, in 1953.

life and time, a questionable carelessness in this era when youth-worship threatens to erupt into an epidemic of mass-hysteria. Upon turning forty in 1972, she surprised millions of time-burying women (and men) with the comment, "I think it's fantastic! I've always wanted to be older. So I find actually being forty very appealing."

In 1975, aged forty-three and already four years a grandmother by her son Michael, Elizabeth Taylor has lived enough to equal a lifetime for most women. Her acting ability, once dismissed as summarily by herself as by others, has garnered, among other laurels, two Academy Awards, five Oscar nominations, and a citation from the New York Film Critics. If her more recent movies have proved passably entertaining but ultimately forgettable, then the fact that films of the past decade have offered few noteworthy roles for women can be held largely accountable. Long free from studio contractual obligations and an actress who decides herself what films she'll appear in, Elizabeth Taylor has attracted much criticism for allowing herself to become a veritable camp queen in many of her post-1960 motion pictures. Perhaps her performance in the unlikely role of a blowsy, middle-aged termagant in Edward Albee's *Who's Afraid of Virginia Woolf?,* a performance so unexpectedly effective that it won the star her second Oscar, may have solidified that image. Many of her subsequent

era reveals a woman whose weight fluctuates with her years, her whims, and her health problems—a fact which her journalistic detractors belabor endlessly and needlessly. Perhaps there is a lack of empathy for a woman who risks being called un-American by her disregard for the scars of

On the Texas set of *Giant,* clowning with co-stars Mercedes McCambridge, Rock Hudson and James Dean, at the apparent expense of director George Stevens.

vehicles have revealed colorfully amusing aspects of the snarling, conniving shrew, the perfect bitch who's capable of anything to get her way or hold her man, while titillating an audience with her vocal mannerisms, her attire, and the methods of her attack. Like Rosalind Russell in *Auntie Mame* and Judy Holliday in *Born Yesterday*, Elizabeth Taylor has preserved and kept enough of the successful ingredients of one great role (Martha in *Virginia Woolf*) to remind her critics so thoroughly of this artistic borrowing as to make her detractors consider each successive Taylor performance as a mere further adventure of Albee's Martha, a role which few thought she could bring off successfully. A more careful study of her post–*Virginia Woolf* performances might indicate otherwise, despite her all-too-obvious miscasting in *Boom!*, a role Tennessee Williams had written for Tallulah Bankhead, and the amusing bitch-wife of Edna O'Brien's *Zee & Co.* (*X Y & Zee*). (For contrast, study Taylor's understated performance as the quietly desperate, aging wife who undergoes head-to-toe rejuvenation in *Ash Wednesday*).

Plagued with serious and recurring health problems and possessed of a charismatic physiognomy that consistently attracts writers and

photographers, Elizabeth Taylor is a gorgeous feline who, while seeming to have nearly exhausted her nine lives, continues to defy her detractors by surviving, by prevailing, and by silently promising to keep the elusive and now nearly obsolete profession of movie queen extant for years to come. She may be the last of a dying breed, but she is not to be underestimated. Elizabeth Taylor is what the word *Star* is all about.

She was born in London on February 27, 1932, and named Elizabeth Rosemond Taylor. Despite the locale of her birth, her parents, Francis and Sara (Warmbraten) Taylor, were Americans then in Europe indefinitely on business. Under the name Sara Sothern, Elizabeth's mother had pursued an acting career with stock companies and had later played on Broadway where, in 1926, she met and married Taylor, the nephew of a successful art dealer with whom he was associated. Their first child, Howard, who preceded Elizabeth by three years, showed no interest in a show-business career, though he later appeared, for a lark, in bit roles in two of his sister's movies.

Elizabeth's formative years were spent in London, where her mother saw to it that the child studied the performing arts at the Vaccani Dancing Academy, as well as at the various English private schools to which she was sent. In the summer of 1939, with Europe on the brink of war, Francis Taylor dispatched his family to California, where he later joined them, assuming the management of an art gallery housed in the Beverly Hills Hotel. Howard and Elizabeth were now enrolled in the Hawthorne School in Beverly Hills.

At seven, Elizabeth Taylor was a child of sufficient beauty to interest movie talent-scouts, and although Sara Taylor sought screen tests and a movie career for her daughter, Francis Taylor remained opposed to the notion. Had he not done so, it seems that little Elizabeth, because of a resemblance to Vivien Leigh, would have been engaged by David O. Selznick for the small role of Bonnie Blue, the child of Scarlett O'Hara and Rhett Butler, who falls from her pony and dies, in *Gone With the Wind*.

Eventually Sara Taylor had her way when

Out on the town with her third husband, Mike Todd.

one of her daughter's classmates, whose father was a producer at Universal Pictures, touted Elizabeth's beauty to such an extent that she was signed to a contract on the basis of her appearance, as well as her song-and-dance talents. Had Universal had any notions of promoting Elizabeth Taylor as a successor to their youthful money-maker Deanna Durbin, they showed little incentive. At ten, the little girl with the big beautiful violet eyes and the little-woman features made her film debut in a near-forgotten program comedy called *There's One Born Every Minute,* although Elizabeth—and some of her biographers—continue to call this 1942 effort by its working title, *Man or Mouse.* In it, she and Carl "Alfalfa" Switzer, late of the "Our Gang" series, played mischievous brats. The powers at Universal were unimpressed with their debutante starlet and so, apparently, was the public, for Elizabeth was allowed to remain idle for the duration of her short contract with that studio.

Elizabeth Taylor's association with Metro-Goldwyn-Mayer came about when her father happened to meet a studio executive named Samuel Marx, who made mention of MGM's then-current search for a dog-loving English girl who could qualify for a small role in *Lassie Come Home* (1943), then already in production. Cast opposite the popular English child actor, Roddy McDowall (with whom the actress has maintained a close friendship over the years), she managed to catch the eye of a number of critics whose comments on her preadolescent beauty impressed the MGM executives sufficiently to secure her a twelve-month contract and an immediate loan-out to 20th Century-Fox for the tragic part of Helen, the childhood friend who catches pneumonia and dies in *Jane Eyre* (1944).

Early in 1974, ninety-two-year-old actor Donald Crisp, interviewed in retirement, had pleasant recollections of working with young Elizabeth and Roddy McDowall during those years: "They were the nicest little kids you'd ever want to meet. They were always on time and worked like little professionals. Liz was the prettiest little girl and she often told me that she hoped she would become as beautiful as her mother."

At Metro, Elizabeth played another small role in *The White Cliffs of Dover* (again opposite McDowall). She then secured the part that

Elizabeth and her fourth husband, Eddie Fisher, visit Judy Garland backstage at New York's Metropolitan Opera House, following Judy's show, in May of 1959.

made her famous, in *National Velvet* (1944), although not without the well-known story of her famous three-month weight-gaining, height-stretching campaign. This, along with her horseback-riding skills, eventually convinced Pandro S. Berman, that film's producer, that she was capable of the role. Particularly instrumental in these efforts was Sara Taylor who, to secure the coveted part for her child, had to sign a contract that, Elizabeth later recalled, "made me an MGM chattel until I did *Cleopatra.*" All of Metro's considerable stars, she has stated, "were born or died more or less at the whim of Louis B. Mayer, who was an absolute dictator."

Elizabeth's recollections of Mayer are anything but sentimental. "I thought he was a beast," she said in a 1972 David Frost interview. "He was inhuman. He used his power over people to such a degree that he no longer became a man; he became an instrument of power, and he had no scruples. He didn't care whom he cut down or whom he hurt. He never hurt me, because I think maybe I was too young."

At fourteen, Elizabeth recalls a rather traumatic encounter with Mayer that could have spelled *finis* to her career at that studio. When reports had circulated that Elizabeth's next picture would have her singing and dancing in something entitled *Sally in Our Alley,* Mrs. Taylor took her daughter to Mayer's office with the sug-

[19]

gestion that he give his permission for Elizabeth to have musical training. According to Elizabeth, he exploded at her mother, "Don't you tell me how to run my business! You and your daughter are both guttersnipes! Get out of here!" To which fourteen-year-old Elizabeth screamed back at him, "You and your studio can both go to hell!" In tears, the child ran from Mayer's office, while her mother stayed behind to pacify him. Though told by Metro VIPs that she must apologize to the chief executive, Elizabeth refused because she was offended by the way he'd spoken to her parent. "I never saw him or spoke to him again," she says. Nor did she make *Sally in Our Alley*.

Carefully protected by her mother from any adolescent connection with the so-called wild life of a Hollywood starlet, Elizabeth further developed a natural love of animals that resulted in her writing, at fourteen, a slim, photo-illustrated children's book, *Nibbles and Me* (published in 1946), about her life with a pet chipmunk. "I didn't start to date until I was sixteen," she recalls. "The people in MGM's press department would suggest that I date somebody, and I would immediately rebel. Nobody was going to decide for me whom to date, what to wear, or put words in my mouth."

After *National Velvet*, the young star's public had to be content with *Nibbles and Me* and reading about her in publications like *Calling All Girls*, which revealed how she dressed and what she did at home. In fact, nearly a year and a half passed before Elizabeth's fans saw her subsequent picture, *Courage of Lassie* (1946). It was the last time she co-starred with an animal. The following year, Metro cast her in her own starring vehicle, a bittersweet comedy-drama called *Cynthia,* in which she was the sickly daughter of overprotective parents (Mary Astor and George Murphy) who rebelled, overcame her ailments, and even won herself a boyfriend (James Lydon, the screen's Henry Aldrich), who gave her her first screen kiss. MGM then lent her to Warner Brothers to play sweetly crinolined Mary Skinner, who takes a shine to young Clarence Day (James Lydon again) in *Life With Father,* a "prestige" film released initially as a reserved-seat, road-show attraction.

Back at Metro, she played the rich chum of Jane Powell, stealing handsome-older-man Robert Stack away from the latter, in the juvenile musical-comedy *A Date With Judy,* and then shared love scenes with Peter Lawford, an actor whom she secretly worshiped, in the Greer Garson–Walter Pidgeon comedy *Julia Misbehaves.* Both films were released in 1948. The following year she was an effectively affected Amy in Mervyn LeRoy's sugary remake of Louisa May Alcott's *Little Women,* and then went to England for her first really grown-up part—in *Conspirator,* a suspense drama in which the teenage actress played the wife of Robert Taylor, a star some

Signing to play *Cleopatra,* under the watchful eye of Fox studio chief Buddy Adler (left) and the film's producer, Walter Wanger.

twenty years her senior. Despite her poise and beauty, it was nevertheless clear that Elizabeth Taylor still had a lot to learn about acting.

Having "grown up" on the screen, Elizabeth now felt sufficiently mature in her private life to evade the protective arms of her family long enough to date football hero Glenn Davis, and to become engaged to wealthy young William Pawley, Jr. However, her fiancé proved more demanding than the actress could bear and, faced with a decision between him and her career, she elected to retain the latter.

While her film roles had not been noteworthy, Elizabeth had, with Metro's assistance, crossed over the often-difficult period which has defeated the careers of so many former child performers. And her loan-out to Paramount for the coveted role of the young heiress in that studio's remake of Theodore Dreiser's *An American Tragedy* proved an important milestone for her. Under the new title of *A Place in the Sun*, this strong drama about a lowborn youth (Montgomery Clift) who falls for a rich beauty (Taylor) and lets his pregnant girlfriend (Shelley Winters) drown to gain his freedom, was so well handled by producer-director George Stevens that Elizabeth was, for the first time in her young career, put on her mettle as an actress. Clift and Winters had stage experience behind them, and Taylor at first felt her lack, although she credits Clift with being of great help to her. With this film, she claims to

have begun for the first time to really enjoy the challenge of acting, a factor which extended to that movie's critics, suddenly made aware that Elizabeth Taylor might have something more to offer the screen than mere physical beauty. *A Place in the Sun* garnered Academy Award nominations for Clift and Winters, but not for Taylor. However, it did pick up six Oscars, recipients including director George Stevens and its Michael Wilson-Harry Brown screenplay.

Recalling his association with the young Elizabeth on this film, George Stevens has said, "She had enormous beauty but she wasn't charmed by it. It was there. It was a handicap and she discouraged people being overimpressed with it. She was seventeen and she had been an actress all her life. So there was no problem there. The only thing was to prod her a bit into realizing her dramatic potential."

While MGM publicists linked her name romantically with everyone from Roddy McDowall and Montgomery Clift to millionaire industrialist Howard Hughes, Elizabeth played opposite Van Johnson in a slight romantic comedy called *The Big Hangover* (1950) and once more became engaged—this time to Conrad Nicholson ("Nicky") Hilton, Jr., of the hotel Hiltons. She was just eighteen and busy filming one of her best comedies, *Father of the Bride*, opposite Spencer Tracy and Joan Bennett. Metro used every means of exploiting her subsequent wedding (May 6, 1950) in tandem with the film—which centered on the problems of an upper-middle-class couple whose only daughter is being married.

While the movie was a big success, the Taylor-Hilton marriage was not, and the following January Elizabeth won an uncontested divorce. She has admitted that she was not then sufficiently mature to cope with marital responsibility. Meanwhile, her studio followed up with a film sequel, *Father's Little Dividend*, in which she went through the problems of young motherhood. It was an experience that the off-screen Elizabeth Taylor would not know for two more years.

In between the two *Father* comedies, Elizabeth had also played an uncredited "extra" role

A rare shot with her children, Liza Michael and Christopher, on the *Cleopatra* set.

in Mervyn LeRoy's *Quo Vadis* (1951), whose set she and Hilton had visited in Rome during an extended honeymoon. It was a film in which MGM, at one time, had planned to star Elizabeth—in the role played by Deborah Kerr—and Gregory Peck.

Despite the combined popular and critical success of *A Place in the Sun* (filmed in 1949, but not released until 1951), MGM continued casting their beautiful young star in roles requiring little more than that she be decorative. In 1952, she was seen in the minor romantic comedy entitled *Love Is Better Than Ever,* opposite Larry Parks, and as the persecuted Jewess Rebecca in the historical spectacle *Ivanhoe.* During its production in England, Elizabeth met and married (February 21, 1952) her second husband, British actor Michael Wilding, age thirty-nine, by whom she had two sons, Michael Howard (born January 6, 1953) and Christopher Edward (born February 27, 1955). Their union, which suffered because in America she was a bigger star than he, lasted five years, during which the actress decorated such glossy Metro mediocrities as *The Girl Who Had Everything* (1953), *Rhapsody* (1954), and *Beau Brummell* (1954). Ten years later, reflecting on this period of her career, Elizabeth told an interviewer for *Life* magazine, "Much of my life, I've hated acting. I was doing the *most* awful films—walking around like Dracula's ghost in glamorized B movies. I wore pretty clothes. But it was either that or be suspended by MGM, and I needed money."

In addition, she was lent to Paramount to replace the ailing Vivien Leigh, who had suffered a nervous breakdown in the midst of making *Elephant Walk* (1954). Though Ceylon-filmed long-shots of Leigh were retained, Taylor was then of a size and shape to fit the British star's role and wardrobe, with minor alterations. Unlike her previous sojourn at Paramount, *Elephant Walk* added few laurels to the Taylor career. Somewhat more demanding was her role as the tragic, party-loving rich girl of *The Last Time I Saw Paris,* who marries an alcoholic writer (Van

Johnson) and dies of pneumonia. Though the character she played dies some time before the film's conclusion, Elizabeth got top billing over Johnson, Donna Reed, and Walter Pidgeon. Of his association with Taylor on this film, director Richard Brooks recalls, "What impressed me was that the real Elizabeth was not the publicity figure that had been created. She had a knack of looking at herself in two lights—at what she was supposed to be according to the press, but also with the honesty and cynicism that comes from disappointment. Her disappointment was that she was not regarded as an actress, but merely as a beautiful girl."

In 1955, George Stevens again borrowed Taylor for an important film he was directing, Edna Ferber's *Giant,* a none-too-flattering portrait of one wealthy Texas family in the years when the cattle barons were being overtaken by the oil tycoons. The role required her and co-stars Rock Hudson and James Dean to age from romantic youth to their graying mid-fifties, a

With Richard Burton at England's Wembley Stadium for the fight between Cassius Clay and British heavyweight champion, Henry Cooper.

transformation accomplished with varying results. There were some who opined that the *mature* Elizabeth Taylor was more convincing than the youthful one. "In *Giant,*" says George Stevens, "we gave her a very difficult part; she is the pivot of the whole picture, and she plays five different ages, including a grandmother. Beauty of her kind is hard to overcome in characterization—we put a real burden on her shoulders."

Again, Stevens's great success with actors was reflected in Oscar nominations for Hudson and Dean (who died tragically just a few days after his last scene was filmed)—but none for Elizabeth. And once more Stevens walked away with an Academy Award for his direction. Although the film, too, was nominated as Best Picture, that honor went to *Around the World in 80 Days,* a mammoth extravaganza produced by Mike Todd, the extravagant showman who had, by then, swept the twice-wed Elizabeth Taylor off her impressionable feet and made her his bride. They were married in Mexico on February 21, 1957, just three days after her divorce from Wilding became final. Their only child, Elizabeth ("Liza") Frances Todd, arrived on August 6, 1957. Because Todd (born Avram Hirsch Goldbogen) was Jewish, Elizabeth converted to Judaism, a religion which she has continued to embrace through two subsequent marriages and despite the harm this factor has done to her box-office potential in Arab countries, where her films have been banned altogether.

During her marriage to Todd (again, a much older man, though as extroverted as Wilding had been reserved), Elizabeth made the expensive Civil War costume drama *Raintree County,* in which she finally played a role that won her enough acclaim to get an Oscar nomination. Teamed again with Montgomery Clift, she played Susanna Drake, a conniving Southern belle who tricks her man into marriage but later deteriorates into insanity, derived from her fear of family miscegenation. Although the 1957 Best Actress Academy Award went to Joanne Woodward for *The Three Faces of Eve,* Taylor had once again made some impression as a serious actress, and henceforth her professional partisans would frequently outrank her detractors.

On March 22, 1958, during production of Tennessee Williams's *Cat on a Hot Tin Roof* at

Enjoying life with Richard while he was in Mexico to film *The Night of the Iguana.*

MGM, Mike Todd was killed when his private plane, *The Liz,* crashed near Grants, New Mexico, en route to New York, where he was to have been toasted as "Showman of the Year" by the National Association of Theater Owners. Bronchitis and a temperature of 102 were the only factors that kept Elizabeth from accompanying the forty-nine-year-old Todd on his fatal journey.

Todd's death proved a tremendous blow to Elizabeth, and her emotional state at that time undoubtedly accounts for much of the effectiveness of her Maggie in *Cat on a Hot Tin Roof,* the demands of which helped ease her through a sad and difficult time. "She was remarkable," her producer Lawrence Weingarten told a reporter. "She was working on a string for the first two weeks after her return, but you can't see a flaw in her performance." Burl Ives, who had previously played opposite three different stage Maggies, termed Elizabeth "the best of the bunch." Paul Newman, her co-star, admits that he was "aston-

With Richard during rehearsals for *Who's Afraid of Virginia Woolf?*

ished to find her a real pro," and adds, "She's not afraid to take chances in front of people. Usually stars become very protective of themselves and very self-indulgent, but she's got a lot of guts. She'd go ahead and explore and risk falling on her face." Again Elizabeth won an Academy Award nomination, losing out this time to Susan Hayward's powerful emoting in the downbeat dramatics of *I Want to Live!*

Scandal then clouded Elizabeth's life for the first time when, in her grief over Mike Todd's sudden death, she transferred her emotions to Eddie Fisher, then married to Debbie Reynolds, by whom he had fathered two children. Debbie and Eddie had been close friends of Mike and Elizabeth, but now the gossip columnists pictured the Widow Todd as a scarlet woman destroying an ideal marriage. Each side had its innings. Elizabeth's comment to the press: "No woman can steal a happily married man."

Fisher pressed Debbie for a divorce, to which she eventually consented. He and Elizabeth were wed on May 12, 1959. Eddie's singing career then took a downward turn from which it never fully recovered. His wife was later to term their union "the biggest mistake of my life," adding, "We both tried very hard, but the marriage was untenable for both of us."

Taylor's first film after this, her fourth trip to the altar, was another Tennessee Williams drama, *Suddenly, Last Summer,* produced independently for Columbia release. Under Joseph L. Mankiewicz's direction, Elizabeth gave what many consider her finest performance as the traumatized Catherine Holly, whose aunt (Katharine Hepburn) arranges a lobotomy to prevent Catherine's revealing the truth about her late homosexual son, Sebastian. Particularly impressive was the lengthy, climactic sequence in which a truth serum enables Catherine, in long monologues, to

Elizabeth and a young fan visit Richard on the set of *The Spy Who Came in From the Cold.*

With Richard and director Mike Nichols on the set of *Who's Afraid of Virginia Woolf?*

recall the horrible events of the previous summer, when her cousin met a grisly end during the European vacation they had shared. For this, Mankiewicz alternates between close-ups of Taylor's face and silent flashbacks to the actual events, while the actress's voice describes them on the soundtrack. Mankiewicz was sufficiently impressed with his star to report, "She is close to being the greatest actress in the world, and so far she has done it mostly by instinct. She is still a primitive, sort of the Grandma Moses of acting." Released in 1959, the film earned Elizabeth her third Oscar nomination. The fact that she lost to Simone Signoret's poignant acting in the English-made *Room at the Top* may be attributed as much to the French actress's ability as to the fact that both Taylor and Hepburn were in the running for *Suddenly, Last Summer*. Customarily, this sort of same-picture rivalry redirects the awards to another performer altogether. In the case of Taylor, her off-screen behavior hadn't helped.

Fisher announced plans to turn producer and showcase his new wife's talents in a remake of Tolstoy's *Anna Karenina*. Instead, she now received an offer to star in *Cleopatra* for 20th Century-Fox—for the sum of a million dollars. Elizabeth claims that this unprecedented salary came about in response to her flip reply to producer Walter Wanger, "Tell him it will cost him a million dollars." She admits being amazed when Fox agreed. But Metro interfered, contending that she was still under contract to them, that they wanted her to perform first in John O'Hara's

Butterfield 8, and that, if she did not do so, they'd keep her off the screen for two years.

Elizabeth hated the script of *Butterfield 8* and demanded rewrites to soften the story's cheapness and deemphasize the sexual aspects of her role, that of a high-class call girl named Gloria Wandrous. (In the resultant film, interestingly, it is difficult to pinpoint Gloria's profession or identify the source of her income). Reluctantly, the actress went ahead with *Butterfield 8,* filmed in New York to pacify her, but only as a means of finishing out her long-term contract with MGM and ending her obligations to that studio. "Making this film gripes the hell out of me," she told the press. "It's a piece of shit."

And then came *Cleopatra,* a movie plagued with incredible setbacks that would help make it the costliest ever filmed. Elizabeth went to England in September, 1960, to begin filming, under the direction of Rouben Mamoulian, with Stephen Boyd as Antony and Peter Finch as Caesar. To begin with, bad weather hampered the production's start, there were problems with the script, and both Finch and Boyd had other commitments that demanded their scenes be completed without delay. Almost immediately, Elizabeth contracted a virus infection, resulting from an abscessed tooth. When this developed into meningism, Fox stopped production on the picture while their star returned to California for a lengthy recovery.

But the delay had cost the film its two male stars, so Rex Harrison was engaged to replace Finch as Julius Caesar, while Richard Burton

As Helen of Troy in the Oxford Playhouse production of Marlowe's *Doctor Faustus*. (1966).

assumed Boyd's Mark Antony gear. While script improvements were made constantly, Joseph L. Mankiewicz took over the directorial reins from Mamoulian, as well as putting his experienced hand to the troubled screenplay.

Fully recovered, Elizabeth Taylor joined the company in Rome, to which the production had shifted, at no small expenditure. But, on March 4, 1961, she was taken ill with staphylococcus pneumonia, from which she nearly died. When her lung congestion became critical, doctors performed a tracheotomy, cutting a hole in her windpipe. With the aid of a newly developed electronic lung, her life, which had hung in the balance for days, was saved. According to a doctor's report, she was, at one point, only fifteen minutes from death. Eventually, she was well enough to return to Hollywood in time to appear at the 1961 Academy Awards ceremony, where she was amazed to win an Oscar for *Butterfield 8,* the movie she had loathed making. Helped to the podium by Eddie Fisher, and obviously overcome with emotion, Elizabeth said, "I don't really know how to express my great gratitude. I guess I will just have to thank you with all my heart." Afterward, posing for photographers along with that year's other winners—Burt Lancaster, Shirley Jones, and Peter Ustinov—she remarked, "I feel weak but wonderful."

"The reason I got the Oscar," Elizabeth later explained, "was that I had come within a breath of dying of pneumonia. Nevertheless, I was filled with gratitude when I got it, for it meant being considered an actress and not a movie star. But

With Richard Burton during filming of *The Taming of the Shrew.*

With Richard and director Joseph Losey on the set of *Boom!*

it was for the wrong picture. Any of my three previous nominations was more deserving. I knew it was a sympathy award, but I was still proud to get it."

Returning to Rome and *Cleopatra,* the star was soon again in the news. The press reported that her health was fine, though her marriage was not. Elizabeth, it soon developed, was romantically involved with her also-married co-star Richard Burton. When Eddie phoned her from New York, seeking a denial, she confirmed the rumors to him. Eddie promptly filed for divorce, demanding half of her *Cleopatra* salary. During *Cleopatra's* expensive months of filming, Fox's president, Darryl F. Zanuck accepted the immense publicity accorded the Taylor-Burton-Fisher scandal as "quite constructive for our organization."

By the time that mammoth historical epic was completed in 1962 (at a reported record cost of $40 million), Elizabeth and Richard were considered the hottest team in movies, and Metro, which had long since signed Burton for *The V.I.P.s,* now hastened to contract with Elizabeth to play his adulterous wife in the film. She had been off the screen some two and a half years by the time *Cleopatra* was finally released, in June, 1963. Critical reaction was not overly kind to the epic movie; few thought Elizabeth well-suited for Egypt's great queen, citing the shrillness of her

voice and the lack of passion (oddly enough) with which she and Burton approached their on-screen love scenes. The best notices went to Rex Harrison's Caesar.

Of *Cleopatra,* Elizabeth has said, "It must be the most eccentric film ever made. I was finally forced to see it in London, knowing full well, after what I'd heard, that I'd be sick to my stomach. They had cut out the heart, the essence, the motivations, the very core, and tacked on all those battle scenes. It should have been about three large people, but it lacked reality and passion. I found it vulgar."

Quick to cash in on Fox's headaches and the Burton-Taylor publicity, MGM premiered *The V.I.P.s* before the end of that summer, and this *Grand Hotel*–like multidrama met with great and immediate success. While Burton joined Deborah Kerr and Ava Gardner in Mexico for Tennessee Williams's *The Night of the Iguana,* Elizabeth stayed by his side awaiting his divorce from his wife Sybil and her own from Fisher. Eventually, on March 15, 1964, they were married in Montreal, where Richard was trying out his *Hamlet.* Signing formal adoption papers, he gave his surname to Maria, the little German girl Elizabeth and Eddie Fisher had adopted.

On June 7, 1964, during the subsequent, successful Broadway revival of *Hamlet,* the famous

Enjoying a visit from Richard and one of his sons, on the *Secret Ceremony* set.

couple made a joint live appearance in *World Enough and Time,* a one-performance evening of prose and poetry readings staged and introduced by Philip Burton, the actor's foster father. It was a high-priced event with all proceeds benefiting the elder Burton's American Musical and Dramatic Academy in New York. Two years later, at England's Oxford Playhouse, Elizabeth essayed the role of Helen of Troy, opposite her husband, in a production of Christopher Marlowe's classic, *Doctor Faustus.*

Taylor's occasional TV appearances have ranged from a tribute to the late Mike Todd to her 1963 special, *Elizabeth Taylor in London,* and a stint with Burton on Lucille Ball's *Here's Lucy* show, in a script fabricating humorous events surrounding Elizabeth's celebrated 69-carat $1.5-million diamond ring (a 1969 gift from Richard), to add to her other treasures—the $305,000 Krupp diamond and "La Peregrina," the world's most famous pearl, purchased for a mere $37,000.

In April of 1975, the ABC network aired a 90-minute, late-night tribute entitled *Elizabeth Taylor: Hollywood's Child,* hosted by her old friend and co-star, Peter Lawford. Among those interviewed about Elizabeth were Rock Hudson, Roddy McDowall, Vincente Minnelli, and even her mother, who made the curious statement, "We didn't *want* her in pictures."

Richard Burton had long enjoyed a reputa-

tion as a ladies' man during his earlier marriage to Sybil Williams, and Elizabeth was seldom separated from him (she later told a reporter, "Maybe we loved each other too much"). Often, they co-starred in the same film; at other times, Elizabeth turned down roles in order to be with Richard on the locations of *his* movies. On few occasions did she let him get far from her sight. Their only serious marital split occurred in the summer of 1973, followed by formal announcements that the marriage, they regretted to report, was at an end. However, by Christmastime they had reconciled, with Richard flying from the Roman location of *The Voyage,* a film he was shooting with Sophia Loren, to visit the Los Angeles hospital bed where his wife was recovering from abdominal surgery.

The reunion was short-lived; by May, formal divorce proceedings had been started and, on June 26, 1974, the ten-year marriage was officially ended in Gstaad, Switzerland. Listed as grounds for the divorce were "mutual incompatibility" and "irreconcilable differences," though insiders credited Burton's ego, his endless stories and, especially, his drinking. "Life with Richard," Elizabeth told the judge, "became intolerable."

Reportedly, she received custody of their adopted daughter, Maria, and rights to all her property, including their yacht and her considerable jewelry collection.

Soon thereafter, Elizabeth was seen in the

constant company of Henry Wynberg, a former Los Angeles used-car dealer who had been a close pal during her 1973 estrangement from Burton. For a time it was erroneously rumored that they had wed. They never did. When Taylor returned to the States on a visit, then went to Leningrad to film *The Blue Bird,* Wynberg accompanied her.

Burton, meanwhile, became engaged to, then disengaged from, the already-married Princess Elizabeth of Yugoslavia, and later took up with black American model Jeanne Bell, who credits her influence with helping him quit drinking, undoubtedly an important factor in the Taylor-Burton reconciliation.

In August 1975, directly after completing her various roles in the trouble-plagued *Blue Bird* film and returning to her Swiss home, Elizabeth was back in newspaper headlines again. Quite unexpectedly, it was announced that she and Burton had not only patched up their differences, but were back together again and planned to re-marry. "This is not a trial reconciliation," pro-claimed their press agent, John Springer. "It is permanent." A subsequent announcement said that the couple would live together, but had no immediate plans to re-legalize their arrangement.

While speculation quite naturally circulated as to the *real* reasons behind it all, the press revealed that Taylor had kept in close touch with Burton ever since their divorce and had been quite concerned about his welfare. One rumor even had it that Richard was seriously ill and that this factor was Elizabeth's chief motivation. Whatever the personal details were, no one could deny the obvious fact that both parties were still very much in love. And on Friday, October 10, 1975, in a mud-hut village on a Botswana (Africa) game preserve, they were officially re-wed. But it was not to last long.

Unlike some *au pair* professionals, the Burtons seemed always to enjoy their limelight, reinforcing Richard's statement that "publicity is always good for an actor." Countless newspaper pictures showed them disembarking at airports, holding press conferences, arriving at public

Enjoying a frug with ballet star Rudolf Nureyev at a London party she hosted.

With Lucille Ball and Richard Burton in an episode of the TV show, "Here's Lucy."

functions—and always smiling, outgoing, basking in their fame and good fortune. They were the beautiful couple who, for a decade, lived the fabulous life and never ceased to hold the interest of a celebrity-worshipping public who'd purchase every magazine and newspaper featuring news of them.

Burton bought his wife priceless gems and the world took note. Accompanied by an entourage of children, animals and personal retainers, the couple vacationed on their yacht or at one of their various worldwide homes, and the press reported it all. Whatever Elizabeth Taylor did was news. She was Richard Burton's woman, but she was also very much her own person. In an age of relaxed morality and increased female freedom, there was little that was shocking—much less her well-reported friendship with Henry Wynberg, first while she was separated from Burton, then again during the 14 months between the divorce and their reconciliation.

If Richard and Elizabeth seemed good for one another in their personal lives, there were those who pondered on the progress of their respective careers since *Cleopatra*. Together, they co-starred in no less than nine theatrical movies and one for television. Of these, only *Who's Afraid of Virginia Woolf?* (1966) could be termed an unqualified success, winning Academy Award nominations for both stars and a second Oscar for Elizabeth. This role she considers the most difficult and challenging she has ever had. In *The Taming of the Shrew* (1967), the Burtons had a lot going for them, thanks to the genius of Franco Zeffirelli. Richard won the best notices for his acting, while Elizabeth received credit merely for *attempting* Shakespeare. *The Sandpiper* and *The Comedians* were far more popular with moviegoers than the critics, while *Boom!* and *Doctor Faustus* (based on their Oxford stage production) proved too pretentious and misguided to completely satisfy *anyone*.

The arty, offbeat *Under Milk Wood*, while enthusiastically embraced by a small coterie of critics, failed to interest the general public at all. Nor did *Hammersmith Is Out*, for which Elizabeth unexpectedly won a Silver Bear as best actress at the Berlin Film Festival. Their 1973 TV-movie, a double-header called *DIVORCE; his/DIVORCE; hers,* and designed to cover both sides of a marital break-up, proved a complete fiasco in every way but one: their sizable fees, reportedly, went to charity.

In March of 1970, Elizabeth made London headlines when she unceremoniously replaced bit-player Charlotte Selwyn as virtual set-dressing for *Anne of the Thousand Days,* in which Burton played Henry VIII. In reply to Miss Selwyn's

While her costume gets attention, Elizabeth enjoys a joke with co-star Michael Caine and director Brian Hutton on the set of *Zee & Co.*

complaint, a spokesman for Universal Pictures said: "Miss Taylor happened to be on the set and thought it would be amusing for her to do this scene. She didn't get a credit for it. It was just a fun thing." But no fun for Miss Selwyn, who lost a day's pay.

During her years with Burton, Taylor starred on her own in seven films. While some of these had their partisans, none were unqualified blockbusters, either with press or public. Many books and articles of recent vintage have suggested or stated that Richard Burton and Elizabeth Taylor were the Great Loves of one another's lives. Whatever the case, their second attempt at marital happiness culminated in a second split. And, while she resumed her friendship with Henry Wynberg and spent some time in the company of Maltese ad executive Peter Darmanin, Burton became the constant companion of British model Susan Hunt. He also made a triumphant return to the Broadway stage in *Equus*. The year was 1976, and after Richard and Elizabeth were divorced for the second time, he married Susan Hunt and Elizabeth took yet another husband (her last to date), John W. Warner, former Secretary of the Navy and soon to become Republican Senator from Virginia. That union would last six years, during which Elizabeth settled into suburban domestic life, helping her husband campaign. She also gained considerable weight,

ballooning up to a formidable 180 pounds. During a 1977 Barbara Walters TV interview in their Virginia home, Taylor asserted that she didn't mind at all "being fat," a statement she would later admit had been a lie.

Elizabeth Taylor's acting assignments were now few and far between. The Soviet/American remake (filmed in Russia) of *The Blue Bird*—in which she played four different roles—proved a fiasco, despite the eminent directorial presence of George Cukor. Her silent-cameo role in the trouble-ridden *Winter Kills* couldn't be advertised, due to mysterious contractual obligations, and the film adaptation of Broadway's *A Little Night Music*, in which Elizabeth got to sing that musical hit's show-stopping "Send in the Clowns," was another quiet bomb. On television, she was a guest star on the daytime "soap" *General Hospital*, the nighttime series *Hotel* and the miniseries *North and South*, and she had uneven results with dramatic parts in TV-movies that ranged from the mostly exploitative (*Victory at Entebbe*) to the pleasantly diverting (*Poker Alice*). But there was at least one meaty vehicle: the made-for-cable comedy-drama *Between Friends*, in which she and Carol Burnett enjoyed roles of substance and favorable reviews, as well as obvious personal rapport. To date, Taylor's last theatrical film, the Italian-made *Young Toscanini*, has met with derision in Europe and has been reported to be "almost unreleasable" here, with its American debut most likely to be via videocassette. In May 1989, Elizabeth began filming for television a new production of Tennessee Williams' *Sweet Bird of Youth,* with her and Mark Harmon cast in the showy roles made famous on stage and screen by Geraldine Page and Paul Newman.

Having successfully dieted away most of the excess weight that had provided material for comedians like Joan Rivers, Elizabeth made her Broadway stage debut in a 1981 revival of Lillian Hellman's *The Little Foxes* in a role that had well served Tallulah Bankhead and Bette Davis in its respective stage and screen incarnations. Although the reviews were somewhat mixed, Taylor earned some praiseworthy notices—and a Tony nomination. And her salary for the 126-performance run is said to have broken all Broadway records. After New York, the production visited New Orleans, Los Angeles and, in 1982, London. As Elizabeth later admitted, "I loved performing for a live audience."

In partnership with producer Zev Bufman, Elizabeth Taylor teamed with Richard Burton for the last time in 1983's ill-starred tour and Broadway revival of Noel Coward's sophisticated comedy, *Private Lives,* which she later admitted was not the best choice of a vehicle for them. Plagued by poor reviews and Elizabeth's recurring ill health, it lasted only 63 performances. During its run, Burton finalized his divorce from Susan Hunt and married his then-current companion, Sally Hay. And Elizabeth suddenly announced her engagement to Mexican lawyer Victor Luna—a fiancé destined to remain just that. Burton's untimely death in 1984, at 58, affected her profoundly.

As she wrote in her best-selling 1987 diet book, *Elizabeth Takes Off*—in which she tells of fighting back from 180 pounds to a mere 120—"At 50 years of age, I had to recreate or reinvent myself, and in my case because of extra problems, it eventually meant entering the Betty Ford Center." Pills and alcohol led to a 1983 sojourn there that was

With husband John Warner and Barbara Walters on TV (1977).

strongly encouraged by her family. Without their support, she has admitted, "I'm sure I would have wound up dead."

In 1985, before she managed to shed 25 unwanted pounds, Taylor was confined to bed for five months with recurring back problems. In the spring of 1986, New York's Film Society of Lincoln Center honored Elizabeth with a tribute in a glittering evening of film clips and the accolades of her colleagues. Soon afterwards, reduced to a svelte size-six, she talked freely in TV interviews about her new-found emotional tranquility: "I'm much more secure with myself than I was before. I used to drink because I thought it would help my shyness. It didn't; it only accentuated it." Of her last marriage, she said, "I tried very hard to make it work. I love John; he's a wonderful man, and a wonderful politician. There just wasn't room in his life for me . . . for family. The Senate is a very hard mistress to fight."

In a March 1987 Barbara Walters TV Special, Elizabeth—whose name was now being linked with publisher Malcolm Forbes, actor George Hamilton, and a perfume called "Elizabeth Taylor's Passion"—admitted enjoying the single life and seemed reluctant to discuss Richard Burton, other than admitting, "They're wonderful memories, they're warm memories and they're *my* memories."

Early in 1988, amid rumors of extensive plastic surgery, the now gorgeous-looking Elizabeth Taylor strongly denied the gossip, while revealing, "I did have a chin tuck because there was some loose skin. And that is all!" Later that year, though, she was again a patient at the Betty Ford Center, where a roving photographer cruelly snapped a picture of her in a wheelchair looking puffy. A summer fracture of her already-fragile back had led to a dependence on painkillers—and an addiction sufficient to make her once again seek help. By February of 1989, however, Elizabeth was healthy enough to make a rare public appearance. Looking beautiful, if a trifle heavier than when last seen by her fans, she was present at the Bob Hope Cultural Center in Palm Desert, California, where—in a celebrity-packed event taped for TV—she received the second annual America's Hope Award for "her humanitarian efforts and all of the problems she has had to face in overcoming drug and alcohol addiction."

In Paris in April to launch her "Passion for Men" fragrance, Elizabeth spoke of her health: "I'm hobbling along, I'm OK." Calling her lumbar vertebrae fracture "inoperable," she added, "I've learned to live with the pain. It hasn't been easy."

Of her much-publicized work in helping stamp out AIDS—a dedication activated by the 1985 death of her friend and co-star, Rock Hudson—she said: "I remain national chairman of the AIDS Foundation, and we're soon going international. Unfortunately, there's no cure on the horizon. There's still a lot of work to be done. I give part of my perfume earnings to the AIDS Foundation; I have from the beginning."

As Helena Cassadine on "General Hospital" (1981).

As a New Orleans madam in the miniseries "North and South" (1985).

With Roddy McDowall on the ABC-TV series "Hotel" (1984).

Talking about the turn in her career from the cinema screen to television, Elizabeth explains, "The time schedule is easier for me. It takes six weeks to do a TV picture, and you can more or less choose what you want to do. Frankly, I'm at the age where it's not easy to find movies. It's much easier to find vehicles for TV."

Of her craft, she has said: "I never had an acting lesson in my life, but I've learned by experience and by working with some wonderful professionals. I learned most from Spencer Tracy. He had a marvelous way of underplaying a character and taught me how to concentrate so I could work intensely." And she added, "I concentrate on my role at the studio, but I shed it like an overcoat when I go home to my personal life."

In the months before this volume went to press, Elizabeth Taylor's personal life had, according to gossip-column and tabloid reports, included a man described as "a 37-year-old ex-truck driver she had met at the Betty Ford Center," one Larry Fortensky. Some sources even had him lined up as her next husband.

Whatever the future holds for this charismatic and unsinkable superstar, there will be many another chapter to her story before she'll call it a career—and a life.

Gloria Twine

With Carl "Alfalfa" Switzer and Catherine Doucet

There's One Born Every Minute

A Universal Picture / 1942

CAST

Lemuel P. Twine: Hugh Herbert; *Jimmie Hanagan:* Tom Brown; *Helen Twine:* Peggy Moran; *Lester Cadwalader, Sr.:* Guy Kibbee; *Minerva Twine:* Catherine Doucet; *Moe Carson:* Edgar Kennedy; *Lester Cadwalader, Jr.:* Scott Jordan; *Quisenberry:* Gus Schilling; *Gloria Twine:* Elizabeth Taylor; *Trumbull;* Charles Halton; *Miss Phipps:* Renie Riano; *Junior:* Carl "Alfalfa" Switzer.

CREDITS

Director: Harold Young; *Associate Producer:* Ken Goldsmith; *Screenwriters:* Robert B. Hunt and Brenda Weisberg; *Based on a Story by:* Rob-

With Hugh Herbert, Catherine Doucet, Carl "Alfalfa" Switzer, Peggy Moran and Tom Brown

[37]

ert B. Hunt; *Cinematographer:* John W. Boyle; *Art Director:* Jack Otterson; *Sound Director:* Bernard B. Brown; *Musical Director:* H. J. Salter; *Gowns:* Vera West; *Running Time:* 59 minutes.

THE FILM

Through the years, Elizabeth Taylor has consistently referred to this little program comedy, in which she made her movie début, as *Man or Mouse,* its title during production. As she remarked on a David Frost TV interview, "I remember I played a beastly child who slung rubber bands at ladies' and gentlemen's bottoms."

There's One Born Every Minute was decidedly a minor entry in the then-dwindling taste for "screwball" comedy. Its plot centers on the wacky family of Lemuel P. Twine, owner of the Twine Tasty Pudding Company. Lester Cadwalader, the town's political boss, is promoting Twine for mayor, but only to keep a more likely candidate out of the running. When laboratory tests reveal that Twine's pudding is loaded with Vitamin Z, the resultant publicity insures Twine's election to office, whereupon Cadwalader does an about-face, pronouncing the pudding a fake and Twine himself a fraud. But Twine fights back, exposing Cadwalader as the real fraud. And he wins the election.

Elizabeth was nine years old when she made her screen bow as the Twines' bratty youngest child. This was her only Universal picture during the entire year she was under contract to that

Catherine Doucet, Tom Brown and Hugh Herbert

studio, whose pressbooks heralded her as a "nine-year-old singer and dancer." *There's One Born Every Minute* was deemed so unimportant that it was not even screened for (or reviewed by) the trade press, much less newspaper and magazine critics.

Carl "Alfalfa" Switzer, Elizabeth's fellow rubber-bandit and former member of the *Our Gang* comedies, was killed in a gun brawl January 21, 1959. He was thirty-two.

With Peggy Moran, Catherine Doucet and Carl "Alfalfa" Switzer

With Nigel Bruce

Lassie Come Home

A Metro-Goldwyn-Mayer Picture / 1943
In Technicolor

CAST

Joe Carraclough: Roddy McDowall; *Sam Carraclough:* Donald Crisp; *Rowlie:* Edmund Gwenn; *Dolly:* Dame May Whitty; *Duke of Rudling:* Nigel Bruce; *Mrs. Carraclough:* Elsa Lanchester; *Priscilla:* Elizabeth Taylor; *Hynes:* J. Patrick O'Malley; *Dan'l Fadden:* Ben Webster; *Snickers:* Alec Craig; *Buckles:* John Rogers; *Jock:* Arthur Shields; *Andrew:* Alan Napier; *Butcher:* Roy Parry; *Allen:* George Broughton; *Cobbler:* Howard Davies; *Miner:* John Power; *Teacher:* Nelson Leigh; *Fat Woman:* May Beatty; *Tom:* Charles Irwin; *Lassie:* Pal.

CREDITS

Director: Fred M. Wilcox; *Producer:* Samuel Marx; *Screenwriter:* Hugh Butler; *From the Novel by:* Eric Knight; *Cinematographer:* Leonard Smith; *Art Director:* Cedric Gibbons; *Special Effects:* Warren Newcombe; *Musical Score:* Daniele Amfitheatrof; *Editor:* Ben Lewis; *Lassie's Trainer:* Rudd Weatherwax; *Running Time:* 88 minutes.

THE FILM

Lassie Come Home was derived from a 1938 short story published in the *Saturday Evening Post* and two years later expanded into novel form. Its 1943 movie version proved ideal·family entertainment, charming adults as well as small fry. In essence, it's about the mutual love affair between Joe Carraclough, a poor Yorkshire schoolboy, and Lassie, the beautiful brown-and-

Roddy McDowall, Lassie and Donald Crisp

white collie that his father must sell to make ends meet. The dog's new owner, a wealthy duke, finds it difficult to keep her from running off and returning to her former master. Finally, the duke takes Lassie far away to his estate in Scotland, where he will train her for exhibition. But his little daughter Priscilla, whose sympathies lie with Joe, helps the collie escape from her father's kennels, and Lassie begins the long and arduous trek home—nearly a thousand miles to Yorkshire. Eventually boy and dog are reunited, and Joe's father is offered the job of kennel-keeper on the duke's estate, thus pointing to a happy-ever-after conclusion.

Eric Knight's childhood classic became one of the most popular and sentimental animal stories ever brought to the screen. Its success fostered no less than seven sequels and a network television series that ran for nineteen years.

This was Elizabeth Taylor's first movie at MGM, the studio to which she would be contractually bound for the next seventeen years. As twelve-year-old Priscilla, Elizabeth made a Tech-

nicolor début that revealed an extraordinary blend of coloring, hair texture, and thickly lashed violet eyes that predicted a promising career as one of the all-time great beauties of the cinema. On the set of *Lassie Come Home,* so naturally impressive was the child's face that cameraman Leonard Smith tried to get her to remove "the false eyelashes and eye make-up." Elizabeth, of course, wasn't wearing any.

Lassie, a female dog, has been played by a total of five canines, all male and each descended from the other. The first Lassie, actually named Pal, lived to the ripe old age of nineteen, although he was "retired" from the movies at five, to be replaced on the screen by his son.

CRITICS' CORNER

"The story of a boy and a dog, told with such poignance and simple beauty that only the hardest heart can fail to be moved. But it is really the collie, Lassie, which is the most remarkable performer in the film. The beauty of this dog and her responsiveness go far to make the picture a thorough delight."

Bosley Crowther, THE NEW YORK TIMES

"Juvenile actors of first-rate quality are so scarce that the movies seldom have possessed more than one of them at a time. This picture re-emphasizes that Roddy McDowall is easily the best of the current lot. The set of character actors surrounding Roddy and Lassie were thoughtfully chosen, and the result is a set of acting gems."

Alton Cook, NEW YORK WORLD-TELEGRAM

"It is one of the best boy and dog stories to reach the screen, as it carefully turns away from bathos and tells an emotional story with simple and poignant sincerity.

"Lassie and Roddy have a good supporting cast, with Donald Crisp and Elsa Lanchester as stalwart parents, May Whitty and Ben Webster as two old people who learn to love Lassie, Edmund Gwenn as a traveling peddler, Nigel Bruce as the kindly, comical duke and vivid little Elizabeth Taylor as his granddaughter. *Lassie Come Home* is a picture for anyone who has ever loved a boy or a dog."

Eileen Creelman, NEW YORK SUN

"A richly sentimental story about a collie dog and her several human environments. Among the best dog pictures, it can be ranked below *To the Victor* (1938) and above *The Biscuit Eater* (1940), the two leaders on the list."

Archer Winsten, NEW YORK POST

"Elizabeth Taylor, a pretty moppet, shows up to good advantage."

VARIETY

With Elsa Lanchester, Donald Crisp, Nigel Bruce and Lassie

With Peggy Ann Garner

Jane Eyre

A 20th Century-Fox Picture / 1944

CAST

Edward Rochester: Orson Welles; *Jane Eyre:* Joan Fontaine; *Adele Varens:* Margaret O'Brien; *Jane (as a child):* Peggy Ann Garner; *Dr. Rivers:* John Sutton; *Bessie:* Sara Allgood; *Brocklehurst:* Henry Daniell; *Mrs. Reed:* Agnes Moorehead; *Colonel Dent:* Aubrey Mather; *Mrs. Fairfax:* Edith Barrett; *Lady Ingram:* Barbara Everest; *Blanche Ingram:* Hillary Brooke; *Grace Poole:* Ethel Griffies; *Leah:* Mae Marsh; *Miss Scatcherd:* Eily Malyon; *Mr. Briggs:* Erskine Sanford; *Mason:* John Abbott; *Beadle:* Yorke Sherwood; *John:* Ronald Harris; *Auctioneer:* Charles Irwin; *Helen:* Elizabeth Taylor.

CREDITS

Director: Robert Stevenson; *Producer:* William Goetz; *Screenwriters:* Aldous Huxley, Robert Stevenson, and John Houseman; *Based on the Novel by:* Charlotte Brontë; *Cinematographer:* George Barnes; *Art Directors:* James Basevi and Wiard B. Ihnen; *Special Effects:* Fred Sersen; *Musical Score:* Bernard Herrmann; *Editor:* Walter Thompson; *Costumes:* René Hubert; *Running Time:* 96 minutes.

THE FILM

Jane Eyre's early scenes take place at Lowood, a cruelly operated institution where the orphaned young Jane spends a dreary childhood under the sadistic eye of Mr. Brocklehurst. Her only friend is a beautiful little girl named Helen, whose death from pneumonia (the two are forced to stand in the rain as punishment for a minor rebellion) has a traumatic effect on Jane's life.

Grown to adulthood, the spinsterish Jane secures a position as governess to young Adele Varens, the ward of enigmatic Edward Rochester at Thornfield Hall. In time, a series of strange and frightening events at Thornfield draw Jane and her employer together. But their wedding

With Henry Daniell and John Sutton

ceremony is disrupted by a stranger who bursts in to announce that Rochester already has a wife, insane and confined to a tower room of the estate. Jane leaves, returning years later to find a blind, now-widowed Rochester, wandering through the ruins of Thornfield. They are reunited.

This was the fifth screen version of Charlotte Brontë's nineteenth-century Gothic classic. In previous adaptations, Ethel Grandin and Irving Cummings portrayed the leads in 1913; two years later Louise Vale and Alan Hale co-starred in this story; in 1921, a third silent version featured Mabel Ballin and Norman Trevor; and in 1934, Virginia Bruce and Colin Clive were in its first appearance as a talkie.

Jane Eyre has twice been filmed in color for television: in 1957, a low-budget telefeature paired British actors Joan Elan and Patrick Macnee; the more lavish 1971 version starred Susannah York and George C. Scott in a lush

With Eily Malyon, Henry Daniell and Peggy Ann Garner

production filmed in Yorkshire and shown theatrically outside of the United States.

Fox's 1944 *Jane Eyre* emphasized the original novel's Gothic aspects, a factor particularly underscored by George Barnes's shadowy black-and-white photography and the atmospheric background music composed by Bernard Herrmann, who later wrote an opera based on *Emily* Brontë's *Wuthering Heights*. To suit Orson Welles, who received top billing over the titular star Joan Fontaine, the role of moody Edward Rochester was enlarged in a fashion that, while taking some liberties with the Brontë novel, nevertheless maintained its morose tone and setting. Although favorably disposed toward this production, most of the critics had some reservations about Welles's oft-mumbled speech, a trait which has frequently plagued his acting career.

Despite the fact that Elizabeth Taylor appeared in several scenes in the Lowood sequences, most cast lists omit her entirely. Once, when the film was shown on British TV, the actress tells of gathering her children around to watch for her scenes, only to find that she had been completely eliminated from that print: "They'd cut my entire part out!"

CRITICS' CORNER

"Charlotte Brontë's Victorian novel has again reached the screen in a drama that is as intense on celluloid as it is on the printed page. There is some excellent photography by George Barnes, practically all in light and shadow to emphasize the eeriness of the story, and the direction by Robert Stevenson has heightened the illusion of action where, frequently, none existed. But, basically, *Jane Eyre*, the novel, remains something for the high-school classroom, a study in the literature of another day. The picture is something else again. It is intriguing entertainment."

"Kahn," VARIETY

"Jane Eyre is interesting, sometimes chilling and even moving. The supporting players are invariably excellent at creating atmosphere or dramatic embellishments to the continuity."

Howard Barnes, NEW YORK HERALD TRIBUNE

"Mr. Welles's ferocious performance doesn't limn Miss Brontë's hero, but it does strike off a figure which is interesting to observe. Miss Fontaine's performance is so modest and subdued that one comprehends from it only anxiety and awe. Peggy Ann Garner is desperately appealing as the tortured child Jane. The settings are heavy and sombre, and Robert Stevenson has directed in a style that suggests the romantic extravagance of dark Victorian prose.

"The early part of the film, which gives a very moving comprehension of Jane's sad childhood at Lowood School, seems remote from the rest of the picture. It is almost a separate tale."

Bosley Crowther, THE NEW YORK TIMES

John Abbott, Orson Welles and Joan Fontaine

With Roddy McDowall

The White Cliffs of Dover

A Metro-Goldwyn-Mayer Picture / 1944

CAST

Susan Ashwood: Irene Dunne; *Sir John Ashwood:* Alan Marshal; *Hiram Porter Dunn:* Frank Morgan; *John Ashwood II (as a boy):* Roddy McDowall; *Nanny:* Dame May Whitty; *Colonel:* C. Aubrey Smith; *Lady Jean Ashwood:* Gladys Cooper; *John Ashwood II (age twenty-four):* Peter Lawford; *Sam Bennett:* Van Johnson; *Reggie:* John Warburton; *Rosamund:* Jill Esmond; *Gwennie:* Brenda Forbes; *Mrs. Bland:* Norma Varden; *Betsy (age ten):* Elizabeth Taylor; *Betsy (age eighteen):* June Lockhart; *Farmer Kenney:* Charles Irwin; *Mrs. Kenney:* Jean Prescott; *American Soldier:* Tom Drake; *Mrs. Bancroft:* Isobel Elsom; *Major Bancroft:* Edmund Breon; *Major Loring:* Miles Mander; *Miss Lambert:* Ann Curzon; *Gerhard:* Steven Muller; *Dietrich:* Norbert Muller; *Helen:* Molly Lamont; *The Vicar:* Lumsden Hare; *Benson:* Arthur Shields; *Plump Lady in Boarding House:* Doris Lloyd; *Immigration Officer:* Matthew Boulton; *Woman on Train:* Ethel Griffies; *Footman:* Herbert Evans; *Duke of Waverly:* Keith Hitchcock; *Duchess:* Vera Graaff; *Miller:* Anita Bolster; *Skipper:* Ian Wolfe; *Billings:* Alec Craig; *Jennings:* Clyde Cook.

CREDITS

Director: Clarence Brown; *Producer:* Sidney Franklin; *Screenwriters:* Claudine West, Jan Lustig, and George Froeschel; *Based on the Poem "The White Cliffs" by:* Alice Duer Miller; *Cinematographer:* George Folsey; *Art Director:* Cedric Gibbons; *Special Effects:* A. Arnold Gillespie and Warren Newcombe; *Musical Score:* Herbert Stothart; *Editor:* Robert J. Kern; *Running Time:* 126 minutes.

THE FILM

The White Cliffs of Dover was another of MGM's wartime tributes to England and the English, following on the heels of its much-honored *Mrs. Miniver*. With its screenplay developed from Alice Duer Miller's epic poem "The White Cliffs," it spanned two world wars in its story about Susan Dunn, an American girl who becomes the bride of a dashing Briton, Sir John Ashwood, bears him a son, is widowed in the Great War and lives to see her son wounded in World War II. At the story's close, young John dies of his war wounds as his mother recites a noble speech about faith and fortitude.

Elizabeth Taylor's role in this two-hours-plus family chronicle is so brief that it has often been excised completely for television. Again appearing opposite young Roddy McDowall, she plays a flirtatious country girl with a crush on him. The sequence is charming, if expendable.

CRITICS' CORNER

"*The White Cliffs of Dover* seems overlong for such a plotless picture. It runs for more than two hours, but most of the two hours are interesting and often poignant. Clarence Brown has directed the picture so skillfully that the emotion never becomes excessive."

Eileen Creelman, NEW YORK SUN

"There is no lack of fine acting in *The White Cliffs of Dover*. There is no want of production finish. Unfortunately, it misses being an outstanding motion picture."

Howard Barnes, NEW YORK HERALD TRIBUNE

"This sterling-silver picture is such a tribute to English gentility as only an American studio would dare to make. Miss Dunne gives to her character a nice glow of American charm, and Mr. Marshal makes Sir John Ashwood a thoroughly pleasant and graceful Britisher.

"For such folks as like to think of England and America being symbolically bound by such ties, say, as Lady Astor's, *The White Cliffs of Dover* should be a comforting film."

Bosley Crowther, THE NEW YORK TIMES

"The picture is, among other things, a powerful but intelligent approach to a better understanding between the English and the Yanks.

"Strongly a woman's picture, but not singu-

With Roddy McDowall

Alan Marshal and Irene Dunne

larly for them only, the movie is much more a distillate of romantic elements than it is of war."

"Char," VARIETY

"It would be very easy to make fun of *The White Cliffs of Dover,* but for some reason I don't care to. On the whole, I like the film. It is sentimental, class conscious, and a little complacent; it fondles England in a way that would be inconceivable to a Briton. But the impulse is honest, the love story seems often sincere, and the message of mutual understanding can do nothing but good in both our countries. Irene Dunne, in the trickiest part she has ever tackled, seems to me to give a flawless performance.

"I have not the smallest doubt that *The White Cliffs of Dover* will repeat the popular success of *Random Harvest* in British cinemas, and I feel it would be the poorest taste on the part of a British critic to reject a gesture so opportunely tendered and so generously made."

C. A. Lejeune, LONDON OBSERVER

With Roddy McDowall

With Jackie "Butch" Jenkins, Juanita Quigley, Anne Revere and Angela Lansbury

National Velvet

A Metro-Goldwyn-Mayer Picture / 1944
In Technicolor

CAST

Mi Taylor: Mickey Rooney; *Mr. Brown:* Donald Crisp; *Velvet Brown:* Elizabeth Taylor; *Mrs. Brown:* Anne Revere; *Edwina Brown:* Angela Lansbury; *Malvolia Brown:* Juanita Quigley; *Donald Brown:* Jackie "Butch" Jenkins; *Farmer Ede:* Reginald Owen; *Ted:* Terry Kilburn; *Tim:* Alec Craig; *Mr. Taski:* Eugene Loring; *Miss Sims:* Norma Varden; *Mr. Hallam:* Arthur Shields; *Mr. Greenford:* Dennis Hoey; *Entry Official:* Aubrey Mather; *Stewart:* Frederic Worlock; *Man with Umbrella:* Arthur Treacher; *Van Driver:* Harry Allen; *Constable:* Billy Bevan; *Townsman:* Barry Macollum; *Entry Clerk:* Matthew Boulton; *First Pressman:* Leyland Hodgson; *Second Pressman:* Leonard Carey; *Cockney:* Colin Campbell; *Englishman:* Frank Benson; *Jockey:* Wally Cassell; *Valet:* Alec Harford; *Reporter:* William Austin; *Cameraman:* Gerald Oliver Smith; *First Villager:* Olaf Hytten; *Second Villager:* George Kirby; *Woman:* Moyna MacGill; *American:* Donald Curtis; *Schoolboy:* Howard Taylor.

CREDITS

Director: Clarence Brown; *Producer:* Pandro S. Berman; *Screenwriters:* Theodore Reeves and Helen Deutsch; *Based on the Novel by:* Enid Bagnold; *Cinematographer:* Leonard Smith; *Art Directors:* Cedric Gibbons and Urie McCleary; *Set Decorators:* Edwin B. Willis and Mildred Griffiths; *Costumes:* Irene; *Men's Wardrobe:* Valles; *Special Effects:* Warren Newcombe; *Musical Score:* Herbert Stothart; *Editor:* Robert J. Kern; *Running Time:* 125 minutes.

With Mickey Rooney and Anne
Revere

THE FILM

MGM had owned the screen rights to Enid Bagnold's most successful novel, published in 1935,
for some five years before they actually filmed it.
Reportedly, this was because they couldn't find
the right child actress to portray Velvet Brown.
Elizabeth Taylor was eleven years old and under
a twelve-month contract to Metro when she and
her mother appealed to producer Pandro S.
Berman to consider her for the coveted part.
National Velvet was, at that time, her favorite
book and, although small for her age, Elizabeth
had the appropriate English accent and horseback-riding experience required for Velvet. Producer Berman measured her, but declared her too
short and too slight for the role. The child was,
however, sufficiently undaunted to embark on
a three-month weight-gaining, height-stretching
program that paid off. In twelve weeks, she grew
three inches and won the title part in what she
refers to as "still the most exciting film I've ever
done."

The story is set in Sussex, England, where
Velvet Brown, a butcher's daughter, teams with a
vagabond teenager named Mi Taylor to train for
competition a horse she's won in a raffle. With
some difficulty, Velvet manages to enter "The
Pie" in the Grand National, in which she rides
him disguised as a boy and with her long hair cut

short. Although her horse wins, Velvet is dis-
qualified, though happy in the knowledge that
"The Pie" is a true champion. Having helped
Velvet train her horse to victory, Mi leaves to
make his way in the world.

Despite excellent notices, the movie drew
audiences through the fame of its literary predecessor, as well as Mickey Rooney's popularity.
However, once they'd seen the film, it was young
Elizabeth Taylor audiences talked about. Her
charm and beauty were extraordinary, and what
she lacked in talent and experience was well
hidden in a fine production that boasted a topnotch supporting cast and solid direction by the
veteran Clarence Brown. The film won Academy
Awards for Anne Revere's performance as Elizabeth's mother and for Robert J. Kern's editing,
which drew critical raves for the exciting steeple-
chase sequences. Oscar nominations were earned
by director Brown; Leonard Smith, for his color
photography; and those responsible for art direction and set decoration.

To get the part of Velvet, Elizabeth Taylor
had to sign a long-term contract that, in her
words, made her "their chattel" for the next
eighteen years. For this film, Elizabeth displayed
fine form as a horsewoman. As a reward for her
performance and the picture's immense popularity, Metro made their new young star a gift,

on her thirteenth birthday, of the horse used in the film.

CRITICS' CORNER

"In *National Velvet* Metro has one of the top b.o. clicks of the year. It's a horse picture with wide general appeal, a potent draw for femme and juve attendance, in particular. The production also focuses attention on a new dramatic find—moppet Elizabeth Taylor, who plays Velvet. Anne Revere does another fine job—restrained and excellently modulated. Rooney's part is a difficult one, hampered by a lack of motivation, but he handles it well. Clarence Brown, who directed, has used the asset of color superbly, capturing the charm of English countrysides and, above all, reproducing Aintree, the Grand National course, with fidelity."

"Merr," VARIETY

"That beautiful child of *Lassie Come Home,* a dark-haired, blue-eyed girl named Elizabeth Taylor, plays the dreamy Velvet and makes her one of the screen's most lovable characters."

Eileen Creelman, NEW YORK SUN

"A more exciting horse race than that shown in this film has never been represented on the screen, in our memory, anyhow.

"Mr. Brown has also drawn some excellent performances from his cast, especially from little Elizabeth Taylor, who plays the role of the horse-loving girl. Her face is alive with youthful spirit, her voice has the softness of sweet song and her whole manner in this picture is one of refreshing grace."

Bosley Crowther, THE NEW YORK TIMES

"The performance of Elizabeth Taylor is a lovely conception, a burning eagerness tempered with sweet, fragile charm."

Alton Cook, NEW YORK WORLD-TELEGRAM

"Elizabeth Taylor is as natural and excellent a little actress as you would ever hope to see."

Archer Winsten, NEW YORK POST

"It makes a star of twelve-year-old Elizabeth Taylor."

PIC MAGAZINE

"Elizabeth is admirably suited to the role. She gives a glowing performance that actually over-

With Mickey Rooney

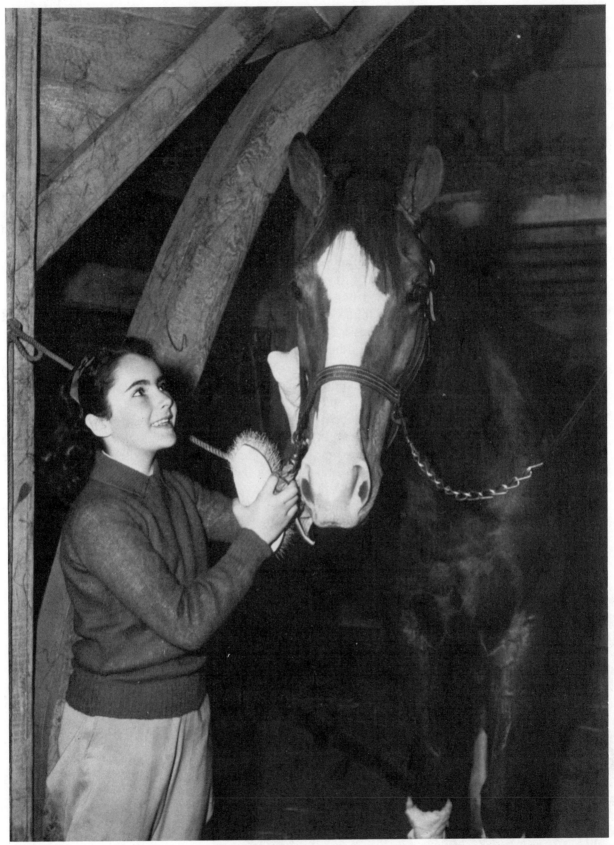

With Pi

shadows her vis-à-vis, Mickey Rooney, who is one of Hollywood's prime scene-stealers."

Kate Cameron, NEW YORK DAILY NEWS

"A beguiling young newcomer named Elizabeth Taylor emerges as one of the outstanding discoveries of the year."

Rose Pelswick, NEW YORK JOURNAL-AMERICAN

"Frankly, I doubt I am qualified to arrive at any sensible assessment of Miss Elizabeth Taylor. Ever since I first saw the child, two or three years ago, in I forget what minor role in what movie, I have been choked with the peculiar sort of adoration I might have felt if we were both in the same grade of primary school.

"I wouldn't say she is particularly gifted as an actress. She seems, rather, to turn things off and on, much as she is told, with perhaps a fair amount of natural grace and of a natural-born female's sleep-walking sort of guile, but without much, if any, of an artist's intuition, perception or resource. She strikes me, however, if I may resort to conservative statement, as being rapturously beautiful. I think she also has a talent, of a sort, in the particular things she can turn on: which are most conspicuously a mock-pastoral kind of simplicity, and two or three speeds of semi-hysterical emotion, such as ecstasy, an odd sort of pre-specific erotic sentience, and the anguish of overstrained hope, imagination and faith. Since these are precisely the things she needs for

her role in *National Velvet,* and since I think it is the most hopeful business of movies to find the perfect people rather than the perfect artists, I think that she and the picture are wonderful, and I hardly know or care whether she can act or not."

James Agee, THE NATION

NOTE

In 1946, Enid Bagnold's stage adaptation of her novel was performed in London. *Variety*'s critic "Clem" wrote of Tilsa Page, who played Velvet, "She is second best to the earnest, tense performance projected by Elizabeth Taylor."

AND A RETROSPECTIVE REVIEW FROM THE 1960s:

"The high point in Elizabeth Taylor's acting career came when she was twelve: under Clarence Brown's direction, she gave her best performance to date as Velvet Brown, the heroine of Enid Bagnold's account of a little girl's sublime folly. Quite possibly the role coincided with the child's own animal-centered universe.

"In lots of ways *National Velvet* isn't a very good movie, but it has a rare and memorable quality. It's one of the most *likable* movies of all time."

Pauline Kael

With Matthew Boulton, Mickey Rooney and Aubrey Mather

With Lassie

Courage of Lassie

A Metro-Goldwyn-Mayer Picture / 1946
In Technicolor

CAST

Kathie Merrick: Elizabeth Taylor; *Harry Mac-Bain:* Frank Morgan; *Sergeant Smitty:* Tom Drake; *Mrs. Merrick:* Selena Royle; *Judge Payson:* Harry Davenport; *Farmer Crews:* Morris Ankrum; *Gil Elson:* Mitchell Lewis; *Alice Merrick:* Catherine Frances McLeod; *Pete Merrick:* David Holt; *Old Man:* George Cleveland; *Sheriff Ed Grayson:* Minor Watson; *Mrs. Elson:* Jane Green; *Sergeant Mac:* William Wallace; *First Youth:* Carl "Alfalfa" Switzer; *Second Youth:* Conrad Binyon.

CREDITS

Director: Fred M .Wilcox; *Producer:* Robert Sisk; *Screenwriter:* Lionel Hauser; *Co-Director of Animal Sequences:* Basil Wrangel; *Cinematographer:* Leonard Smith; *Art Directors:* Cedric Gibbons and Paul Youngblood; *Musical Score:* Bronislau Kaper; *Editor:* Conrad A. Nervig; *Costumes:* Irene; *Running Time:* 93 minutes.

THE FILM

Elizabeth Taylor received top billing for the first time in this girl-and-collie film, released nearly a year and a half after her great success in *National Velvet.* Presumably, Metro was hard put to find an appropriate vehicle for their new adolescent star, and reasoned that they would do well to exploit Elizabeth's own natural love for animals by teaming her again with their canine favorite. Although released as *Courage of Lassie,* the film contains no mention of "Lassie" per se. Indeed, throughout the movie, Elizabeth's collie co-star is called "Bill," a factor which must have caused MGM's advertising department endless migraines. During production, this picture was originally known as *Hold High the Torch,* a title later changed to *Blue Sierra,* which is how it's listed in the Library of Congress Catalog of Copyright Entries. Obviously, *Courage of Lassie* was a last-minute, play-it-safe (if inaccurate) title-change to reassure Lassie fans that this was

[53]

With Harry Davenport

neither a Western nor a romantic drama. Nor was it in any way related to *Lassie Come Home* or its 1945 sequel, *Son of Lassie,* which took the 1943 film's hero Joe Carraclough into young manhood (in the person of twenty-two-year-old Peter Lawford) and World War II.

Courage of Lassie centers on a collie pup that fate separates permanently from his mother in the wilderness of Washington State. A pretty teenager named Kathie Merrick finds the dog after he's been accidentally shot by two boys hunting birds, and she nurses the animal back to health with the aid of an elderly, neighboring sheep rancher, Harry McBain. Grown to full size, Bill, as he is named, proves useful in rounding up stray sheep, but one day he's struck by a car, an accident that leads the collie into an unusual series of adventures, separating him for a long time from his young mistress. He becomes a war dog and serves in combat against the Japanese. But in so doing, he turns "mean and vicious," or so it seems. Eventually, Bill and Kathie are reunited, and she saves him from being destroyed by pleading his case in court, assuring the judge

that Bill is a victim of shell-shock, like any soldier, and that her love will return him to normal.

CRITICS' CORNER

"The plot is not likely to give you pause. Neither is the acting by the bipeds. Lassie walks off with all the acting honors, which is as it should be."

Joe Pihodna, NEW YORK HERALD TRIBUNE

"Young Miss Taylor does a pleasant enough job, although her dialogue is limited to endless cries of 'Oh, Bill!' "

Alton Cook, NEW YORK WORLD-TELEGRAM

"The principal human actors are excellent in their simple roles. Elizabeth Taylor is refreshingly natural as Lassie's devoted owner, and Frank Morgan, as her elderly confidant, makes pleasant the characterization of a philosophical sheep farmer. Selena Royle, as Miss Taylor's mother, and Tom Drake carry off their assignments easily and competently. But it is Lassie's, or Bill's, picture. And, despite some improbabili-

With Lassie

With Catherine McLeod

ties in the plot, it is his 'acting' and the polychromatic setting which are the chief delights of this offering."

A. H. Weiler, THE NEW YORK TIMES

"I hope the ASPCA can't get me for being unkind to animal pictures when I warn fans that it is unreal and slightly tedious. There is a great deal of scenic beauty in this Technicolor production, and parts of the story are delightful and some of it is touching. Altogether, it is not a successful blending of humor and pathos.

"Elizabeth Taylor, very beautiful and charmingly sincere, has the leading role as Bill's devoted mistress."

Wanda Hale, NEW YORK DAILY NEWS

With Frank Morgan and Selena Royle

With Mary Astor and George Murphy

Cynthia

A Metro-Goldwyn-Mayer Picture / 1947

CAST

Cynthia Bishop: Elizabeth Taylor; *Larry Bishop:* George Murphy; *Professor Rosenkrantz:* S. Z. Sakall; *Louise Bishop:* Mary Astor; *Dr. Fred I. Jannings:* Gene Lockhart; *Carrie Jannings:* Spring Byington; *Ricky Latham:* James Lydon; *Will Parker:* Scotty Beckett; *Fredonia Jannings:* Carol Brannan; *Miss Brady:* Anna Q. Nilsson; *Mr. Phillips:* Morris Ankrum; *McQuillan:* Kathleen Howard; *Stella Regan:* Shirley Johns; *Alice:* Barbara Challis; *J. M. Dingle:* Harlan Briggs; *Gus Wood:* Will Wright.

CREDITS

Director: Robert Z. Leonard; *Producer:* Edwin H. Knopf; *Screenwriters:* Harold Buchman and Charles Kaufman; *Based on the Play* "The Rich, Full Life" *by:* Viña Delmar; *Cinematographer:* Charles Schoenbaum; *Musical Score:* Bronislau Kaper; *Musical Numbers:* Johnny Green; *Editor:* Irvine Warburton; *Costumes:* Irene; *Running Time:* 98 minutes.

THE FILM

In *Cynthia,* fifteen-year-old Elizabeth had her second lead, this time as a sickly teenager whose physical frailties have not been helped by over-protective parents. Eventually she rebels against being coddled, gains a boyfriend, and attends the school prom, proving her ability to lead a normal adolescent life.

Cynthia was derived from Viña Delmar's un-successful play, *The Rich, Full Life,* which had lasted a mere twenty-seven performances on Broadway in 1945. Coincidentally, the stage version had featured, as Cynthia, Virginia Weidler, a talented and promising former MGM juvenile, who had scored in *The Philadelphia Story* and retired from the screen in 1943, after *The Youngest Profession* and *Best Foot Forward,* at age sixteen.

In this film, Elizabeth Taylor not only got to sing but received her first movie kiss—from James Lydon, perhaps best-known as star of Paramount's Henry Aldrich series. In her autobiog-

With James Lydon

raphy, Elizabeth reports that, in prospect, this scene terrified her. Amusingly, she erroneously refers to the osculator as "Marshall Thompson," a youthful Metro contemporary with whom, however, she *never* worked in a film!

During production, *Cynthia* retained the original title of the play, *The Rich, Full Life*. Then Metro decided that *First Kiss* would be more appropriate. Characteristically, that, too, was altered before the movie's September, 1947, release —some fourteen months after her previous *Courage of Lassie*.

Due to Elizabeth's youthful talent for charming her audiences and a physical beauty perhaps precocious for her fifteen years, *Cynthia* became one of the films most often requested at United

With S. Z. Sakall

States military bases, both here and overseas.

CRITICS' CORNER

"Miss Taylor breathes plenty of life into the title role as a sheltered young girl who has never had a date or other fun generally accepted as matter of fact by teen-agers."

VARIETY

"Played by Elizabeth Taylor in a dewy-eyed, fluttery style, little Cynthia will chew her way softly, like a moth, into susceptible hearts.

"*Cynthia* is a synthetic morsel—right out of the Metro candy box."

Bosley Crowther, THE NEW YORK TIMES

"Able acting and a few moments of emotional intensity do not keep *Cynthia* from being a fragmentary screen drama. Mary Astor and Elizabeth Taylor portray a mother-daughter relationship with appealing reticence.

"What the production lacks is a cohesion of plot and the cumulative urgency that might have made it something more than a sentimental domestic comedy.

"Miss Taylor does a brilliant job with the title role. In vivid contrast to Hollywood's general conception of the bobby-soxer, she plays an unwilling invalid with grave charm. The scenes in which she has her first taste of the rich, full life are interpreted with subtle authority. At the same time, Miss Astor is a staunch foil as the woman who rebels against her husband and her in-laws to send her frail daughter off to a prom in a blinding rainstorm. Together they have scenes of considerable force. The ending, in which the girl is miraculously cured by being the belle of the ball, is hard to take, but it is slapped on in a hurry.

"As a matter of fact, the whole work veers closer to tragedy than to teen-age comedy. *Cynthia* generates snatches of realism and feeling, but not enough of them to sustain the film."

Howard Barnes. NEW YORK HERALD TRIBUNE

With Mary Astor

With ZaSu Pitts and Irene Dunne

Life With Father

A Warner Brothers Picture / 1947
In Technicolor

CAST

Father (Clarence Day): William Powell; *Vinnie:* Irene Dunne; *Mary Skinner:* Elizabeth Taylor; *Reverend Dr. Lloyd:* Edmund Gwenn; *Cora:* ZaSu Pitts; *Clarence:* James Lydon; *Margaret:* Emma Dunn; *Dr. Humphries:* Moroni Olsen; *Mrs. Whitehead:* Elisabeth Risdon; *Harlan:* Derek Scott; *Whitney:* Johnny Calkins; *John:* Martin Milner; *Annie:* Heather Wilde; *The Policeman:* Monte Blue; *Nora:* Mary Field; *Maggie:* Queenie Leonard; *Delia:* Nancy Evans; *Miss Wiggins:* Clara Blandick; *Dr. Somers:* Frank Elliott; *Scrubwoman:* Clara Reid; *Milkman:* Philo McCullough; *Corsetière:* Lois Bridge; *Salesman:* George Meader; *Mr. Morley:* Douglas Kennedy; *Clerk:* Phil Van Zandt; *Stock Quotation Operator:* Russell Arms; *Hilda:* Faith Kruger; *François:* Jean Del Val; *Twins:* Michael and Ralph Mineo; *Father of Twins:* Creighton Hale; *Mother of Twins:* Jean Andren; *Ellen:* Elaine Lange; *Perkins (Clerk):* John Beck; *Chef:* Jack Martin; *Girl in Delmonico's:* Arlene Dahl.

CREDITS

Director: Michael Curtiz; *Producer:* Robert Buckner; *Screenwriter:* Donald Ogden Stewart; *Based on the Play by:* Howard Lindsay and Russel Crouse; *Cinematographers:* Peverell Marley and William V. Skall; *Art Director:* Robert Hass; *Sets:* George James Hopkins; *Special Effects:* William McGann; *Sound:* C. A. Riggs; *Musical Score:* Max Steiner; *Editor:* George Amy; *Costumes:* Milo Anderson; *Technical Advisor:* Mrs. Clarence Day; *Running Time:* 118 minutes.

With William Powell

THE FILM

For many years *Life With Father,* at 3,224 performances, was Broadway's longest-running show. In 1972, *Fiddler on the Roof* beat that record by eighteen performances. The Lindsay-Crouse comedy, based on the book of reminiscences by Clarence Day, Jr., about his family, ran from 1939 to 1947, and inspired a less-successful sequel, *Life With Mother,* as well as a 1955 TV series.

This elaborate Warner Brothers film version retained the fun and spirit of the stage play, chronicling in episodic style the humorous events that detailed life in the Clarence Day household in late nineteenth-century New York City. Although she received third billing, following the movie's actual stars, William Powell and Irene Dunne, Elizabeth Taylor, on loan from MGM, played a relatively minor role as Mary Skinner, the pretty young household visitor. Again she was cast romantically opposite James Lydon, who played the Day family's eldest son, and again their on-screen romance was shy and tentative.

Although a rare departure from the usual custom of motion-picture release patterns in 1947, *Life With Father* bowed as a high-priced road-show movie before its eventual general release at popular prices.

CRITICS' CORNER

"Life With Father recaptures all the nostalgia and affection which went into the original Clarence Day sketches and charges the material with far more comic delight. With William Powell giving the greatest performance of a highly distinguished career, Donald Ogden Stewart's canny script and the superb direction of Michael Curtiz, this photoplay is something to cheer for.

"Powell's impersonation of an irascible Manhattan home-owner in the horsecar period is a magnificent piece of make-believe. He has had valuable assistance in recreating the mood and atmosphere in what amounts to a high period of American life. Irene Dunne is excellent as Mrs. Day. Edmund Gwenn and ZaSu Pitts contribute revealing portrayals, and Jimmy Lydon and Elizabeth Taylor and others concerned with mirroring a vanished era never miss a trick."

Howard Barnes, NEW YORK HERALD TRIBUNE

With ZaSu Pitts

With Irene Dunne, unidentified player, William Powell, Jean Del Val and ZaSu Pitts

"Elizabeth Taylor is alternately kittenish, silly and coquettish, as she is romantically involved with Clarence, Jr."

THE FILM DAILY

"All that the fabulous play had to offer in the way of charm, comedy, humor and gentle pathos is beautifully realized in this handsomely Technicolored picture.

"William Powell is every inch Father, from his carrot-patched dome to the tip of his button-up shoes. His is not merely a performance; it is character delineation of high order and so utterly dominates the picture that even when he is not on hand, his presence is still felt.

"Irene Dunne interprets Vinnie Day with charm, wit and an exactness that perfectly compliments Mr. Powell's Father. Elizabeth Taylor is very appealing as Mary Skinner, and other fine performances are contributed by Edmund Gwenn and ZaSu Pitts."

Thomas M. Pryor, THE NEW YORK TIMES

"This faithful reproduction of the enormously successful stage play retains all the charm, gentle humor and nostalgic appeal of the original.

"The well-known story is a warm and engaging slice of American family life replete with those intensely human and heart-warming touches that will endear it to the hearts of film patrons. The action of the film is confined to the Day household, except for brief episodes on the quiet, horse-carted streets, in fashionable Delmonico's and in McCreery's Department Store—all of them quaintly pictured. It will be a boxoffice winner in any type of theatre."

BOXOFFICE

"Elizabeth Taylor is sweetly feminine."

VARIETY

With William Powell, Irene Dunne, Martin Milner, Johnny Calkins, Derek Scott, James Lydon, Elisabeth Risdon and Clara Blandick

With Jane Powell

A Date With Judy

A Metro-Goldwyn-Mayer Picture / 1948
In Technicolor

CAST

Melvin R. Foster: Wallace Beery; *Judy Foster:* Jane Powell; *Carol Pringle:* Elizabeth Taylor; *Rosita Conchellas:* Carmen Miranda; *Xavier Cugat:* Himself; *Stephen Andrews:* Robert Stack; *Mrs. Foster:* Selena Royle; *Ogden "Oogie" Pringle:* Scotty Beckett; *Lucien T. Pringle:* Leon Ames; *Gramps:* George Cleveland; *Pop Scully:* Lloyd Corrigan; *Jameson:* Clinton Sundberg; *Mitzie:* Jean McLaren; *Randolph Foster:* Jerry Hunter; *Jo-Jo Hoffenpepper:* Buddy Howard; *Nightingale:* Lillian Yarbo; *Miss Clarke:* Eula Guy; *Professor Green:* Francis Pierlot; *Olga:* Rena Lenart; *Little Girl in Drugstore:* Sheila Stein; *Girl:* Alice Kelley; *Elderly Woman:* Polly Bailey; *Miss Sampson:* Fern Eggen; *Headwaiter:* Paul Bradley.

CREDITS

Director: Richard Thorpe; *Producer:* Joe Pasternak; *Screenwriters:* Dorothy Cooper and Dorothy Kingsley; *Based on the Characters Created by:* Aleen Leslie; *Cinematographer:* Robert Surtees; *Art Directors:* Cedric Gibbons and Paul Groesse; *Musical Director:* George Stoll; *Editor:* Harold

With Wallace Beery

F. Kress; *Songs:* "Judaline" by Don Raye and Gene DePaul; "It's a Most Unusual Day" by Harold Adamson and Jimmy McHugh; "I'm Strictly on the Corny Side" by Stella Unger and Alec Templeton; "I've Got a Date with Judy" and "I'm Gonna Meet My Mary" by Bill Katz and Calvin Jackson; *Running Time:* 113 minutes.

THE FILM

Aleen Leslie's successful juvenile radio series of

With Scotty Beckett

With Leon Ames

the 1940s, tricked out by MGM with songs and Technicolor, made a pleasant vehicle for their young musical star Jane Powell, although the fabulous Carmen Miranda stole the movie every time she appeared in her typically malaprop supporting comedy role.

Elizabeth Taylor had the secondary part of poor-little-rich-girl Carol Pringle, best friend of

With Jane Powell and Robert Stack

the movie's nominal heroine, Judy Foster (Powell). Amid subplots and teenage crises, Carol's brother (Scotty Beckett) worships Judy, while she has eyes only for a handsome older man (Robert Stack). Eventually everything is straightened out: Powell loses Stack to the more sophisticated Taylor and is reunited with her musical partner, Beckett.

In 1951, *A Date With Judy* became a television series. However, it did not enjoy the immense success of the prior radio show and film.

CRITICS' CORNER

"One of its more amusing songs, "Strictly on the Corny Side," just about epitomizes *A Date With Judy*. Hollywood has developed an extensive and rigid set of conventions for its unceasing stream of comedies of adolescence, and *Judy* adheres carefully to all of them. But within the limits of this familiar pattern, the picture is pleasantly entertaining."

Thomas F. Brady, THE NEW YORK TIMES

"Casting is particularly apt, both in youthful and character assignments, and each member delivers strongly under skillful direction by Richard Thorpe.

"Elizabeth Taylor makes a talented appearance. Her breathtaking beauty is complimented by the Technicolor lensing."

"Brog," VARIETY

"The big surprise in *A Date With Judy* is Elizabeth Taylor as the petulant, dark-eyed banker's daughter. The erstwhile child star of *National Velvet* and other films has been touched by Metro's magic wand and turned into a real, 14-carat, 100-proof siren with a whole new career opening in front of her. Judging from this picture, Hedy Lamarr had better watch out, with Miss Taylor coming along."

Otis L. Guernsey, Jr.,
NEW YORK HERALD TRIBUNE

With Carmen Miranda, Xavier Cugat and Jane Powell

Julia Misbehaves

A Metro-Goldwyn-Mayer Picture / 1948

CAST

Julia Packett: Greer Garson; *William Packett:* Walter Pidgeon; *Ritchie:* Peter Lawford; *Fred:* Cesar Romero; *Susan Packett:* Elizabeth Taylor; *Mrs. Packett:* Lucile Watson; *Colonel Willowbrook:* Nigel Bruce; *Mrs. Gennochio:* Mary Boland; *Bennie Hawkins:* Reginald Owen; *Hobson:* Ian Wolfe; *Daisy:* Phyllis Morris; *Jamie:* Edmond Breon; *Pepito:* Fritz Feld; *Gabby:* Marcelle Corday; *Louise:* Veda Ann Borg; *Vicar:* Aubrey Mather; *Lord Pennystone:* Henry Stephenson; *Lady Pennystone:* Winifred Harris; *Woman in Pawn Shop:* Elspeth Dudgeon; *Pawn Shop Clerk:* Stanley Fraser; *Bill Collector:* James Finlayson; *Postman:* Victor Wood; *Piano Player in Pub:* Herbert Wyndham; *Waiter in Pub:* Sid D'Albrook; *Drunk:* Jimmy Aubrey; *French Messenger:* Roland Dupré; *Bellhop:* Alex Goudavich; *Stage Doorman:* André Charlot; *The Head:* Joanee Wayne; *Train Official:* Mitchell Lewis; *Mannequins:* Joi Lansing, Lola Albright; *Commissar:* Torben Meyer.

CREDITS

Director: Jack Conway; *Producer:* Everett Riskin; *Screenwriters:* William Ludwig, Harry Ruskin, and Arthur Wimperis; *Adaptation:* Gina Kaus and Monckton Hoffe; *Based on the Novel* "The Nutmeg Tree" *by:* Margery Sharp; *Cinematographer:* Joseph Ruttenberg; *Art Directors:* Cedric Gibbons and Daniel B. Cathcart; *Musical Score:* Adolph Deutsch; *Editor:* John Dunning; *Song:* "When You're Playing with Fire" by Jerry Seelen and Hal Borne; *Running Time:* 99 minutes.

THE FILM

Margery Sharp's 1937 best-seller, *The Nutmeg Tree,* introduced the delightfully amoral character of Julia Packett, who was subsequently impersonated on Broadway in 1940 by Gladys Cooper in a stage version entitled *Lady in Waiting.* MGM had owned the rights to the Sharp property for some time when they decided to give the waning career of their Oscar-winning Greer Garson a light change of pace by making it a comedy vehicle in which to reunite her with her co-star of four previous dramas, Walter Pidgeon.

After adverse public reaction to Garson in the 1946 *Adventure* ("Gable's Back and Garson's Got Him!") and the really disastrous 1947 *Desire Me,* Metro was reluctant to give *Julia Misbehaves* the full Technicolor treatment. Consequently, although they gave their once-top dramatic star Pidgeon and an excellent supporting cast, the vehicle for her fling at champagne farce was a modest black-and-white production which the critics praised but faintly. For the most part, they thought Garson ill-advised and out of her element.

Julia Misbehaves is a slender comedy about an insolvent music-hall actress who returns to the society husband she left years ago, because her eighteen-year-old daughter is to be married and has sent for her. At the family estate, Julia discovers that her daughter Susan loves not her in-

With Peter Lawford

tended, but rather a young artist named Ritchie, and Julia maneuvers to bring them together before it's too late. A series of frantic misadventures results in the young couple's elopement and an unexpected romantic reunion for Julia and her estranged spouse.

Because of Elizabeth's convincing love scenes with Peter Lawford, MGM began to seriously consider her for more grown-up roles. *Julia Misbehaves* provided Elizabeth with her second screen kiss. Speaking of the experience, she has said, "Peter to me was the last word in sophistication. He was terribly handsome, and I had a tremendous crush on him." Although the couple teamed again the following year in *Little Women* and have remained great friends ever since, there was reportedly no off-screen romance between them. In 1948, Lawford was twenty-five, while Elizabeth was only sixteen and still very much under her mother's eye.

CRITICS' CORNER

"When Metro finally surrendered to Greer Garson's agonized pleas that it let her play something less lofty than the stuff she's accustomed to, it certainly capitulated with a rush to the opposite extreme. *Julia Misbehaves,* the obligement, is a fantastic knockabout farce which discovers Miss Garson in a bathtub and leaves her in a puddle of mud. And what makes it all the more embarrassing is that Metro has also required that she work in a little of her usual rendering of 'Hearts and Flowers.' A weepy scene with the daughter, Elizabeth Taylor, sees Miss Garson again being her customary noble and high-minded self.

"Maybe Miss Garson's wild adorers will think it the giddiest sort of lark, but it looks to this anxious observer like a fall on her beautiful face."

Bosley Crowther, THE NEW YORK TIMES

"The picture receives a most valuable decoration in the presence of Elizabeth Taylor, former child star, who has developed into one of the cinema's reigning queens of beauty and talent. She plays Julia's daughter with both sincerity and charm."
Otis L. Guernsey, Jr., NEW YORK HERALD TRIBUNE

"Although obvious in outline, the comedy bounces

With Peter Lawford, Walter
Pidgeon and Greer Garson

with merriment and is played strictly for laughs. Miss Garson's support is first-rate: husband Walter Pidgeon, daughter Elizabeth Taylor, junior romantic lead Peter Lawford, and elderly Lothario Nigel Bruce. Cesar Romero as a lovelorn acrobat contributes one of the funniest characterizations of the year, with Mary Boland doing a grand job as the mother of the Cockney acrobatic brood."

CUE

"A riot of screwball slapstick that never takes itself seriously for a single moment. Jack Conway's direction is fast and vigorous in walloping over the comedy.

"Elizabeth Taylor is the daughter who upsets her rich relatives when she elopes with an eager painter, elegantly portrayed by Peter Lawford. They shape up as a strong team of juves.

"The usual Metro elegance is found in production trappings that give smart physical framing to the comedy. Class lensing by Joseph Rutten-berg, art direction and settings, Adolph Deutsch's music score, tight editing and special effects are among contributions that lend production polish."

"Brog," VARIETY

"This semi-farcical rehash of *Madame X* might have been an entertaining movie, but it is done without gaiety, irony, style or even simple fun. MGM, long the world's number one star-polisher, has mishandled the stars in the show. Elizabeth Taylor, who is just beginning to move into grown-up roles, is one of the loveliest girls in movies; but here she is made-up and hair-done and directed into tired, tiresome conventional prettiness. Miss Garson has beauty, vitality and professional know-how. These are all visible, yet the performance is almost never joyous or even convincing. It looks as if she herself is trying her level best to be everything that Metro has made of her, and nothing that she really is."

TIME

With Walter Pidgeon

With Will Wright, June Allyson, Margaret O'Brien and Janet Leigh

Little Women

A Metro-Goldwyn-Mayer picture / 1949
In Technicolor

CAST

Jo March: June Allyson; *Laurie Laurence:* Peter Lawford; *Beth March:* Margaret O'Brien; *Amy March:* Elizabeth Taylor; *Meg March:* Janet Leigh; *Professor Bhaer:* Rossano Brazzi; *Marmee March:* Mary Astor; *Aunt March:* Lucile Watson; *Mr. Laurence:* Sir C. Aubrey Smith; *Hannah:* Elizabeth Patterson; *Mr. March:* Leon Ames; *Dr. Barnes:* Harry Davenport; *John Brooke:* Richard Stapley; *Mrs. Kirke:* Connie Gilchrist; *Sophie:* Ellen Corby; *Storekeeper:* Will Wright; *Schoolteacher:* Olin Howlin.

CREDITS

Director/Producer: Mervyn LeRoy; *Screenwriters:* Andrew Solt, Sarah Y. Mason, and Victor Heerman; *Based on the Novel by:* Louisa May Alcott; *Adaptation:* Sally Benson; *Cinematographers:* Robert Planck and Charles Schoenbaum; *Art Directors:* Cedric Gibbons and Paul Groesse; *Set Decorators:* Edwin B. Willis and Jack D.

Moore; *Musical Score:* Adolph Deutsch; *Editor:* Ralph E. Winters; *Costumes:* Walter Plunkett; *Running Time:* 122 minutes.

THE FILM

This was the third version of Louisa May Alcott's durable classic to reach the screen. In 1919, a silent adaptation featured the now-forgotten cast of Lillian Hall, Dorothy Bernard, Florence Flimm, and Isabel Lamon, for Paramount Artcraft. A far more distinguished sound version was produced for RKO in 1933 by David O. Selznick, with Katharine Hepburn, Joan Bennett, Jean Parker, and Frances Dee as, respectively, Jo, Amy, Beth, and Meg. In the mid-forties, Selznick began shooting a remake starring Jennifer Jones and Shirley Temple but inexplicably closed down production after three weeks of filming and abandoned the project altogether.

Mervyn LeRoy's 1949 production makes up,

in lush, Technicolored slickness, what it lacks in the finely honed characterizations of Selznick's 1933 black-and-white film. The familiar story of four Massachusetts girls who during their father's Civil War absence learn to grow up and find direction in their lives, was sweet and sentimental, played out against pretty Hollywood back-lot settings that were as unreal as the prismatic rainbow arching over the March homestead at the picture's finale. Although no Hepburn, June Allyson was well cast as Jo March, and played her dedicated-young-writer role with a tomboyish attractiveness that was not fully appreciated by the film's critics. As her selfish, conceited younger sister Amy, who snaps up Jo's rejected suitor Laurie for her *own* husband, Elizabeth Taylor (in a becoming blond wig) seemed perfectly cast —a logical variation on her Carol Pringle of *A Date with Judy*.

The 1949 *Little Women* bowed at New York's Radio City Music Hall and proved very successful for MGM, although it's not nearly so well remembered or respected as is the Selznick version. However, it did win Oscars for the four men responsible for its settings, as well as a nomination for its cameramen.

With June Allyson

With June Allyson, Janet Leigh and Margaret O'Brien

also arises a question whether or not the saccharine had to be piled on so heavily and so embarrassingly. LeRoy did not miss a single trick nor did he indulge in any oversights. There are no shadings. When things are bright, they practically dazzle. When they are dark, they are as unrevealing as the night."

MOTION PICTURE HERALD

"Louisa May Alcott's sentimental classic parades a new set of heroines in Mervyn LeRoy's episodic screen version. They labor in a generally unrewarding remake. Although the film has had the aid of three scenarists and is bright with Technicolor, it breaks into a series of tableaux, instead of being a warm and humorous recreation of family life in Concord at the time of the Civil War.

"Miss Allyson is not the best of Jo's. She is overly emphatic, both in her attempts to hold the March family together and her lachrymose outbursts. Elizabeth Taylor is lovely and properly spoiled in the part of Amy. As Marmee, Mary Astor turns in a sympathetic and honest characterization, which is of vast assistance in the recurring family groupings.

"LeRoy has spent great attention to period costumes and bric-à-brac. He has handled color well in his direction. What he has failed to do is to give *Little Women* the inherent vitality and

emotional sweep which has kept it a perennial favorite."

Howard Barnes, NEW YORK HERALD TRIBUNE

"Metro's fidelity to the book incorporates its strength and weakness. The sentiment is too meticulously preserved, a bit out of joint with our times.

"Playing the part which won critical plaudits for Katharine Hepburn back in '33, June Allyson shows that there is meat in the role for more than one actress. Her thesping dominates the film: it is well-paced, aptly touched with humor and it gets under the skin of the winning, restless and uncertain girl who is imbued with a little too much *joie-de-vivre* for her own peace of mind. On the basis of this pic, Miss Allyson is ready for major dramatic assignments.

"Direction of Mervyn LeRoy is sensitive and tasteful, if a bit too reverent of the sentimentalities of Victoriana. Sharper editing could have shipped up a faster start for *Women*, which flounders somewhat on a tedious and overly whimsical opening reel or two."

"Wit," VARIETY

"It is, of course, possible (as some cynics contend) that the calculated coyness and naiveté of

With Peter Lawford and June Allyson

this candy-tinted Technicolor tear-jerker may meet with some forthright resistance from our modern, hard-boiled Young Lollipop Set.

"The entire cast does nobly by Mrs. Alcott's venerable tome, with the exception of recent Italian-import Rossano Brazzi, who is inexcusably miscast as the German professor who loves and finally wins courageous, indomitable, starry-eyed Jo."

CUE

With Richard Stapley, Elizabeth Patterson, Margaret O'Brien, Janet Leigh, June Allyson, Mary Astor and Peter Lawford

With Robert Flemyng

Conspirator

A Metro-Goldwyn-Mayer Picture / 1950

CAST

Major Michael Curragh: Robert Taylor; *Melinda Greyton:* Elizabeth Taylor; *Captain Hugh Ladholme:* Robert Flemyng; *Colonel Hammerbrook:* Harold Warrender; *Joyce Penistone:* Honor Blackman; *Aunt Jessica:* Marjorie Fielding; *Broaders:* Thora Hird; *Lord Penistone:* Wilfrid Hyde-White; *Lady Penistone:* Marie Ney; *Henry Raglan:* Jack Allen; *Mrs. Hammerbrook:* Cicely Paget-Bowman; *Mark Radek:* Karel Stepanek; *Alek:* Nicholas Bruce; *Detective Inspector Weldon:* Cyril Smith; *Lady Witherington:* Helen Haye.

CREDITS

Director: Victor Saville; *Producer:* Arthur Hornblow, Jr.; *Screenwriter:* Sally Benson; *Based on the Novel by:* Humphrey Slater; *Adaptation:* Sally Benson and Gerard Fairlie; *Cinematographer:* F. A. ("Freddie") Young; *Art Director:* Alfred Junge; *Photographic Effects:* Tom Howard; *Musical Score:* John Wooldridge; *Editor:* Frank Clarke; *Running Time:* 87 minutes.

THE FILM

In 1949, at age seventeen, Elizabeth went to England to film *Conspirator,* in which she played her first really grown-up dramatic role—opposite thirty-eight-year-old Robert Taylor. Though obviously a bit younger than her co-star, she was then sufficiently mature and sophisticated to make this

With Honor Blackman and Robert
Flemyng

teaming believable, even though the script was
not.

Conspirator is among those of her early films
that Elizabeth claims she now wants to forget. In
fairly conventional terms, it relates the story of
an American girl visiting in London who is romantically swept off her feet by a British Guards
officer, whom she stays to marry, only to find out
that he's a steadfast Communist who's more inclined to kill her to pacify his party allegiances
than to change his way of life. In the end, once
she's finally come to see the kind of person he
really is, the major shoots himself.

For the most part, Conspirator is an ordinary
little black-and-white melodrama that could just
as well have been filmed in a Hollywood studio
as in Britain. However, the film does benefit by
some excellent English actors in the supporting
roles.

Elizabeth has commented on the irony of
alternating passionate love scenes with Robert
Taylor in tandem with the on-the-set school les-
sons then required of her by law.

CRITICS' CORNER

"An attempt to make capital of a topical theme
has failed dismally on the screen. Robert Taylor
is playing the traitor, so Elizabeth Taylor, natu-

rally, is the victim who falls for him. At no point
does Conspirator achieve the melodramatic impact which was evidently the intent of the film.
The hero is handsome and the heroine is pretty.
The script merely serves as a background for another screen romance."

Joe Pihodna, NEW YORK HERALD TRIBUNE

"Apart from its unconvincing treatment, the pic,
notwithstanding two box-office names in Robert
Taylor and Elizabeth Taylor, falls down in its
departure from normal convention. Here is a boy-
meets-girl plot without the familiar happy ending,
and this will inevitably disappoint many of the
younger fans.

"Taylor gets to grips with the starring role,
but the script doesn't allow wide scope and re-
stricts his performance within a limited frame.
Elizabeth Taylor is given a big opportunity for
an emotional and romantic lead, and comes out
with flying colors."

"Myro," VARIETY

"The anguish of a young wife who discovers that
her husband is a Soviet spy becomes an occasion
of torment for all of us before the film runs its
course. Conspirator is a lugubrious affair in which
Robert Taylor and Elizabeth Taylor are paired.

With Robert Taylor

Beyond sharing a common name and demonstrating a capacity for acting which shows obvious limitations in this instance, these particular Taylors are otherwise unrelated.

"Whatever its merits were as a book, *Conspirator* is a disappointment in film form, and since Sally Benson and Gerard Fairlie wrote the script in an uninspired mood, it should be recognized that the actors were working under a considerable handicap. Miss Taylor and Mr. Taylor are capable of doing better."

Thomas M. Pryor, THE NEW YORK TIMES

With Robert Taylor

With Rosemary DeCamp, Leon Ames and Van Johnson

The Big Hangover

A Metro-Goldwyn-Mayer Picture / 1950

CAST

David Maldon: Van Johnson; *Mary Belney;* Elizabeth Taylor; *John Belney:* Percy Waram; *Martha Belney:* Fay Holden; *Carl Bellcap:* Leon Ames; *Uncle Fred Mahoney:* Edgar Buchanan; *Kate Mahoney:* Selena Royle; *Charles Parkford:* Gene Lockhart; *Clare Bellcap:* Rosemary De-Camp; *Dr. Lee:* Phillip Ahn; *Williams:* Gordon Richards; *Mr. Rumlie:* Matt Moore; *Samuel C. Lang:* Pierre Watkin; *Steve Hughes:* Russell Hicks.

CREDITS

Director/Producer/Screenwriter: Norman Krasna; *Cinematographer:* George Folsey; *Art Directors:* Cedric Gibbons and Paul Groesse; *Set Decorators:* Edwin B. Willis and Henry W. Grace; *Special Effects:* Warren Newcome; *Musical Score:* Adolph Deutsch; *Editor:* Frederick Y. Smith; *Women's Costumes:* Helen Rose; *Running Time:* 82 minutes.

THE FILM

Directly upon her return from London and *Conspirator,* Metro put Elizabeth into this trivial romantic comedy with Van Johnson. The imminent prospect of a reunion with her then fiancé, ex-footballer and serviceman Glenn Davis, occupied the actress's mind more than did her role in this movie. Anticipating the end of a career that had ceased to matter to her, Elizabeth was more concerned with thoughts of marriage than with movies.

As a result of a wartime accident (he nearly drowned in brandy stored in the wine cellar of a monastery), young lawyer David Maldon (Van Johnson) is allergic to alcohol. The merest whiff makes him intoxicated. Mary Belney (Elizabeth Taylor), his boss's daughter, helps him to conquer his odd problem and sees him overcome some career problems brought on by his lofty idealism.

CRITICS' CORNER

"Norman Krasna has brewed a curious, cloudy mixture of farce, sociology and romance in *The Big Hangover.* He has directed it as though he expected the script and the stars to carry the ball on a team that cannot quite decide which goal

With Van Johnson, Percy Waram and Fay Holden

With Van Johnson and friend

to head for. Part clowning and part lesson, it is a disunified and hesitant piece of work.

"Elizabeth Taylor hovers on the edges of this comedy, dressed up like a mannequin. She has merely to appear interested or affectionate, while Johnson, on the comic side of things, is clean-cut and plaintive. There are a few laughs here, though the picture tends to repeat the same pieces of business."

Otis L. Guernsey, Jr., NEW YORK HERALD TRIBUNE

"This is a light, beguiling comedy with a great deal of charm. Norman Krasna has done a good job on his one-man show. Film gets a little too cute at times, and has a few dull stretches, but neither happens often enough to be serious.

"Miss Taylor is warm and appealing as the amateur psychiatrist, in a role more mature and adult than is usual for her. Johnson, too, is rather subdued and serious here, to just as warming effect."

"Bron," VARIETY

"Van Johnson gives a rather agreeable, if at times somewhat forced, performance. The boss's lovely daughter is most engagingly represented by Elizabeth Taylor.

"*The Big Hangover,* although it runs an uneven course, still is good for some laughs and is deserving of attention."

Thomas M. Pryor, THE NEW YORK TIMES

With Van Johnson, Fay Holden, Percy Waram, Anna Q. Nilsson and Gene Lockhart

With Spencer Tracy

Father of the Bride

A Metro-Goldwyn-Mayer Picture / 1950

CAST

Stanley T. Banks: Spencer Tracy; *Kay Banks:* Elizabeth Taylor; *Ellie Banks:* Joan Bennett; *Buckley Dunstan:* Don Taylor; *Doris Dunstan:* Billie Burke; *Mr. Massoula:* Leo G. Carroll; *Herbert Dunstan:* Moroni Olsen; *Mr. Tringle:* Melville Cooper; *Tommy Banks:* Rusty Tamblyn; *Warner:* Taylor Holmes; *The Reverend A. I. Galsworthy:* Paul Harvey; *Joe:* Frank Orth; *Ben Banks:* Tom Irish; *Delilah:* Marietta Canty; *Dixon:* Willard Waterman; *Fliss:* Nancy Valentine; *Effie:* Mary Jane Smith; *Peg:* Jacqueline Duval; *Miss Bellamy:* Fay Baker; *Duffy:* Frank Hyers;

Usher: Chris Drake; *Organist:* Douglas Spencer; *Fat Man:* Paul Maxey; *Young Man (Usher):* Peter Thompson; *Young Man With Coke (Usher):* Carleton Carpenter; *Timid Guest:* Frank Cady; *Teacher:* Lillian Bronson; *Stranger:* Thomas Browne Henry; *Movers:* Dewey Robinson, Ed Gargan, Ralph Peters, Dick Wessel, Dick Alexander, Joe Brown, Jr., Jim Hayward, Gil Perkins; *Foreman of Movers:* William "Bill" Phillips.

CREDITS

Director: Vincente Minnelli; *Producer:* Pandro

With Spencer Tracy and Joan Bennett

S. Berman; *Screenwriters:* Frances Goodrich and Albert Hackett; *Based on the Novel by:* Edward Streeter; *Cinematographer:* John Alton; *Art Directors:* Cedric Gibbons and Leonid Vasian; *Set Decorators:* Edwin B. Willis and Keogh Gleason; *Musical Score:* Adolph Deutsch; *Editor:* Ferris Webster; *Costumes:* Helen Rose and Walter Plunkett; *Running Time:* 93 minutes.

THE FILM

With a good script, Vincente Minnelli to direct, and the incomparable Spencer Tracy in the title role, *Father of the Bride* was a pleasant experi-ence that Elizabeth thoroughly enjoyed. When in an event almost simultaneous with the film's release in May, 1950, she and Nicky Hilton were married, the resultant publicity helped make the movie a box-office winner for MGM.

Father of the Bride is short on plot but long on amusing observations of character as a well-to-do family goes through the painful procedure of planning and executing a fully catered wedding and reception for their only daughter. Although Spencer Tracy blithely stole the film from everyone else, he had excellent support from Joan Bennett, in top comedy form as his wife, as well

With Tom Irish, Spencer Tracy, Don Taylor, Joan Bennett and Rusty Tamblyn

With Spencer Tracy

as from Elizabeth Taylor, perfectly cast as the daughter who threatens to upset all the family plans by not going through with her marriage after all. In *Father of the Bride,* everything finally *does* go off as planned, but not without a massive comedy-of-errors with which almost any audience could readily identify.

CRITICS' CORNER

"There is in this picture every episode of any consequence in the book, all constructed to illustrate completely the vast hilarity of preparing a girl to wed. And all of them add up to something that is grandly funny, sharp and just a bit sad.

"As a father, torn by jealousy, devotion, pride and righteous wrath, Mr. Tracy is tops. And right

beside him are Joan Bennett as the typical mother of the bride, Elizabeth Taylor as the happy little lady and Don Taylor as the overshadowed groom.

"*Father of the Bride* is a honey of a picture of American family life. It shouldn't discourage matrimony, but—well, this reviewer is certainly happy to have all sons."

Bosley Crowther, THE NEW YORK TIMES

"It's the second strong comedy in a row for Spencer Tracy, and he socks it. There's also the timely casting of Elizabeth Taylor as the bride (a role she just assumed in real life) to help stir wicket interest, and Joan Bennett completes the star trio with an elegant performance as the mother.

With Marietta Canty, Spencer Tracy, Tom Irish, Rusty Tamblyn and Joan Bennett

"The screenplay provides director Vincente Minnelli with choice situations and dialog, sliced right from life and hoked just enough to bring out the comedy flavor.

"On the critical side, but more or less minor quibbles: Minnelli could have timed many of the scenes so that laughs would not have stepped on dialog tag lines. Also he permits the wedding rehearsal sequence to play too long, lessening the comedic effect."

"Brog," VARIETY

"Specializing in situations and dialogue rather than story, the film is hilariously humorous. While limitless credit is the due of the writers, producer Pandro Berman and director Vincente Minnelli, it is a finely shaded, ingratiating performance by Spencer Tracy that sparkplugs the refreshingly wholesome mirth marathon."

BOXOFFICE

"Miss Taylor demonstrates that she is still in the promising-young-actress stage of her career. For quite a time to come, she is likely to stir up more fuss off screen than on."

Alton Cook, NEW YORK WORLD-TELEGRAM

"The picture accomplished a hard task stylishly and with airy confidence. It was no mean trick to keep the pre-matrimonial incidents coming along fast enough to sustain the gaiety, or to translate the written barbs into visual action. Under the direction of Vincente Minnelli, the whole problem has been worked out into irresistible good fun.

"Tracy is a fine figure of a man living hopelessly in what has suddenly become an alien woman's world. He holds the show together with a sure grip on his character. Elizabeth Taylor's good looks aid her in creating the illusion that in each succeeding scene the audience, like father, is seeing her for the first time."

Otis L. Guernsey, Jr.,
NEW YORK HERALD TRIBUNE

With Joan Bennett, Rusty Tamblyn, Spencer Tracy, Melville Cooper, Chris Drake, Carleton Carpenter, Charles Smith, Peter Thompson and unidentified player

With Joan Bennett, Don Taylor and Spencer Tracy

Father's Little Dividend

A Metro-Goldwyn-Mayer Picture / 1951

CAST

Stanley Banks: Spencer Tracy; *Ellie Banks:* Joan Bennett; *Kay Dunstan:* Elizabeth Taylor; *Buckley Dunstan:* Don Taylor; *Doris Dunstan:* Billie Burke; *Herbert Dunstan:* Moroni Olsen; *Delilah:* Marietta Canty; *Tommy Banks:* Rusty Tamblyn; *Ben Banks:* Tom Irish; *Dr. Andrew Nordell:* Hayden Rorke; *The Reverend Galsworthy:* Paul Harvey; *Police Sergeant:* Richard Rober; *Policeman:* Frank Faylen; *Nurse:* Beverly Thompson; *Taxi Driver:* Dabbs Greer; *Officer:* Robert B. Williams; *Diaper Man:* Frank Sully; *Mike:* James Menzies; *Red:* Thomas Menzies; *Old Man:* Harry Hines; *Bridesmaids:* Nancy Valentine, Wendy Waldron; *Elderly Man on Porch:* Lon Poff; *Gym Instructor:* George Bruggeman; *The Dividend:* Donald Clark.

CREDITS

Director: Vincente Minnelli; *Producer:* Pandro S. Berman; *Screenwriters:* Frances Goodrich and Albert Hackett; *Based on Characters Created by:* Edward Streeter; *Cinematographer:* John Alton; *Art Directors:* Cedric Gibbons and Leonid Vasian; *Musical Score:* Albert Sendrey; *Editor:* Ferris Webster; *Set Decorators:* Edwin Willis and Keogh Gleason; *Women's Costumes:* Helen Rose; *Running Time:* 82 minutes.

THE FILM

Filmed after *A Place in the Sun,* but released months before that George Stevens drama, *Father's Little Dividend* used the same cast and production crew of *Father of the Bride* to repeat the box-office formula of Spencer Tracy, true-to-life family foibles, and Elizabeth Taylor, whose off-screen marital break-up contrasted with the on-screen expectant-mother plot of the film. Although her private life fascinated the public, as it has always continued to do, Elizabeth's divorce from a Roman Catholic did nothing to harm her box-office attraction in an amusing, if predictable, movie like this one. Once again, Spencer Tracy

With Spencer Tracy, Don Taylor, Moroni Olsen, Billie Burke and Joan Bennett

stole the picture as he reluctantly came to face grandfatherhood. And again the mixture reaped financial rewards for Metro.

CRITICS' CORNER

"It is not very often that the sequel to a successful film turns out to be even half as successful or re-warding as the original picture was. But we've got to hand it to Metro: its sequel to *Father of the Bride* is so close that we'll willingly concede it to the humor and charm of that former film."

Bosley Crowther, THE NEW YORK TIMES

"All the players are just right in the roles to which they have become accustomed, but once again Spencer Tracy wraps the picture up with a grand comedy performance as an innocent bystander turned baby-sitter."

NEWSWEEK

"These further family adventures do not have the solid core of satire that the marriage saga en-joyed, but most of the vignettes are staged and acted with a light and pleasant touch. *Father's Little Dividend* is a buoyant, if not a hearty,

With Joan Bennett, Spencer Tracy and Don Taylor

With Moroni Olsen, Billie Burke,
Joan Bennett and Spencer Tracy

comedy—a cut above most attempts to follow on the footsteps of a popular act.

"Once again Vincente Minnelli has directed with a sensitive feeling for the humorous battle-ground of family affections. The script uses a lot of familiar parenthood jokes, telegraphing some of its laughs, but managing to maintain a satisfactory standard of fresh and wholesome entertainment."

Otis L. Guernsey, Jr., NEW YORK HERALD TRIBUNE

"*Dividend* does what few sequels are able to manage—measure up to the first. The glib script by Albert Hackett and Frances Goodrich, based on the characters created by Edward Streeter, misses none of the situations that make for laughs among those about to become grandparents or parents for the first time.

"Miss Bennett is good as Tracy's wife. Elizabeth Taylor beautifies her scenes as the new mother, and Don Taylor catches the right shading as the new father. Vincente Minnelli's direction races the film along neatly, playing strictly for laughs without going too far below the surface of the characters. Trouping, however, makes up for this, as does the scripting."

"Brog," VARIETY

With Spencer Tracy

With Montgomery Clift

A Place in the Sun

A Paramount Picture / 1951

CAST

George Eastman: Montgomery Clift; *Angela Vickers:* Elizabeth Taylor; *Alice Tripp:* Shelley Winters; *Hannah Eastman:* Anne Revere; *Marlowe:* Raymond Burr; *Charles Eastman:* Herbert Heyes; *Earl Eastman:* Keefe Brasselle; *Anthony Vickers:* Shepperd Strudwick; *Mrs. Vickers:* Frieda Inescort; *Dr. Wyeland:* Ian Wolfe; *Marsha Eastman:* Lois Chartrand; *Bellows:* Fred Clark; *Jansen:* Walter Sande; *Boatkeeper:* Douglas Spencer; *Coroner:* John Ridgely; *Mrs. Louise Eastman:* Kathryn Givney; *Judge:* Ted de Corsia; *Kelly:* Charles Dayton; *Reverend Morrison:* Paul Frees; *Mr. Whiting:* William Murphy; *Joe Parker:* John Reed; *Frances Brand:* Marilyn Dialon; *Secretary to Charles Eastman:* Josephine Whittell; *Truck Driver:* Frank Yaconelli; *Policeman:* Ralph A. Dunn; *Eagle Scout:* Bob Anderson; *Maid:* Lisa Golm; *Mrs. Roberts (Landlady):* Mary Kent; *Warden:* Ken Christy; *Martha:* Kathleen Freeman; *Butler at Eastman House:* Hans Moebus; *Butler:* Eric Wilton; *Motorcycle Officer:* Mike Mahoney; *Bailiff:* Al Ferguson; *Tom Tipton:* James W. Horne; *Miss Harper:* Laura Elliot; *Miss Newton:* Pearl Miller; *Jailer:* Major Philip Kieffer; *Man:* Major Sam Harris.

CREDITS

Director/Producer: George Stevens; *Screenwriters:* Michael Wilson and Harry Brown; *Based on the Novel "An American Tragedy" by:* Theodore Dreiser *and the stage adaptation of* Patrick Kearney; *Cinematographer:* William C. Mellor; *Art Directors:* Hans Dreier and Walter Tyler; *Musical Score:* Franz Waxman; *Editor:* William Hornbeck; *Costumes:* Edith Head; *Running Time:* 122 minutes.

THE FILM

In 1931, Josef von Sternberg directed an unsuccessful version of the Dreiser novel for Para-

With Montgomery Clift

mount, with Phillips Holmes and Sylvia Sidney in the leading roles portrayed in the remake by Montgomery Clift and Shelley Winters. In the early adaptation, Elizabeth Taylor's role of Angela (then called "Sondra" and played by Frances Dee, at the start of her career) is much smaller in size and importance than those of Holmes and Sidney. Indeed, in all but the basic story line, there is hardly any basis for comparison between the two films, only twenty years apart in copyright but eons distant in artistry.

The now-familiar story was Theodore Dreiser's first great success as a novelist in 1925. Based on an actual 1906 murder case, it told of a young man from lowly midwestern background who longs for the better things in life and is swept off his feet when he comes into contact with wealth and success. His love for a beautiful young society girl is threatened by the factory girl he's already made pregnant. The latter wants marriage, but the boy wants out. One day he takes her out on a lonely mountain lake, fully

With Montgomery Clift

intending to drown her and free himself of his past. When their boat capsizes, the fellow leaves his passenger to her fate while he swims for shore and escapes from the scene.

Eventually, he's caught and put on trial for murder (this part consumes the bulk of Dreiser's novel). And, although this antihero is eventually convicted of guilt by intent, he goes to his death uncertain of his degree of involvement in the crime. He only knows that he *wanted* to kill the deceased.

When MGM lent Elizabeth Taylor to Paramount for this film, she realized the importance of working with George Stevens and was very much in awe of Montgomery Clift, a former Broadway actor who enjoyed high praise and popular success in his first movies, especially Howard Hawks's *Red River* (1948). *A Place in the Sun* offered him a role so compatible with his offbeat, hesitant style of Method acting that it won him an Oscar nomination, as it also did Shelley Winters, pathetically impressive as his drab victim. The film itself won a Best Picture nomination. But none of them won. Instead, *A Place in the Sun* scored in its technical categories, sweeping away Academy Awards for director George Stevens, as well as its excellent screenplay, cinematography (black-and-white), score, editing, and costume design.

Elizabeth has called this movie, "The first time I even faintly considered acting, when I was young." Impressed with Clift's kindness in the face of being cast romantically opposite "a cheap movie star," she claims to have learned a lot from this professional alliance: "I watched Monty. I watched how much time he spent on concentration—which has since become the key to my kind of acting, if you can call it acting."

George Stevens has drawn from Elizabeth Taylor some of her best work. *A Place in the Sun* remains a high point in her career, and his 1956 *Giant* offered her a different kind of challenge, which she met with unexpected success. Much of the Dreiser story was filmed on location in wintry Lake Tahoe, where the snow had to be force-melted away with hoses to depict scenes at a summer lake. Despite the temperatures, Elizabeth swam, water skied, and played a love scene with Clift—as though it were summer. The film won her no acting prizes, but it did win Elizabeth her

With Shepperd Strudwick, unidentified player, Montgomery Clift and Frieda Inescort

With Montgomery Clift and Shepperd Strudwick

first critical praise and respect as an adult actress.

CRITICS' CORNER

"In the early 1930s, Paramount made a movie of Theodore Dreiser's 900-page novel, *An American Tragedy,* and Mr. Dreiser disliked the film treatment of his book to such a degree that he sought, unsuccessfully, in court to restrain the producers from showing it. If Mr. Dreiser were alive today, it is possible that he would have less to quarrel with in Paramount's second screen treatment of his work. This one is, by and large, an honest job of picture-making and one that sticks pretty close to the values of a story that has become an American classic.

"In the main, the success of *A Place in the Sun* is probably attributable to George Stevens, who produced and directed it with workmanlike, powerful restraint and without tricks or sociological harangue. He has drawn excellent performances from Montgomery Clift, who is thoroughly believable as the young man; Elizabeth Taylor, who is remarkably well cast as the daughter of a wealthy social clan; and Shelley Winters, who is particularly moving in the role of the unwanted sweetheart."

G. A., NEW YORK HERALD TRIBUNE

"This is Stevens's first picture in several years,

and it's first-class in every department and by every approach."

MOTION PICTURE HERALD

"It gives three young actors the chance to give the most natural performances of their careers. Until it sinks into a sentimental quagmire at the end, the second movie excels the first in being remarkably faithful to Dreiser's tale of three pitiful youngsters and in telling the story with the same earnestness and breadth that have made the novel survive as a classic."

LIFE

"Montgomery Clift, Shelley Winters and Elizabeth Taylor give wonderfully shaded and poignant performances. For Miss Taylor, at least, the histrionics are of a quality so far beyond anything she has done previously that Stevens' skilled hands on the reins must be credited with a minor miracle."

"Herb," VARIETY

"Miss Taylor deserves an Academy Award for her work. Raymond Burr, as the district attorney, dominates the final reels with a powerful portrayal."

BOXOFFICE

"This second screen edition of Theodore Dreiser's

With Montgomery Clift

monumental novel is a work of beauty, tenderness, power and insight. And, though Mr. Stevens, his scenarists and cast have switched its time and setting to the present and avoided extreme concentration on the social crusading of the book, *A Place in the Sun* emerges as a credit to both the motion-picture craft and, we feel reasonably certain, the author's major intentions. Out of Dreiser's often murky and turgid tale of the Twenties, scenarists Michael Wilson and Harry Brown have distilled the essence of tragedy and romance that is both moving and memorable. Retained too, in this two-hour drama—representing the painstakingly edited end-result of hundreds of thousands of feet of material shot—are characterizations which cleave to the Dreiser originals. Elizabeth Taylor's delineation of the rich and beauteous Angela is the top effort of her career. It is a shaded, tender performance and one in which her passionate and genuine romance avoids the pathos common to young love as it sometimes comes to the screen."

A. H. Weiler, THE NEW YORK TIMES

"Lacking the deeper significance that pervaded the book, *A Place in the Sun,* although frequently absorbing, is marred by a vague superficiality that causes it to lose any higher significance as drama, and fall somewhere in the area of a romantic triangle that devolves into a murder melodrama."

Jesse Zunser, CUE

"George Stevens' most highly respected work is an almost incredibly painstaking movie derived from Dreiser's *An American Tragedy.* It is full of meaning-charged details, murky psychological overtones, darkening landscapes, the eerie sounds of a loon, and overlapping dissolves designed to affect you emotionally without your conscious awareness.

"Whatever one thinks about it, it is a famous and impressive film. The performances by Montgomery Clift, Shelley Winters and Elizabeth Taylor are good enough (and Clift is almost too good, too sensitive), though they appear to be over-directed pawns. If Elizabeth Taylor had played the victim in this production, then the poor could at least be shown to have some natural assets. But Shelley Winters makes the victim so horrifyingly, naggingly pathetic that Clift hardly seems to be contemplating a crime: it's more like euthanasia."

Pauline Kael

Dorothy McGuire, Howard Keel,
Fred MacMurray and Ben Strobach

Callaway Went Thataway

A Metro-Goldwyn-Mayer Picture / 1951

CAST

Mike Frye: Fred MacMurray; *Deborah Patterson:* Dorothy McGuire; *"Smoky" Callaway/ "Stretch" Barnes:* Howard Keel; *Georgie Markham:* Jesse White; *Tom Lorrison:* Fay Roope; *Martha Lorrison:* Natalie Schafer; *The Drunk:* Douglas Kennedy; *Marie:* Elisabeth Fraser; *Johnny Terrento:* Johnny Indrisano; *Marvin:* Stan Freberg; *Director:* Don Haggerty; *Guest Stars:* June Allyson, Clark Gable, Dick Powell, Elizabeth Taylor, and Esther Williams.

CREDITS

Directed, Produced, and Written for the Screen by: Norman Panama and Melvin Frank; *Cinema-* *tographer:* Ray June; *Art Directors:* Cedric Gibbons and Eddie Imazu; *Musical Score:* Marlin Skiles; *Editor:* Cotton Warburton; *Running Time:* 81 minutes.

THE FILM

Sooner or later, most Hollywood studio contract players of the forties and fifties would appear as themselves, if briefly, in either a musical revue or a film that had a movie-capital background. Just such a story was *Callaway Went Thataway,* a clever and amusing spoof that featured Dorothy McGuire and Fred MacMurray as a pair of advertising promoters involved with the resurrection

[93]

of a movie cowboy's career through the showings of his early Westerns on television. In this case, Elizabeth Taylor appeared in a night-club sequence as herself, being introduced to the *real* cowboy (Howard Keel), who's brought in to impersonate screen-cowboy Callaway, whose penchant for dames and booze have temporarily clouded his whereabouts.

Although, for a lark, Elizabeth filled in as an "extra" in two other films, *Quo Vadis* and *Anne of the Thousand Days,* and played a surprise "cameo" role in *Scent of Mystery,* this was the only occasion in which she appeared in a movie as Elizabeth Taylor.

CRITICS' CORNER

"The gags fall thick and fast, the lines bounce off the screen bright and shiny and funny, and the whole adds up to good fun for all concerned."

Jesse Zunser, CUE

"Those who have had their fill of cowboys, TV style, should head this one off at Loew's State."

Bosley Crowther, THE NEW YORK TIMES

"Let it be said that this is a really hilarious comedy with situations that range from broad farce to very subtle humor. As a takeoff on television Westerns and, for that matter, on Hollywood and regular Westerns too, it can't be beat. The dialogue is crisp, witty and very funny, and no one is going to care whether or not the story makes sense.

"In some of the sequences, well-known stars on the Metro lot, like Clark Gable and Elizabeth Taylor, appear in a natural Hollywood setting. All concerned, from Keel, who has a dual role, to the beautiful Miss McGuire and the very capable MacMurray, are excellent. The accent is on laughs."

MOTION PICTURE HERALD

With unidentified player, Dorothy McGuire, Fred MacMurray and Howard Keel

With Larry Parks

Love Is Better Than Ever

A Metro-Goldwyn-Mayer Picture / 1952

CAST

Jud Parker: Larry Parks; *Anastacia Macaboy:* Elizabeth Taylor; *Mrs. Macaboy:* Josephine Hutchinson; *Mr. Macaboy:* Tom Tully; *Mrs. Levoy:* Ann Doran; *Pattie Marie Levoy:* Elinor Donohue; *Mrs. Kahrney:* Kathleen Freeman; *Albertina Kahrney:* Doreen McCann; *Hamlet:* Alex Gerry; *Smittie:* Dick Wessel.

CREDITS

Director: Stanley Donen; *Producer:* William H. Wright; *Screenwriter:* Ruth Brooks Flippen; *Cinematographer:* Harold Rosson; *Art Directors:* Cedric Gibbons and Gabriel Scognamillo; *Musical Score:* Lennie Hayton; *Editor:* George Boemler; *Running Time:* 81 minutes.

THE FILM

This slight romantic comedy about a beautiful young dance teacher from New Haven who is swept off her feet by a big-time talent agent (Larry Parks) while in New York City for a dance teachers' convention is pleasant and unpretentious, but nothing more. Made early in 1951, it was shelved for over a year when its leading man, Parks, was blacklisted for alleged Communist leanings. Freshly divorced from Nicky Hilton, Elizabeth was not in good health during the film's production, a period during which she was nearly inseparable from her director, Stanley Donen, himself newly freed from an unhappy marriage. However, Sara Taylor strongly disapproved of Donen and, by the time the film reached theaters, Elizabeth had married Michael Wilding.

CRITICS' CORNER

"It is strained and artificial comedy that is dispensed here under Stanley Donen's direction. Miss Taylor appears often in rehearsal tights, thereby displaying her physical charms, as well as the warm glow of a feminine personality. Parks gives an amiable performance as a breezy bachelor looking for nothing but a good time and,

With Larry Parks

With Josephine Hutchinson, Larry Parks and Dick Wessel

between them, the stars bring this picture just to the edge of something like romantic comedy.

"In its striving for novelty and local color, *Love Is Better Than Ever* must be credited with worthy aims, but it does not quite come out as scheduled by its creators."

Otis L. Guernsey, Jr., NEW YORK HERALD TRIBUNE

"This is a comedy about show business—the professional and amateur aspects of it. It is a pleasant and frothy concoction, with a light, humorous script that does not strain credulity."

MOTION PICTURE HERALD

"A lagging pace, uncertain direction and a none-too-skillful delivery of lines weakens what might otherwise have turned into a very funny little comedy about a pretty, small-town lambykin and how she outsmarted a bold, bad big-city wolf. It's too bad it missed.

"Quite surprisingly, Elizabeth Taylor indicates a nice talent for underplayed comedy in the role of the dancing-school mistress who braves the dangers of the big city and bags herself a husband. On the other hand, Larry Parks, as the caught-and-skinned Broadway wolf, is certainly not at his best—appearing stiff, uncomfortable and seemingly unhappy in this, his first picture in eighteen months."

Jesse Zunser, CUE

With Josephine Hutchinson

With George Sanders

Ivanhoe

A Metro-Goldwyn-Mayer Picture / 1952
In Technicolor

CAST

Ivanhoe: Robert Taylor; *Rebecca:* Elizabeth Taylor; *Rowena:* Joan Fontaine; *De Bois-Guilbert:* George Sanders; *Wamba:* Emlyn Williams; *Sir Hugh De Bracy:* Robert Douglas; *Cedric:* Finlay Currie; *Isaac:* Felix Aylmer; *Font De Boeuf:* Francis De Wolff; *Prince John:* Guy Rolfe; *King Richard:* Norman Wooland; *Waldemar Fitzurse:* Basil Sydney; *Locksley:* Harold Warrender; *Philip De Malvoisin:* Patrick Holt; *Ralph De Vipont:* Roderick Lovell; *Clerk of Copmanhurst:* Sebastian Cabot; *Hundebert:* John Ruddock; *Baldwin:* Michael Brennan; *Servant to Isaac:* Megs Jenkins; *Norman Guard:* Valentine Dyall; *Roger of Bermondsley:* Lionel Harris; *Austrian Monk:* Carl Jaffe.

CREDITS

Director: Richard Thorpe; *Producer:* Pandro S. Berman; *Screenwriter:* Noel Langley; *Based on the Novel by:* Sir Walter Scott; *Adaptation:* Aeneas McKenzie; *Cinematographer:* F. A. (Freddie) Young; *Art Director:* Alfred Junge; *Musical Score:* Miklos Rozsa; *Editor:* Frank Clarke; *Costumes:* Roger Furse; *Running Time:* 106 minutes.

THE FILM

Richard Thorpe's *Ivanhoe* was, oddly enough, only the third incarnation of Scott's classic to reach the screen. Both previous versions appeared in 1913: an American production, filmed on location in Britain by Herbert Brenon with King Baggott and Leah Baird as, respectively, Ivanhoe and Rebecca; and a British adaptation, hastily thrown together to cash in on the Yankee competition, in which Lauderdale Maitland and Edith Bracewell played the leads. In America, the latter version was retitled *Rebecca the Jewess*. In the

With Robert Taylor

mid-thirties, producer Walter Wanger announced plans to film the story with Gary Cooper, Madeleine Carroll, and Sylvia Sidney, but nothing came of it.

Metro's 1952 *Ivanhoe* represents a happy blend of pageantry, action, romance, and anti-Semitic subplot handled with admirable intelligence. Filmed at England's Boreham Wood Studios, this rousing tale of thirteenth-century Norman-Saxon Britain teamed the studio's two Taylors again as the star-crossed lovers in a film which Elizabeth underrates as "just a big medieval Western." Critics seemed united in commenting on the actress's beauty in this spectacular motion picture, though some deplored her inadequacy as a talent. The resultant performance might be reflected in the fact that Elizabeth was assigned to this overseas production against her will, since she knew that the role was not sizable and that her casting was designed partly to separate her from Stanley Donen. In fact, the studio even announced that Deborah Kerr would replace her as Rebecca, and that Margaret Leighton would likely portray Rowena. But, at the eleventh hour, Elizabeth agreed to do the film, after all, and Joan Fontaine was cast in the other female lead.

With George Sanders, Basil Sydney and Guy Rolfe

CRITICS' CORNER

"If Scott was concerned with the *facts* of history, MGM is clearly more concerned with the *appearance* of history—the court life, the battles, the tournaments of England at the end of the 12th Century, and Richard Thorpe has directed with a sharp eye for the pictorial. His action is full-scale and vigorous, presented with obvious relish. Robert Taylor makes a handsome Ivanhoe, George Sanders is superbly villainous as De Bois-Guilbert, and such accomplished players as Emlyn Williams, Finlay Currie, Felix Aylmer and Guy Rolfe dot the lengthy supporting cast. Only the distaff side is a bit weak. Elizabeth Taylor is beautiful enough as Rebecca, but clearly often beyond her dramatic depths; while Joan Fontaine, the Rowena of the film, has little to do but wait patiently for Ivanhoe to claim her in the final close-up."

SATURDAY REVIEW OF LITERATURE

"Elizabeth Taylor gives a sincere, if unrelieved, study of Rowena's rival in love."

"Myro," VARIETY

With Robert Taylor

"The women are no more successful as flesh-and-blood creatures in this *Ivanhoe* than in most tales of chivalry, but they fill the screen handsomely."

Otis L. Guernsey, Jr., NEW YORK HERALD TRIBUNE

"Meticulous attention to detail, plus a tightly written screenplay pays dividends in this magnificent re-creation of Sir Walter Scott's romantic novel. Curiously, the whole is greater than any of its parts. Critics may find fault with the acting of the principals and with the pace which, at times, is leisurely, but that will not dim the attraction of the stars' names on a marquee, nor lessen the pleasant glow which the over-all effect of the production is guaranteed to give any audience.

"The depiction of the pageantry of 12th-century England is more than fascinating enough to excuse the liberties taken first by Scott and second by the screenwriters with parts of history and some of the facts of life in Saxon-Norman England. The way it is told is better than the way it was.

"Above and beyond the individual perform-ances are the superbly detailed spectacle scenes. Outstanding are the siege and conquest of a Norman castle by English archers, easily the best seen on any screen."

MOTION PICTURE HERALD

"Aeneas McKenzie, who adapted the story, and Noel Langley, who wrote the script, have kept the story of Rebecca, the beautiful Jewess, and Isaac, her father, well to the fore. And they have emphasized such episodes in the novel as the beating of Isaac and the trial of Rebecca as a witch to highlight the sobering implications of the universal injustice of social bigotry. In this aspect of the drama, a remarkable forcefulness is achieved, and the picture brings off a serious lesson in fairness and tolerance not customary in spectacle films. Credit for this may be given to Elizabeth Taylor and Felix Aylmer, as well as to the men who made the film. For both of these able performers handle with grace and eloquence the frank and faceted characters of the rejected Jews."

Bosley Crowther, THE NEW YORK TIMES

With Robert Taylor, Joan Fontaine and Emlyn Williams

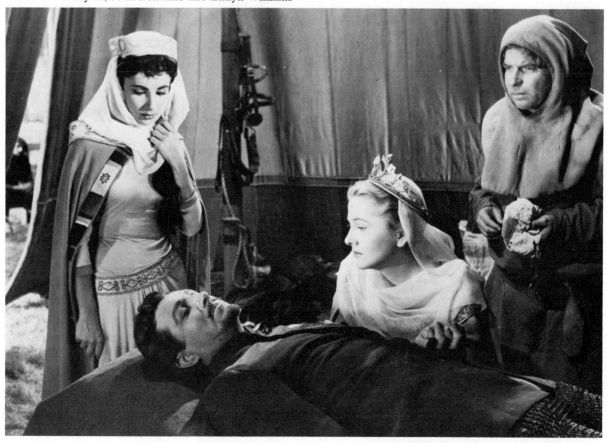

With Fernando Lamas and James
Whitmore

The Girl Who Had Everything

A Metro-Goldwyn-Mayer Picture / 1953

CAST

Jean Latimer: Elizabeth Taylor; *Victor Ramondi:*
Fernando Lamas; *Steve Latimer:* William Powell;
Vance Court: Gig Young; *Charles "Chico" Men-
low:* James Whitmore; *John Ashmond:* Robert
Burton; *Julian:* William Walker.

CREDITS

Director: Richard Thorpe; *Producer:* Armand
Deutsch; *Screenwriter:* Art Cohn; *Based on the
Novel* "A Free Soul" *by:* Adela Rogers St. Johns,
and the Subsequent Play by: Willard Mack; *Cine-
matographer:* Paul Vogel; *Art Directors:* Cedric
Gibbons and Randall Duell; *Musical Score:*
André Previn; *Editor:* Ben Lewis; *Costumes:*
Helen Rose; *Running Time:* 69 minutes.

THE FILM

For Elizabeth Taylor, this watered-down remake
of Metro's 1931 hit, *A Free Soul,* was a glossy
but unexciting programmer. After the expensive
pageantry of *Ivanhoe,* this little sixty-nine-minute
black-and-white melodrama was quite a come-
down. So unimportant was it that MGM didn't
even bother to secure a major New York opening
for it.

Elizabeth played the daughter of a wealthy
criminal lawyer (William Powell, in his last film
at the studio where he had once been an important star) who falls for one of her father's clients,
the crooked boss of a gambling syndicate. On the
eve of her wedding to this shady fellow (Fernando Lamas), the girl learns that her father is
about to bring him before a crime-investigation
committee. Gangster assaults lawyer, and daughter comes to her senses just in time, for her ex-
fiancé is then conveniently murdered by his fellow
mobsters, leaving the young lady to her old beau
(Gig Young).

In the 1928 Broadway play, *A Free Soul,* girl,
gangster, and lawyer were played, respectively, by

With William Powell

With Fernando Lamas and William Powell

Kay Johnson, Melvyn Douglas (his New York debut), and Lester Lonergan. Three years later, Hollywood brought it to the screen with Norma Shearer, Clark Gable, and Lionel Barrymore in these roles. That version was good enough, under Clarence Brown's direction, to win an Oscar for Barrymore and a nomination for Shearer. MGM's 1953 remake was not in the same class at all.

During this film, Elizabeth was signed to a new Metro contract, under the terms of which she would receive $5,000 a week, with 10 percent going to her mother. When it was announced that the actress was pregnant with her first child, this film's shooting schedule was carefully revised to accommodate her more strenuous scenes to release her before her condition might become obvious to the cameras.

CRITICS' CORNER

"Despite some name importance in the casting, it's just a fair program drama that will have to get by mostly with companion-feature bookings for its play-dates. Talents of William Powell, Elizabeth Taylor and Fernando Lamas are more or less wasted in the talky, implausible plot, and the dramatics seem dated, even though such modern touches as telecasts of U.S. crime investigation hearings are used.

"The script is a wild affair, long on dialog, and the characters aren't sufficiently lifelike to provide substance for Richard Thorpe's direction. Under his handling, the performances are smooth and polished, but the players can't do much with the soap opera–ish plotting. Armand Deutsch's production guidance drew on expert technical assists to dress up the physical look of the film,

but short-changed the paying customers on story value and entertainment."

"Brog," VARIETY

"The plot is a trifle sluggish at times, but the melodrama comes across in interesting fashion. Miss Taylor is her usual beautiful self, gracing the screen in formals, bathing suits and sports clothes. Lamas is convincing as the suave king of gamblers. Powell and the rest of the cast also register well."

MOTION PICTURE HERALD

"It is hard to tell which is the more irritating aspect of *The Girl Who Had Everything:* the thoroughly objectionable characters who people the plot or the pseudo-sophisticated air that the film adopts. This Hollywood-lush tale has been handled by Richard Thorpe with routine competence but no imagination; dialogue and incident are of the same monotonous order. Of the cast, William Powell turns in a familiarly wise-slick portrayal and Elizabeth Taylor, decoratively satisfying, plays a limited character with limited skill. The whole adds up to a graceless pattern of screen melodrama."

MONTHLY FILM BULLETIN

With William Powell, Robert Burton and Gig Young

[102]

With Vittorio Gassman and Michael Chekhov

Rhapsody

A Metro-Goldwyn-Mayer Picture / 1954
In Technicolor

CAST

Louise Durant: Elizabeth Taylor; *Paul Bronte:* Vittorio Gassman; *James Guest:* John Ericson; *Nicholas Durant:* Louis Calhern; *Professor Schuman:* Michael Chekhov; *Effie Cahill:* Barbara Bates; *Bruno Fürst:* Richard Hageman; *Otto Krafft:* Richard Lupino; *Frau Sigerlist:* Celia Lovsky; *Dove:* Stuart Whitman; *Mrs. Cahill:* Madge Blake; *Edmund Streller:* Jack Raine; *Madeleine:* Birgit Nielsen; *Yvonne:* Jacqueline Duval; *Student-Pianist:* Norma Nevens.

CREDITS

Director: Charles Vidor; *Producer:* Lawrence Weingarten; *Screenwriters:* Fay and Michael Kanin; *Based on the novel* "Maurice Guest" *by:* Henry Handel Richardson; *Adaptation:* Ruth and Augustus Goetz; *Cinematographer:* Robert Planck; *Art Directors:* Cedric Gibbons and Paul Groesse; *Set Decorators:* Edwin B. Willis and Hugh Hunt; *Special Effects:* A. Arnold Gillespie and Warren Newcombe; *Musical Adaptation:* Bronislau Kaper; *Musical Compositions:* Concerto in D Major for Violin and Orchestra by Peter Ilich Tchaikovsky; Concerto No. 2 in C Minor for Piano and Orchestra by Sergei Rachmaninoff; *Editor:* John Dunning; *Women's Costumes:* Helen Rose; *Running Time:* 115 minutes.

THE FILM

Rhapsody is the sort of glossy romantic drama in which Elizabeth Taylor models an expensive wardrobe, looks stunning, and wastes endless footage fluctuating between her affections for violinist Vittorio Gassman and pianist John Ericson—against beautiful European backgrounds, supplemented by a rich helping of classical music.

With John Ericson

If the film seemed longer than its 115-odd minutes, it might be due to the script by Fay and Michael Kanin, centering on a poor little romantically inclined rich girl who couldn't make up her mind. Indeed, right up to the final fade-out, it's a veritable tennis match between the man she married (Ericson) and the fellow (Gassman) who obsessed her. After a time, the average viewer couldn't care less and settles for the sheer, natural opulence of the movie's leading lady and/or the strains of Tchaikovsky and Rachmaninoff.

CRITICS' CORNER

"Music goes into one of Elizabeth Taylor's shell-like ears and out the other in *Rhapsody*. The dominant theme of this new Technicolor romance is whether Beauty has a right to possess Art or must merely serve it. There is beauty in the picture all right, with Miss Taylor glowing into the camera from every angle, and Art in the persons of Vittorio Gassman and John Ericson, as a pair of students, pretending to give concerts and pretending to love Miss Taylor. The music is fine, but the dramatic pretenses are weak, despite the lofty sentiments and handsome manikin poses.

"The point of the story is to show off Miss Taylor wearing attractive gowns, sobbing in loneliness, or radiant at a concert. It is a ravishing show of feminine charm, in vivid color, but director Charles Vidor has evoked hardly a single honest gesture or expression. Her animation is only the animation of a doll with the strings being pulled behind the scenes. Under these difficult circumstances, without flair in either script or direction, even her evident and genuine beauty seems at times to be a fake."

Otis L. Guernsey, Jr., NEW YORK HERALD TRIBUNE

With Stuart Whitman, Jacqueline Duval, Birgit Nielsen, Richard Lupino and Vittorio Gassman

"It is the type of tears-and-torment drama that has little appeal for the younger set or the male ticket buyer. Thus, despite a lavish presentation in Technicolor, the enduring music of Rachmaninoff and Tchaikovsky, plus a good cast, the picture will not find the boxoffice-going easy.

"The property was acquired from Paramount by Metro. The Culver City lot has given it the 'A' treatment in casting and production budget so that visually the presentation has an outstanding quality. As entertainment, however, it falters often, through stretching its pot-boiler plot over an unnecessarily long one hour and 55 minutes. The story and the characters in it haven't the depth to sustain that much running time.

"Music, of course, is standout as played by Claudio Arrau (Rachmaninoff) and Michael Rabin (Tchaikovsky). These piano and violin solo stints, respectively, are high artistry."

"Brog," VARIETY

"Elizabeth Taylor is always decorative to look at; Vittorio Gassman and John Ericson cope bravely with violin and piano and give sympathetic performances. Claudio Arrau's recordings are particularly to be admired; it seems doubtful, however, if the heroine was aware that she had, in fact, picked the winner from a musical point of view."

MONTHLY FILM BULLETIN

"Miss Taylor never looked lovelier than she does in this high-minded film, which is all wrapped up in music on the starry-eyed classical plane. Her wind-blown black hair frames her features like an ebony aureole, and her large eyes and red lips glisten warmly in the close-ups on the softly lighted screen. Any gent who would go for music with this radiant—and rich—Miss Taylor at hand is not a red-blooded American. Or else he's soft in the head."

Bosley Crowther, THE NEW YORK TIMES

With Vittorio Gassman

With Dana Andrews

Elephant Walk

A Paramount Picture / 1954
In Technicolor

CAST

Ruth Wiley: Elizabeth Taylor; *Dick Carver:* Dana Andrews; *John Wiley:* Peter Finch; *Appuhamy:* Abraham Sofaer; *Dr. Pereira:* Abner Biberman; *Atkinson:* Noel Drayton; *Mrs. Lakin:* Rosalind Ivan; *Strawson:* Barry Bernard; *Ralph:* Philip Tonge; *Gregory:* Edward Ashley; *Chisholm:* Leo Britt; *Rayna:* Mylee Haulani; and the Madhyma Lanka Mandala Dancers.

CREDITS

Director: William Dieterle; *Producer:* Irving Asher; *Screenwriter:* John Lee Mahin; *Based on the Novel by:* Robert Standish; *Cinematographer:* Loyal Griggs; *Art Directors:* Hal Pereira and Joseph MacMillan Johnson; *Set Decorators:* Sam Comer and Grace Gregory; *Special Effects:* John P. Fulton and Paul Lerpae; *Process Photography:* Farciot Edouart; *Musical Score:* Franz Waxman; *Editor:* George Tomasini; *Costumes:* Edith Head; *Running Time:* 103 minutes.

THE FILM

Originally, producer Irving Asher had intended his production of the Robert Standish novel about a triangular romantic situation on a Ceylonese tea plantation as a vehicle for Elizabeth Taylor, whom he hoped to borrow from MGM. However, the actress's pregnancy prevented her from accepting the role, and Asher then decided *Elephant Walk* would be well served by the joint abilities of Laurence Olivier and his then wife, Vivien Leigh. Olivier was still too busy with *The Beggar's Opera,* filming in London, but his wife was signed, with the understanding that a month's location shooting in Ceylon would precede Hollywood studio interiors at Paramount. The hackneyed script failed to deter Vivien Leigh; she was pleased at the prospect of a role not requiring the extremes of neurotic behavior to which she was usually driven professionally. Although considered completely recovered from a bout with tuberculosis, the British actress found the heat and humidity of Ceylon overpowering, and she suffered from insomnia. After a month of location work, very close to exhaustion, she journeyed to Hollywood with the company but managed only two weeks of studio work before collapsing completely with a nervous breakdown.

Forced to accept the fact that Vivien Leigh could not finish the film, Irving Asher reasoned that, if he now obtained Elizabeth Taylor—the two actresses were similar in height and build—he could still use most of the Ceylon footage. In fact, only about 10 percent of his location shooting had to be scrapped.

Elizabeth cost Paramount a pretty penny for this role, because Metro, which had a new Taylor vehicle ready to start, put her services at a stiff price: the outright sum demanded was $150,000, plus a penalty of $3,500 a day for delaying their own production. Of the twenty-six costumes made for Leigh, Edith Head had to let out twenty to accommodate Elizabeth's somewhat fuller measurements. The remaining six had to be remade.

But production problems on the film had not yet ended: Elizabeth nearly lost the sight in one eye when a steel splinter from a wind machine lodged there, requiring her hospitalization.

CRITICS' CORNER

"The novelty of the Ceylon backgrounds and pictorial beauty are recommendable points in *Elephant Walk,* an otherwise leisurely paced romantic drama that strolls through an hour and 42 minutes. There's not enough dramatic wallop in the yarn to carry that much footage so, overall, the film's appeal and b.o. chances appear moderate. Had both screenwriter Mahin and director Dieterle concentrated more on the dramatic points along the way and less on unnecessary detail, it would have been a better show. Of interest, tradewise, is the fact that in some of the Ceylon-filmed longshots, Vivien Leigh is still seen, although not noticeably so. Noteworthy among the production values are Loyal Griggs' color lensing, Franz Waxman's score and the dazzling Edith Head costumes that complement Miss Taylor's natural beauty."

"Brog," VARIETY

"The story about the rich, powerful planter who brings a tender female into the jungle as his bride has cropped up again in *Elephant Walk.* The plantation, of course, must always be endangered by some kind of wildlife. Recently, in *The Naked Jungle,* it was ants. In the new one it is elephants.

With Dana Andrews, Abner Biberman and Abraham Sofaer

Thus, Miss Taylor is threatened by the echoed will of a ghost, by a herd of wild animals and by the bad temper of her husband, played by Peter Finch. Dana Andrews, as the plantation overseer, admires her beauty and lends her a helping hand occasionally. Most of the time, though, Miss Taylor must go it alone, knitting her symmetrical eyebrows over a cholera epidemic, drunken house guests and a disobedient native major-domo.

"Trick photography gives you the illusion that human beings are mixed up with a herd of

With Abner Biberman and Peter Finch

rampaging elephants in the finale, and William Dieterle has staged a game that looks like quite a lot of fun: polo on bicycles indoors on a polished marble floor. Otherwise, there is nothing stimulating going on in *Elephant Walk*."

Otis L. Guernsey, Jr., NEW YORK HERALD TRIBUNE

"This sort of menace melodrama has to be done awfully well to hold. Unfortunately, the script that John Lee Mahin prepared from the Robert Standish book is lengthy and hackneyed in the build-up, and William Dieterle's direction does not provide anything more than gaudy panoramas of a tropical palace to fascinate the eye.

"Miss Taylor's performance of the young wife is petulant and smug. Mr. Andrews is pompous as the manager. And Mr. Finch, as the husband, is just plain bad."

Bosley Crowther, THE NEW YORK TIMES

"Elizabeth Taylor, though pretty and charming, fails to convey much in the way of character."

MONTHLY FILM BULLETIN

"The producers of MGM's *Rhapsody* and Paramount's *Elephant Walk* have placed Elizabeth Taylor, the star of both films, in the incredible position of being rejected by a total of four men she chooses to love. Elizabeth puts up a game fight, though. She wins their reluctant hearts by means of sheer grit, rather than through her natural charms—a most unsatisfactory arrangement for any girl. These woeful tales, however, have a curious power in the hands of Miss Taylor—an indication of her growing talents as an adult and honest actress, who can make an audience believe just about anything."

LOOK

With Peter Finch

With James Donald

Beau Brummell

A Metro-Goldwyn-Mayer Picture / 1954
In Eastman Color

CAST

Beau Brummell: Stewart Granger; *Lady Patricia:* Elizabeth Taylor; *Prince of Wales:* Peter Ustinov; *King George III:* Robert Morley; *Lord Edwin Mercer:* James Donald; *Mortimer:* James Hayter; *Mrs. Fitzherbert:* Rosemary Harris; *William Pitt:* Paul Rogers; *Lord Byron:* Noel Willman; *Midger:* Peter Dyneley; *Sir Geoffrey Baker:* Charles Carson; *Doctor Warren:* Ernest Clark; *Mr. Fox:* Peter Bull; *Mr. Burke:* Mark Dignam; *Colonel:* Desmond Roberts; *Thurlow:* David Horne; *Sir* *Ralph Sidley:* Ralph Truman; *Mr. Tupp:* Elwyn Brook-Jones; *Doctor Dubois:* George De Warfaz; *Dr. Willis:* Henry Oscar; *Mayor:* Harold Kasket.

CREDITS

Director: Curtis Bernhardt; *Producer:* Sam Zimbalist; *Screenwriter:* Karl Tunberg; *Based on the play by:* Clyde Fitch; *Cinematographer:* Oswald Morris; *Art Director:* Alfred Junge; *Photographic Effects:* Tom Howard; *Musical Score:* Richard

With Rosemary Harris and Peter Ustinov

Addinsell; *Editor:* Frank Clarke; *Costumes:* Elizabeth Haffenden; *Running Time:* 111 minutes.

THE FILM

Clyde Fitch's 1890 play had been written expressly as a vehicle for stage star Richard Mansfield. In 1924, Warner Brothers brought it to the screen as a vehicle for John Barrymore. Mary Astor co-starred as "Lady Margery" (the counterpart of "Lady Patricia," Elizabeth Taylor's role in the 1954 remake).

In essence, *Beau Brummell* is the story of the sartorial dandy who rose by his wits from a servant-class background to become the court favorite of the pleasure-loving Hanoverian Prince of Wales. Popular with the court ladies, Beau has eyes only for the beautiful Lady Patricia, who's engaged to marry the stolid Lord Mercer. But

With Peter Ustinov, Rosemary Harris, Charles Carson, unidentified player and Stewart Granger

With Stewart Granger

With Rosemary Harris, Stewart
Granger and Peter Ustinov

their love is ill-starred: Beau falls into disfavor at
the court and is banished, becomes bankrupt, and
goes to debtors' prison. His pride prevents his
marriage to Lady Patricia, who weds Mercer. In
France, before he dies, Beau is reconciled with
the prince, now King George IV.

The 1954 version of this romantic drama was
filmed entirely in Britain, with interiors largely
shot at MGM's Boreham Wood studios. Location
scenes were photographed in and about Ockwell
Manor, built in the early fifteenth century and
considered one of England's great historic mansions. It is situated near Windsor Castle and still
maintained in perfect condition.

Beau Brummell is not one of Elizabeth Taylor's favorite early movies. Years later, she remarked, "I never saw that film until after Richard
and I were married. It was on television and
Richard turned it on. I had to change stations
after about five minutes—I mean, I was so embarrassing in it."

CRITICS' CORNER

"Beau Brummell is an elaborate Technicolor
period piece, lofty in manner and principle. Many
of the performers in it are china figures, including Elizabeth Taylor as an eligible maiden of
fashion. The notable exception is Peter Ustinov's
performance, which cuts through the high gloss
and rigid poses of fancy-dress history. His lonely,

With James Donald

pompous prince is animate and touching. Granger's Brummell is a standard adventurer, resounding with bravado as he sets out to conquer the world with the color of his hunting coat and the cut of his trousers. As for Miss Taylor, she is decorative, but something less than useful as a heroine who cannot quite make up her mind between Beau and a stolid young lord."

Otis L. Guernsey, Jr., NEW YORK HERALD TRIBUNE

"Mr. Granger is a tall, muscular sort, who seldom permits the demands of his craft to jolt him out of a handsome complacency. But, in his current venture, he runs head-on into a death scene, with all its histrionic requirements. These he meets with some very powerful breathing—so powerful, it's rather a relief when he stops toying noisily with the summons from above and accepts it. Before Mr. Granger wheezes himself into the beyond, he is his usual self—full of a belowstairs hauteur and a general aloofness to his situation. We also have a girl named Lady Patricia, who, as enacted by Elizabeth Taylor, is a misty, if beautiful type."

John McCarten, THE NEW YORKER

"*Beau Brummell* is adapted from Clyde Fitch's earliest success (1890). Despite the admiration of his contemporaries, Fitch's style—the Mansfield style—is now fatally dated, and it is difficult to see why his play should have been taken as the basis for this elaborate new historical romance.

What remains of the play in this film is formless, bodyless and tediously written.

"Out of this unlikely material, Peter Ustinov and Robert Morley alone draw anything of value—the first with a careful, academic portrayal of the Prince as a pettishly benevolent booby, the second in a splendidly suitable barn-storming mad scene. The more formal players are quite overwhelmed, however. Stewart Granger wears his clothes gracefully and dies with dignity; Elizabeth Taylor makes a barely articulate Lady Patricia. For a brief moment, Rosemary Harris is almost touching as Mrs. Fitzherbert.

"On the credit side, it must be admitted that the settings (though not always the costumes) are sumptuous yet tasteful, and the photography and colour most handsome."

MONTHLY FILM BULLETIN

"The lovely young lady with whom Beau Brummell is supposed to be in love—and who is endowed by Miss Taylor with dazzling beauty and the blossoms of appeal—is a foggy creature who is never made sensibly clear. However, the picture is gorgeous and that's the only word—gorgeous—in settings, in costumes and in its photography. Mainly, it is in the taste and artfulness of design, in the exquisite blendings of colors and in the mellow effects achieved through superlative use of the camera that *Beau Brummell* becomes a lovely film."

Bosley Crowther, THE NEW YORK TIMES

With Peter Ustinov, James Donald and unidentified players

With Van Johnson

The Last Time I Saw Paris

A Metro-Goldwyn-Mayer Picture / 1954
In Technicolor

CAST

Helen Ellswirth: Elizabeth Taylor; *Charles Wills:* Van Johnson; *James Ellswirth:* Walter Pidgeon; *Marion Ellswirth:* Donna Reed; *Lorraine Quarl:* Eva Gabor; *Maurice:* Kurt Kasznar; *Claude Matine:* George Dolenz; *Paul:* Roger Moore; *Vicki:* Sandy Descher; *Mama:* Celia Lovsky; *Barney:* Peter Leeds; *Campbell:* John Doucette; *Singer:* Odette.

CREDITS

Director: Richard Brooks; *Producer:* Jack Cummings; *Screenwriters:* Julius J. Epstein, Philip G. Epstein, and Richard Brooks; *Based on the Story* "Babylon Revisited" *by:* F. Scott Fitzgerald; *Cinematographer:* Joseph Ruttenberg; *Art Directors:* Cedric Gibbons and Randall Duell; *Set Decorators:* Edwin B. Willis and Jack D. Moore; *Special Effects:* A. Arnold Gillespie; *Musical Score:* Conrad Salinger; *Song:* "The Last Time I Saw Paris" by Jerome Kern and Oscar Hammer-stein II; *Editor:* John Dunning; *Costumes:* Helen Rose; *Running Time:* 116 minutes.

THE FILM

For this, their reunion film, Elizabeth Taylor and Van Johnson traded places, with the female star now important enough to get top billing, thus reflecting her considerable rise in popularity at the box-office since *The Big Hangover,* just four years earlier.

In a 1964 *New York Times* interview with Howard Thompson, Elizabeth remarked, "Rather curiously, a not-so-good picture, *The Last Time I Saw Paris,* first convinced me I wanted to be an actress, instead of yawning my way through parts. That girl was off-beat with mercurial flashes of instability—more than just glib dialogue." In agreement, quite a few of her critics admired this performance, if not the film itself.

Told in flashback, the story centers on a suc-

With Van Johnson and Sandy
Descher

cessful American novelist (Van Johnson) who returns to Paris and a reunion with the child he left in the custody of his sister-in-law (Donna Reed), since the death of his wife (Elizabeth Taylor). The time then reverts to World War II Europe, where Johnson first met Taylor, romanced her, and married her. Their life is busy and social, among the leisure set. When their daughter is born, things change: the Parisian social life bores Taylor, and Johnson, unhappy in his failure as a writer, takes to the bottle. Taylor contracts pneumonia and dies, and Johnson returns to America, where he eventually finds success as a novelist.

CRITICS CORNER

"While it is too long in the telling, dissipating some of its emotional effect in the process, it features Elizabeth Taylor looking incredibly lovely, in the best performance of her career and Director Richard Brooks has gotten such excellent performances from the rest of the cast that interest is sustained even when the action lags."

THE FILM DAILY

"This is an unhappy example of the sort of travesty that Hollywood can produce when distinguished material is re-shaped and re-written to the supposed dictates of the box-office. The trans-

With Van Johnson and extras

planting of the story from the late twenties to the present is unfortunate, though not disastrous: but disaster comes with the glib sentimentalizing, the confecting of a happy ending and the consequent destruction of the story's whole moral framework.

"Even if one considers the film without reference to the F. Scott Fitzgerald original, it emerges only as a flat and lugubrious affair, reaching vaguely for something altogether outside its grasp. Richard Brooks' direction is slick but insensitive, and neither Elizabeth Taylor nor Van Johnson—though he makes a gallant attempt—prove equal to the demands made on them."

Penelope Houston, MONTHLY FILM BULLETIN

"Performancewise, Miss Taylor's work as the heroine should be a milestone for her. It is her best work to date and shows a thorough grasp of the character, which she makes warm and real, not just beautiful. Brooks' direction also gets a sock response from Johnson. The latter's portrayal of the Fitzgerald hero easily lines up with his best.

"The post-war period of the footage, which

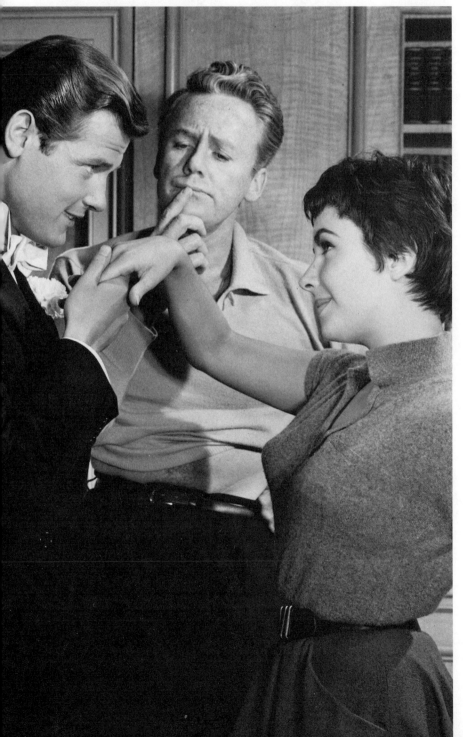

With Roger Moore and Van Johnson

With Van Johnson

occupies most of it, is rich with Parisian flavor, and the script and Brooks' direction are the nearest thing yet to re-creating the reckless gaiety that Fitzgerald caught in his writings."

"Brog," VARIETY

"The story is trite. The motivations are thin. The writing is glossy and pedestrian. The acting is pretty much forced. Mr. Johnson as the husband is too bumptious when happy and too dreary when drunk; Miss Taylor as the wife is delectable, but she is also occasionally quite dull.

"But the soft soap is smeared so smoothly and that sweet old Jerome Kern tune, from which the title is taken, is played so insistently that it may turn the public's heart to toothpaste."

Bosley Crowther, THE NEW YORK TIMES

"F. Scott Fitzgerald's *Babylon Revisited* is now a movie called *The Last Time I Saw Paris*. Incidents and references in this short story have been dramatized into a sprawling, color-splashed drink-by-drink account of a marriage reeling toward a sad conclusion in the mixed-up Paris following World War II. What the story amounts to now is a stylish and handsome tearjerker, full of Parisian glitter and bared emotions, with Van Johnson rising to a magnificent outburst of grief and longing at the end. Richard Brooks' direction has helped to bring out the best in Johnson, and it has done the same for Miss Taylor. She is not only a stunning creature but a vibrant one as she flings herself into the role of an impetuous, alluring, pleasure-loving beauty. She wears yellow and red—the colors of gaiety—but her performance is such that disillusionment is never out of sight. All concerned have done a capable job with the lesser materials at hand."

Otis L. Guernsey, Jr., NEW YORK HERALD TRIBUNE

With Roger Moore

With Rock Hudson, Napoleon Whiting, Carolyn Craig, Judith Evelyn and Paul Fix

Giant

A Warner Brothers Picture / 1956
In WarnerColor

CAST

Leslie Lynnton Benedict: Elizabeth Taylor; *Bick Benedict:* Rock Hudson; *Jett Rink:* James Dean; *Luz Benedict II:* Carroll Baker; *Vashti Snythe:* Jane Withers; *Uncle Bawley:* Chill Wills; *Luz Benedict;* Mercedes McCambridge; *Angel Obregon III:* Sal Mineo; *Jordan Benedict III:* Dennis Hopper; *Mrs. Horace Lynnton:* Judith Evelyn; *Dr. Horace Lynnton:* Paul Fix; *Sir David Karfrey:* Rod Taylor; *Bob Dace:* Earl Holliman; *Pinky Snythe:* Robert Nichols; *Old Polo:* Alexander Scourby; *Judy Benedict:* Fran Bennett; *Whitside:* Charles Watts; *Juana:* Elsa Cardenas; *Lacey Lynnton:* Carolyn Craig; *Bale Clinch:* Monte Hale; *Adarene Clinch:* Mary Ann Edwards; *Gabe Target:* Sheb Wooley; *Angel Obregon I:* Victor Millan; *Sarge:* Mickey Simpson; *Mrs. Obregon:* Pilar del Rey; *Dr. Guerra:* Maurice Jara; *Lorna Lane:* Noreen Nash; *Swazey:* Napoleon Whiting; *Lupe:* Tina Menard; *Watts:* Ray Whitley; *Go-mez:* Felipe Turich; *Mexican Priest:* Francisco Villalobos; *Petra:* Ana Maria Majalca; *Harper:* Guy Teague; *Eusebio:* Nativadid Vacio; *Dr. Walker:* Max Terhune; *Dr. Borneholm:* Ray Bennett; *Mary Lou Decker:* Barbara Barrie; *Vern Decker:* George Dunne; *Clay Hodgins:* Slim Talbot; *Clay Hodgins, Sr.:* Tex Driscoll; *Essie Lou Hodgins:* Juney Ellis.

CREDITS

Director: George Stevens; *Producers:* George Stevens and Henry Ginsberg; *Screenwriters:* Fred Guiol and Ivan Moffat; *Based on the Novel by:* Edna Ferber; *Cinematographer:* William C. Mellor; *Production Designer:* Boris Leven, *with* Ralph Hurst; *Musical Score:* Dimitri Tiomkin; *Editor:* William Hornbeck; *Costumes:* Marjorie Best and Moss Mabry; *Running Time:* 198 minutes.

With James Dean

THE FILM

For *Giant,* Elizabeth Taylor returned to Warner Brothers, the studio where she had filmed *Life with Father,* also on loan from Metro, nine years earlier. This was her second film with George Stevens, a director famous for his painstaking

details, his extravagant shooting methods, and the long gestation periods spent creating his later movies. (In the five-year interlude since *A Place in the Sun,* he had managed to turn out only *Shane;* a sporadic yet distinguished output). Working with Stevens was, according to Taylor,

With Rock Hudson and Mercedes McCambridge

no breeze. Although she describes making her first Stevens film in a state of "hero worship," *Giant* was much harder.

Edna Ferber's mammoth novel about Texas ranchers and oil kings has never set well with certain residents of the Lone Star State, for it's critical of them, of their wealth and their excesses. In three hours and eighteen minutes of screen time, Stevens focused on the major part of this ambitious theme, centering on one young Texan (Rock Hudson) who brings back a bride (Elizabeth Taylor) after a whirlwind trip to Maryland on a horse-buying mission. As the mistress of her husband's vast Reata Ranch, the young Eastern wife has to contend with the jealousy of his unmarried sister, racial prejudice between Texans and Mexicans, and the hesitant attentions of a wild young ranchhand (James Dean), hell-bent on becoming a millionaire.

As the years pass, husband and wife raise two children, see the ex-ranchhand become a powerful oilman, and come face to face with an interracial marriage in the family.

At twenty-three, Elizabeth admirably came

With James Dean

to grips with a time-spanning, plum role for which Stevens had originally—and unsuccessfully —sought Grace Kelly. Having been his second choice seems not to have bothered his eventual female lead in the slightest; realizing the acting talent of Oscar-winner Kelly, in comparison with her own at that time, Elizabeth recalls only the feeling of gratitude and challenge with which she met the test.

With Rock Hudson

[122]

Critical notices were, on the whole, extremely favorable toward the film's three young stars; although there were some who thought each was more successful in the film's earlier portions than in portraying advanced middle age. Elizabeth recalls *Giant* with pride, and it remains among Rock Hudson's personal favorites. While the film was still in production, and only days after the completion of his own scenes, James Dean was killed in a sports-car accident.

Although nominated for a total of ten Academy Awards, including those for best picture, actors Dean and Hudson, actress Mercedes McCambridge, screenplay, and score, *Giant* only managed to cop one award—for George Stevens's direction.

CRITICS' CORNER

"In turning Edna Ferber's Texas novel into a motion picture, Producer-Director George Stevens focuses his camera almost exclusively on personal relationships. Burgeoning oilfields, monstrous hotels, racial conflict—all of these aspects of Texas life are set forth graphically in terms of the people involved.

"Elizabeth Taylor's portrayal of Leslie Bene-

dict . . . is compounded of equal parts of fervor and Ferber, and she grows old with a grace and sweetness that can arouse only admiration and envy. Rock Hudson doesn't plumb any depths as Bick Benedict, but he does play the part with a straight-forward honesty and convincing appearance."

Herbert Kupferberg, NEW YORK HERALD TRIBUNE

"Miss Taylor, required by her role to age 30 years, gives her usual alert, effectual performance in the earlier years of her role, and then displays a new artistry in meeting the sterner demands of parenthood and grandmotherhood. Dean lives up to his past performances in the youthful phase of his portrayal, but is less convincing, later on, as a drunken oil king."

MOTION PICTURE HERALD

"A tremendously vivid picture-drama that gushes a tawdry tragedy. And Mr. Stevens has made it visual in staggering scenes of the great Texas plains and of passion-charged human relations that hold the hardness of the land and atmosphere.

"Under Mr. Stevens' direction, an exception-

With Rock Hudson, Jane Withers, James Dean, Mary Ann Edwards and Noreen Nash

With Rock Hudson and Chill Wills

ally well-chosen cast does some exciting performing. Elizabeth Taylor as the ranchman's lovely wife, from whose point of observation we actually view what goes on, makes a woman of spirit and sensitivity who acquires tolerance and grows old gracefully.

"However, it is the late James Dean who makes the malignant role of the surly ranchhand who becomes an oil baron the most tangy and corrosive in the film. This is a haunting capstone to the brief career of Mr. Dean."

Bosley Crowther, THE NEW YORK TIMES

"Many scenes are distinguished by Stevens' personal qualities: in the quiet scenes of the married couple together, he shows himself as one of the cinema's leading creators of a truly intimate mood, which Rock Hudson and Elizabeth Taylor admirably interpret.

"But nothing can hide the truth that *Giant* would be both more entertaining and compelling if it were an hour shorter."

"D.P.," MONTHLY FILM BULLETIN

"It is, for the most part, an excellent film which registers strongly on all levels, whether it's in its breathtaking panoramic shots of the dusty Texas plains; the personal, dramatic impact of the story itself; or the resounding message it has to impart.

"Many elements have been fused to make *Giant* click. Producers George Stevens and Henry Ginsberg have spent freely to capture the mood of the Ferber novel and the picture is fairly saturated with the feeling of the vastness and the mental narrowness, the wealth and the poverty, the pride and the prejudice that make up the Texas of today and yesterday. Here is an unflattering, vivid portrayal of this rugged state where cattle raising was in part supplanted by oil derricks, and where people scaled the economic ladder from rancher to millionaire almost overnight.

"Miss Taylor, whose talent and emotional ranges have usually seemed limited, turns in a surprisingly clever performance that registers up and down the line. She is tender and yet stubborn. Curiously enough, she's far better in the second half of the film, when her hair begins to show some gray, than in the earlier sequences. Portraying a woman of maturity, who has learned to adjust to a different social pattern, Miss Taylor is both engaging and beautiful.

"Hudson achieves real stature as Bick Benedict. A good deal of understanding goes into his performance as a man who sees a ranching tradition destroyed by oil and whose son prefers medicine.

"Stevens' direction on the whole is topnotch and distinctive. In his hands, *Giant* makes the transition from the old Texas to the new with vivid intensity, catching not only the changes wrought by time and money, but also focusing on the contrasts of modern Texas, where social graces are but skin-deep and distances are covered by the oil-rich ranchers in their private planes.

"Stevens and scripters Fred Guiol and Ivan Moffat did not flinch the discrimination angle. *Giant* isn't preachy—although in the end it comes close to it—but it's a powerful indictment of the Texas superiority complex."

"Hift," VARIETY

With Carroll Baker and Rock Hudson

With Montgomery Clift

Raintree County

A Metro-Goldwyn-Mayer Picture / 1957
In Technicolor and Panavision

CAST

John Wickliff Shawnessy: Montgomery Clift; *Susanna Drake:* Elizabeth Taylor; *Nell Gaither:* Eva Marie Saint; *Professor Jerusalem Webster Stiles:* Nigel Patrick; *Orville "Flash" Perkins:* Lee Marvin; *Garwood B. Jones:* Rod Taylor; *Ellen Shawnessy:* Agnes Moorehead; *T. D. Shawnessy:* Walter Abel; *Barbara Drake:* Jarma Lewis; *Bobby Drake:* Tom Drake; *Ezra Gray:* Rhys Williams; *Niles Foster:* Russell Collins; *Southern Officer:* DeForrest Kelley; *Lydia Gray:* Myrna Hansen; *Bartender:* Oliver Blake; *Cousin Sam:* John Eldredge; *Soona:* Isabelle Cooley; *Parthenia:* Ruth Attaway; *Miss Roman:* Eileene Stevens; *Bessie:* Rosalind Hayes; *Tom Conway:* Don Burnett; *Nat Franklin:* Michael Dugan; *Jesse Gardner:* Ralph Vitti (Michael Dante); *Starter:* Phil Chambers; *Man with Gun:* James Griffith; *Granpa Peters:* Burt Mustin; *Madam Gaubert:* Dorothy Granger; *Blind Man:* Owen McGiveney; *Party Guest:* Charles Watts; *Union Lieutenant:* Stacey Harris; *Jim Shawnessy (age two and a half):* Donald Losby; *Jim Shawnessy (age four):* Mickey Maga; *Pantomimist in Blackface:* Robert Foulk; *Photographer:* Jack Daly; *Old Negro Man:* Bill Walker; *Bearded Soldier:* Gardner McKay.

CREDITS

Director: Edward Dmytryk; *Producer:* David Lewis; *Screenwriter:* Millard Kaufman; *Based on the Novel by:* Ross Lockridge, Jr.; *Cinematogra-*

pher: Robert Surtees; *Art Directors:* William A. Horning and Urie McCleary; *Set Decorators:* Edwin B. Willis and Hugh Hunt; *Musical Score:* Johnny Green; *Songs by* Johnny Green and Paul Francis Webster: "Never Till Now" and "Song of the Raintree" (sung during the credits by Nat King Cole); *Editor:* John Dunning; *Costumes:* Walter Plunkett; *Running Time:* originally 187 minutes (later cut to 166 minutes).

THE FILM

Metro had long owned the movie rights to the gigantic 1948 best-seller of Indiana in the Civil War era by the late Ross Lockridge, Jr., and for six years had kept various writers busy trying to get some kind of filmable screenplay from the colorful book. Obviously, the studio had in mind a big-screen successor to their perennial blockbuster, *Gone with the Wind,* but the eventual 1957 results were as negligible as David O. Selznick's 1939 production is a classic. A lot of money went into the actual filming of *Raintree County,* photographed in a newly developed process called MGM Camera 65, in which a 65-mm. negative is reduced to 35-mm. for release prints. To reproduce Civil War Indiana, Metro took cast and crew to locations near Danville, Kentucky, for the most part, while swamp scenes were shot

With Jarma Lewis and Montgomery Clift

at Reelfoot Lake, Tiptonville, Tennessee. The antebellum Southern mansions were photographed in Natchez and neighboring Port Gibson, Mississippi.

The movie's then-astronomical cost of $5 million was partially occasioned by the near-fatal auto accident, in the midst of shooting, of its male star, Montgomery Clift, teamed with Elizabeth Taylor for the first time since *A Place in the Sun.* This caused many weeks of production delay, during which Clift underwent extensive facial plastic surgery. Indeed, a study of the film's

With Montgomery Clift

stills, in particular, discloses two divergent Clift visages. Sadly, his once-handsome face was never quite the same again—and neither were his performances.

Raintree County's rambling story begins in 1862 when a New Orleans belle, Susanna Drake (Elizabeth Taylor) visiting Raintree County, manages to seduce young John Shawnessy (Montgomery Clift) away from his childhood sweetheart, Nell Gaither (Eva Marie Saint). Feigning pregnancy, Susanna gets John to marry her, and he gradually discovers that her mother died insane, with evidence mounting that Susanna may have inherited negative family traits. Time passes, they have a son, and John becomes a schoolteacher, eventually returning to Indiana. During the Civil War, while John serves with the Union Army, Susanna slips through enemy lines to return South. Years later she's discovered in a mental hospital and is brought home. Later, she runs off again and drowns in a swamp, leaving John free, presumably to marry Nell.

After the success of *Giant*, Elizabeth eagerly met the challenge of her part in *Raintree County*, and although the film was not a notable success with either critics or the public, she won her first

With Montgomery Clift

With Myrna Hansen, Eva Marie Saint, Agnes Moorehead, Montgomery Clift, Walter Abel, Nigel Patrick and Rod Taylor

With Montgomery Clift

Academy Award nomination (though losing the Oscar to Joanne Woodward in *The Three Faces of Eve*). Years later, Taylor recalled the schizophrenic Susanna Drake as an "interesting" role, though she termed the movie "bad."

CRITICS' CORNER

"Adapted from a lengthy novel of the Civil War period, *Raintree County* is a rambling narrative which scarcely allows the main theme—an idealist seeking his destiny—to emerge clearly. Montgomery Clift, in a mannered performance, is unable to establish character or hold attention adequately. The emphasis of the story is constantly shifting and after the mild tone of the sequences showing Shawnessy's youth, the film descends into melodrama during a confused exploration of Susanna's inherited madness. The monotonous high-fever pitch on which she is made to act prevents Elizabeth Taylor from presenting a credible portrait, though Eva Marie Saint manages, in such moments as her renunciation scene with Clift, to achieve a genuine feeling. Dmytryk's competent direction seems unwilling to become involved with the actors, and evokes no sense of period. Only the battle scenes reflect the director's technical skill and vigor."

"*J. C. G.,*" MONTHLY FILM BULLETIN

"There is something wrong with the picture, and it isn't merely the outsized length. In general, it's too good to become offensive or actively boring. The performances are of a piece, lusty, lively and historically human. Montgomery Clift disturbs because he doesn't look quite as he did before his accident. His performance seems to lack the extra something it used always to have. The slack is not completely taken up by Miss Taylor's unusually strenuous efforts, nor by the fine contribution of Lee Marvin. It is not that Clift lets the picture down; it is simply that he fails to lift and carry it on his shoulders alone. And someone does need to carry it."

Archer Winsten, NEW YORK POST

"Instead of spectacle, action and racy narrative,

With Montgomery Clift

Raintree County brings to the cinema a rare gift of allegory, a spacious sense of proportion and a narrative style that, throughout some two hours thirty-six minutes, holds a firm balance between the romantic and the realistic.

"Montgomery Clift and Elizabeth Taylor give outstanding performances, Miss Taylor revealing depths of feeling and intelligence such as we have never seen from her before.

"If, on the surface, it seems long and the canvas too broad, it is because Dmytryk refuses to be concerned with superficialities. As a result, *Raintree County* is the best 'big' film of many months, and infinitely greater than *Gone with the Wind*."

Peter Baker, FILMS AND FILMING

"Millard Kaufman's screenplay is a formless amoeba of a thing, and therein lies the fatal weakness of this costly, ambitious film. But the people here are vaporous creatures, without clear personalities or drives, pasted together with patches of literary clichés and poetic sentiments. And Miss Taylor's daughter of the Deep South is a vain, posey, shallow young thing whose only asset is her beauty."

Bosley Crowther, THE NEW YORK TIMES

"Elizabeth Taylor, as the frightened and pathetic wife, is the best of the actors. The other roles have less variety, as the players well realize. But

vaster than anything else in *Raintree County* is its numbing boredom."

William K. Zinsser, NEW YORK HERALD TRIBUNE

"*Raintree County* is one of the biggest and costliest productions from Metro since its release of David O. Selznick's *Gone with the Wind*. Its three-hour length and a certain vagueness in char-acterizations will create certain b.o. problems. Cast is a strong one, though not uniformly well handled."

"Gene," VARIETY

"It has color, intense dramatic values, stunning performances and is mounted in a superb production."

MOTION PICTURE HERALD

With Montgomery Clift

With Paul Newman

Cat on a Hot Tin Roof

An Avon Production
A Metro-Goldwyn-Mayer Picture / 1958
In Metrocolor

CAST

Maggie Pollitt: Elizabeth Taylor; *Brick Pollitt:* Paul Newman; *Big Daddy Pollitt:* Burl Ives; *Gooper Pollitt:* Jack Carson; *Big Mama Pollitt:* Judith Anderson; *Mae Pollitt:* Madeleine Sherwood; *Dr. Baugh:* Larry Gates; *Deacon Davis:* Vaughn Taylor; *Dixie:* Patty Ann Gerrity; *Sonny:* Rusty Stevens; *Buster:* Hugh Corcoran; *Trixie:* Deborah Miller; *Boy:* Brian Corcoran; *Lacey:* Vince Townsend, Jr.; *Brightie:* Zelda Cleaver.

CREDITS

Director: Richard Brooks; *Producer:* Lawrence Weingarten; *Screenwriters:* Richard Brooks and James Poe; *Based on the Play by:* Tennessee Williams; *Cinematographer:* William Daniels; *Art Directors:* William A. Horning and Urie McCleary; *Set Decorators:* Henry Grace and Robert Priestley; *Special Effects:* Lee LeBlanc; *Editor:* Ferris Webster; *Miss Taylor's Wardrobe:* Helen Rose; *Running Time:* 108 minutes.

THE FILM

Cat on a Hot Tin Roof was the fifth Tennessee Williams play to reach the screen. A Broadway dramatic hit in 1955, it offered Barbara Bel Geddes, Ben Gazzara, Pat Hingle, and Mildred Dunnock in the roles here enacted by, respectively, Taylor, Newman, Carson, and Anderson. Burl Ives and Madeleine Sherwood repeated their stage characterizations.

The film won six Oscar nominations, but no awards. *Gigi* beat it out for Best Picture, and Vincente Minnelli's direction of that musical classic defeated Richard Brooks's nomination for *Cat*. For her hard-hitting portrayal of condemned murderess Barbara Graham, Susan Hayward stole the Best Actress award from Elizabeth Taylor, in her second nomination. By the same token, David Niven's character work in *Separate Tables* triumphed over Paul Newman in the male sweepstakes. Ironically, although Burl Ives won the Best Supporting Actor trophy, it was for *The Big*

With Paul Newman

Country; his superb Big Daddy wasn't even nominated.

Elizabeth Taylor's Maggie the Cat was created under severe hardships. Two weeks into filming, she learned that her third husband, showman Mike Todd, had died in a plane crash, and she credits this acting assignment with "saving" her. It was a role she had chosen for herself, and she reports, "I went slightly round the bend with grief. I was lucky I had somebody else to become. When I was Maggie was the only time I could function. The rest of the time I was a robot."

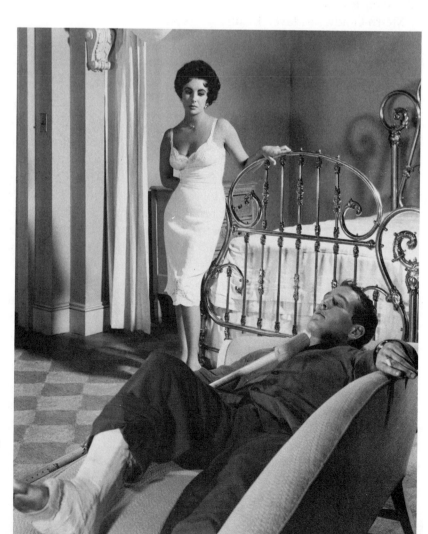

With Paul Newman

With Paul Newman

The Williams play is a corrosive character study of avarice, Southern pride, and seething sexual problems, set on a well-to-do Mississippi plantation where Big Daddy Pollitt, dying of cancer, celebrates his sixty-fifth birthday, doubly disturbed by the strained and childless marriage of his favored son Brick and the overfertile union of his other boy, Gooper, whose wife is about to bring forth another in an endless outpouring of little "no-neck monsters." Brick's wife, Maggie, beautiful and desirable, tries unsuccessfully to coax her husband away from the bottle, while alternately enticing him and taunting him about his "relationship" with a deceased male pal. The steamy tensions reach a climax when the truth of Big Daddy's health is revealed, and he and Brick manage a cathartic reunion of sorts, as, in the fade-out, Maggie and Brick do also. Although Williams's play explores definite questions of

homosexuality, Brooks and Poe, to avoid censorship problems in a climate far less permissive than that of the 1970s, soft-pedal the issue almost to nonexistence.

Many of Elizabeth Taylor's champions consider Maggie the Cat to be the apex of her work as an actress, while others prefer certain of her later performances. However, the critical consensus was heavy in her favor, despite Brooks's glamorization of a gutsy role that had provided theatrical tours-de-force for such stage stars as Barbara Bel Geddes and Kim Stanley (in the London production).

CRITICS' CORNER

"Homosexuality has generally been regarded as a distasteful subject for the motion picture screen, and all reference to it has therefore been eliminated from MGM's adaptation of *Cat on a Hot*

With Paul Newman

Tin Roof. And while this movie is often biting and strongly acted, while it is noisy, virulent and violent, the hullabaloo much of the time seems directionless, like a hurricane without an eye. Mr. Williams, our best contemporary playwright, deserves better than this."

Hollis Alpert, SATURDAY REVIEW

"By no means is this a watered-down version. It is hard-hitting and pointed about sex, though 'immature dependence' has replaced any hint of homosexuality. Motivations remain psychologically sound. Credit producer Lawrence Weingarten's adroit approach and Richard Brooks' direction with achieving a powerful, well-seasoned

With Jack Carson and Burl Ives

With Madeleine Sherwood and
Judith Anderson

film produced within the bounds of good, if 'adults only,' taste.

"Elizabeth Taylor has a major credit with her portrayal of Maggie. The frustrations and desires, both as a person and as a woman, the warmth and understanding she molds, the loveliness that is more than a well-turned nose—all these are part of a well-accented perceptive interpretation. That she performed in this manner under the stress of recent tragedy makes her performance certain to provoke conversation."

"Ron," VARIETY

"Censorship difficulties admittedly make it im-

With Burl Ives and Paul Newman

possible to show homosexuality as the root of Brick's problem, but Brooks does not appear to have the skill to make convincing the motives he has substituted. Most of Williams' exhilarating dialogue has been left out or emasculated, and the screenplay fails to harmonise the revised characterization of Brick with the author's original conception. Elizabeth Taylor, though momentarily successful, has no overall grasp of her part, and Paul Newman, adequate in the cruder moments, has insufficient finesse to make his performance more than an essay in emotional high jinks and repressed anger. Burl Ives' monotonous playing comes gratifyingly alive in the final scenes, but it is left to Jack Carson and Madeleine Sherwood to give the most rewarding performances. Brooks' handling, at its best detached, at its worst chaotically melodramatic, seldom excites and completely lacks attack; it is this, more than anything else, that robs the film of any of the power of the play."

"*T.B.*," MONTHLY FILM BULLETIN

"Such a lot of gross and greedy characters haven't gone by since Lillian Hellman's *The Little Foxes*. As a straight exercise in spewing venom and

With Burl Ives

flinging dirty linen on a line, this fine production would be hard to beat. It is done by superior talents, under the direction of Richard Brooks, making even the driest scenes drip poison with that juicy Williams dialogue.

"Miss Taylor is terrific as a panting, impatient wife, wanting the love of her husband as sincerely as she wants his inheritance."

Bosley Crowther, THE NEW YORK TIMES

"Miss Taylor is unimpeachable at suggesting the poor little rich girl of Hollywood fable, but her Cat, though admirably beautiful, emerges as one more kitten on a plush carpet; the heat, the vital-ity, the intense necessity of Maggie's love are not revealed; it remains thin and tepid, its only impact that of statement."

Rod McManigal, SIGHT AND SOUND

"Newman gives his finest performance to date. Miss Taylor, though not as intense as her role suggests she might be, gives it a great deal of conviction that contributes much to the movie's basic reality."

Paul V. Beckley, NEW YORK HERALD TRIBUNE

"Elizabeth Taylor plays with surprising sureness. Ives is superb."

TIME

With Paul Newman

Suddenly, Last Summer

A Horizon Production
Released by Columbia Pictures / 1959

CAST

Catherine Holly: Elizabeth Taylor; *Mrs. Violet Venable:* Katharine Hepburn; *Dr. Cukrowicz:* Montgomery Clift; *Dr. Hockstader:* Albert Dekker; *Mrs. Holly:* Mercedes McCambridge; *George Holly:* Gary Raymond; *Miss Foxhill:* Mavis Villiers; *Nurse Benson:* Patricia Marmont; *Sister Felicity:* Joan Young; *Lucy:* Maria Britneva; *Hockstader's Secretary:* Sheila Robbins; *Young Blond Intern:* David Cameron; *A Patient:* Roberta Woolley.

CREDITS

Director: Joseph L. Mankiewicz; *Producer:* Sam Spiegel; *Screenwriters:* Gore Vidal and Tennessee Williams; *Based on the Short Play by:* Tennessee Williams; *Cinematographer:* Jack Hild-

With Katharine Hepburn

yard; *Production Designer:* Oliver Messel; *Art Director:* William Kellner; *Set Decorator:* Scot Slimon; *Musical Score:* Buxton Orr and Malcolm Arnold; *Photographic Effects:* Tom Howard; *Editors:* William W. Hornbeck and Thomas G. Stanford; *Costumes:* Joan Ellacott; Running Time: 114 minutes.

THE FILM

Notwithstanding the ersatz Williams of *This Property Is Condemned, Suddenly, Last Summer* represents the greatest expansion for a motion picture of any of the plays of Tennessee Williams. On the stage, this work is a long one-act series of monologues, largely involving two women. It was originally presented Off-Broadway, preceded by a curtain-raiser called *Something Unspoken,* and

offered under the collective title of *Garden District.* In the roles filmed later by Katharine Hepburn, Elizabeth Taylor, and Montgomery Clift, were Hortense Alden, Anne Meacham, and Robert Lansing.

The play has only one set; the film takes the action back to an earlier time and invades the inner workings of a run-down mental hospital, although its most important action still focuses on the veranda and garden of the Venable home in the New Orleans "Garden District." To re-create this hothouse atmosphere, producer Sam Spiegel hired stage designer Oliver Messel, who fashioned an awesome house with tropical garden at London's Shepperton Studios, where the film was made.

For the third time, Taylor and Clift appeared

With Montgomery Clift

With Mercedes McCambridge

together, although in this movie the actor's recurring private bouts of ill health affect his performance to a degree impossible to ignore. Indeed, he would seem better cast as a patient than a doctor. Because of the film's then-shocking (to many) subject matter (cannibalism, homosexuality, and insanity), Elizabeth was strongly advised against doing this film. But her admiration for Williams's work, coupled with the great success of *Cat on a Hot Tin Roof,* contributed toward her acceptance of this new departure from the protective comforts of MGM. She was wise to do so; both she and Hepburn were nominated for Oscar's, but they lost to Simone Signoret's moving performance in *Room at the Top.*

The film has little plot per se. Violet Venable, whose only son had died the previous summer in Spain under rather mysterious circumstances, is determined to stop her niece Catherine Holly, who was with Sebastian when he died, from revealing unpleasant truths about his demise. Mrs. Venable consults Dr. Cukrowicz about performing a lobotomy on Catherine, who's confined to a mental institution, and she promises a much-needed and generous donation if the operation is carried out as soon as possible. Although the girl is still in a state of shock from the violent incident she witnessed in Spain, the doctor has doubts about her condition and, with growing personal interest in his patient, he arranges a family gath-

With Montgomery Clift, Katharine Hepburn, Albert Dekker, Gary Raymond, Mavis Villiers, Patricia Marmont and Mercedes McCambridge

[141]

ering during which, under the influence of a truth serum, Catherine is encouraged to recall in detail the factors surrounding Sebastian's death at the hands of some street boys whose sexual favors he had sought.

CRITICS' CORNER

"Gore Vidal and Mr. Williams have expanded and externalized the play for its movie treatment. Events are seen instead of being presented almost entirely in the girl's long speeches. As in the case of the other Williams movie, *Cat on a Hot Tin Roof,* his homosexual references have been made much less specific on the screen.

"The play might have remained vague without the clarifying influence of three profound performances by Miss Taylor, Miss Hepburn and Montgomery Clift. Each of these roles presents a complex problem that has been met with perceptive intelligence and insight."

Alton Cook, NEW YORK WORLD-TELEGRAM

"Elizabeth Taylor, as the beleaguered heroine of a New Orleans nightmare, works with an intensity beyond belief; hers is unquestionably one of the finest performances of this or any year.

"Mankiewicz, particularly in his telling of the flashback to 'last summer,' with Miss Taylor's face superimposed over the dread events, has given vivid, cinematic life to every facet of Williams' play. It is, in short, a wholly admirable rendering into film of a work that is at once fascinating and nauseating, brilliant and immoral. Its reception at the box office unquestionably will have an important bearing on the future of 'adult' films in this country."

Arthur Knight, SATURDAY REVIEW

"The main trouble with the picture is not its subject or its style, but its length. In the 70-minute, one-act play that Williams wrote, the action slithered about the spectator with the speed of a big snake, crushing in its clammy coils. In the 114-minute movie, it glides along so languidly that the audience has time to wonder about what is happening; and to wonder about this story is to realize that it is nothing more than a psychiatric nursery drama, a homosexual fantasy of guilty pleasure and pleasurable punishment. The dead hero is really no more than a sort of perverted Peter Pan, and the cannibalism itself nothing more than an aggravated case of nail-biting."

TIME

"Tennessee Williams' brooding, probing study of a set of introverted people and how they use each other in a devouring way is here brought to the screen with striking theatrical flair by Sam Spiegel in this major production. He has cast his tale of tormented and obsessed people outstandingly, with Elizabeth Taylor, Montgomery Clift and Katharine Hepburn taking the major honors, and excellent support coming from Albert Dekker and Mercedes McCambridge. It is all memorable."

Mandel Herbstman, THE FILM DAILY

"*Suddenly, Last Summer* goes further than anyone has previously cared, I won't say dared, to go. It will be almost certainly so alien to most audiences I doubt they will be able to show it much sympathy, not because it is poorly done, but rather because of its essentially poetic strength.

"As to Miss Hepburn's performance, it is splendid, as one might expect. And if there were ever any doubts about the ability of Miss Taylor to express complex and devious emotions, to deliver a flexible and deep performance, this film ought to remove them."

Paul V. Beckley, NEW YORK HERALD TRIBUNE

"Possibly the most bizarre film ever made by a major American company. Miss Taylor is most effective in her later scenes, although these scenes have been robbed of their original theatricality in transfer from stage to screen."

"Powe," VARIETY

"Mr. Williams and Gore Vidal have indulged in sheer verbal melodramatics which have small effect on the screen and are barely elevated from tedium by some incidental scenes of inmates of a mental institution. The acting is small compensation. Elizabeth Taylor is rightly roiled as the niece, but her wallow of agony at the climax is sheer histrionic showing off.

"Joseph L. Mankiewicz' direction is strained and sluggish, as is, indeed, the whole conceit of the drama. It should have been left to the Off-Broadway stage."

Bosley Crowther, THE NEW YORK TIMES

"As half of a stage double bill, one may imagine Tennessee Williams' hot-house fantasies of insanity, homosexuality, possessive mother domination and cannibalism administering a short, sharp Grand Guignolish shock. But the film is never short, almost everything in it seeming to happen twice, and although it steps gingerly round the forbidden words, its hints are more wordily explicit than most statements. One episode—the flashback revelation of what really happened to Sebastian on that summer afternoon in Spain—is surprisingly terse and carries its imaginative charge. The playing is dogged (Clift), arrestingly mannered (Hepburn), and courageously wholehearted (Taylor). But the work itself remains a sickly fantasy."

SIGHT AND SOUND

With Albert Dekker and Montgomery Clift

[143]

Peter Arne, Beverly Bentley and
Denholm Elliott

Scent of Mystery *(Holiday In Spain)*

A Michael Todd, Jr. Release / 1960
In the New Todd Color Process
   and Smell-O-Vision

CAST

Oliver Larker: Denholm Elliott; *Smiley:* Peter
Lorre; *The Decoy Sally:* Beverly Bentley; *Baron
Saradin:* Paul Lukas; *Johnny Gin:* Liam Red-
mond; *Tommy Kennedy:* Leo McKern; *Fleming:*
Peter Arne; *Winifred Jordan:* Diana Dors; *Mar-
gharita:* Mary Laura Wood; *Miss Leonard:* Ju-
dith Furse; *Pepi:* Maurice Marsac; *Englishman:*
Michael Trubshawe; *Truck Driver:* Juan Ola-
guivel; *Constance Walker:* Billie Miller; *The
Real Sally Kennedy:* Elizabeth Taylor.

CREDITS

Director: Jack Cardiff; *Producer:* Michael Todd,
Jr.; *Screenwriter:* William Roos; *Based on an*
Original Story by: Kelley Roos; *Additional Situations:* Gerald Kersh; *Associate Producer and
Technical Supervisor:* Ned Mann; *Cinematographer:* John Von Kotze; *Production Supervisor
and Art Director:* Vincent Korda; *Special Effects:*
Cliff Richardson; *Second Unit Photography:* John
Drake; *Musical Score:* Mario Nascimbene; *Additional Music:* Jordan Ramin and Harold Adamson; *Editor:* James Newcom; *Costumes:* Charles
Simminger; *Running Time:* 125 minutes plus in-
termission.

THE FILM

Admittedly a "gimmick" film, *Scent of Mystery*

displayed, in the few engagements for which theaters were properly equipped, a series of odors, sprayed into the air at appropriate turns of the plot. The story centered on a vacationing Englishman (Denholm Elliott) who happens on a plot to kill a young American tourist (Beverly Bentley) in Spain. The girl disappears, and the trail becomes tangled with red herrings and odd types of people before it's discovered that she was an impostor. Eventually, the real girl is found and escorted to safety.

Elizabeth Taylor shared a financial interest in this movie with Michael Todd, Jr., the son of her late third husband, and she consented to make a "surprise appearance" as the missing heiress at the film's conclusion. Of course, to keep the secret, no advance billing or publicity was possible. And no stills were made showing the girl's face. *Scent of Mystery* proved a box-office disaster.

CRITICS' CORNER

"Fortunately for Michael Todd, Jr., he has a diverting and entertaining mystery-chase picture that can stand on its own without odors. Among the smells that clicked were those involving flowers, the perfume of the mystery girl in the film, tobacco, orange, shoe polish, port wine, baked bread, coffee, lavender and peppermint. A fun picture, expertly directed by Jack Cardiff."

VARIETY

"It is an artless, loose-jointed chase picture set against some of the scenic beauties of Spain which, indeed, are the most attractive and rewarding compensations of the show. And whatever novel stimulation it might afford with the projection of smells appears to be dubious and dependent upon the noses of the individual viewers and the smell-projector's whims."

Bosley Crowther, THE NEW YORK TIMES

"With *Scent of Mystery,* Michael Todd, Jr. shows himself to be definitely a chip off the old block. His film is big, noisy, boisterous, suspenseful, very funny and often breathlessly beautiful."

Paul V. Beckley, NEW YORK HERALD TRIBUNE

"Some odors come early, some late, and some not at all, and the whole business made me confused, especially since I was trying to equate the evidence of my eyes with the evidence of my nose.

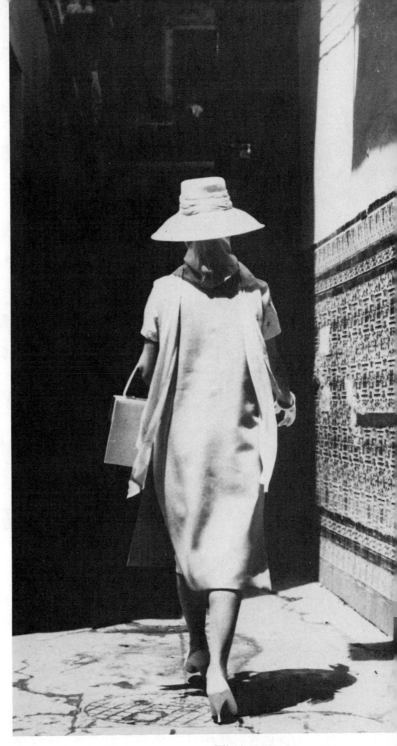

Elizabeth Taylor

"At any rate, what we have in *Scent of Mystery* is a parody of a thriller incidentally exploring the wonders of Spain, caught very nicely in huge-screen color photography. I'm afraid, though, that the director, Jack Cardiff (a former cameraman), handles a view with more finesse than he does actors, and the picture cries out for the deft hand that a Hitchcock might have supplied."

Hollis Alpert, SATURDAY REVIEW

Butterfield 8

A Metro-Goldwyn-Mayer Picture / 1960
In CinemaScope and Metrocolor

CAST

Gloria Wandrous: Elizabeth Taylor; *Weston Liggett:* Laurence Harvey; *Steve Carpenter:* Eddie Fisher; *Emily Liggett:* Dina Merrill; *Mrs. Wandrous:* Mildred Dunnock; *Mrs. Fanny Thurber:* Betty Field; *Bingham Smith:* Jeffrey Lynn; *Happy:* Kay Medford; *Norma:* Susan Oliver; *Dr. Tredman:* George Voskovec; *Clerk:* Virginia Downing; *Mrs. Jescott:* Carmen Mathews; *Anderson:* Whitfield Connor; *Elevator Man:* Dan Bergin; *Cabbie:* Vernon Dowling; *Doorman:* Samuel Schwartz; *Tipsy Man:* Robert Pastene; *Second Doorman:* John Armstrong; *Policeman:* Leon B. Stevens; *Bartender:* Tom Ahearne; *Big Man:* Rudy Bond; *Irate Man:* Victor Harrison; *Chauffeur:* Beau Tilden; *Irate Woman:* Marion Leeds; *Gossip:* Helen Stevens; *Photographer:* Don Burns; *Man:* Philip Faversham; *Messenger:* Joseph Boley; *State Trooper:* Richard X. Slattery.

CREDITS

Director: Daniel Mann; *Producer:* Pandro S. Berman; *Screenwriters:* Charles Schnee and John Michael Hayes; *Based on the Novel by:* John O'Hara; *Cinematographer:* Joseph Ruttenberg;

With Eddie Fisher

Art Directors: George W. Davis and Urie McCleary; *Set Decorators:* Gene Callahan and J. C. Delaney; *Musical Score:* Bronislau Kaper; *Editor:* Ralph E. Winters; *Costumes:* Helen Rose; *Running Time:* 109 minutes.

THE FILM

Butterfield 8 was a script that Elizabeth Taylor at first rebelled against making, because she thought it cheap, commercial, and in bad taste. By accepting it, however, she was thus able to complete her obligations to MGM and end her long contract with that studio. Although she managed to obtain a role for Eddie Fisher, then her husband, the actress filmed the movie in a belligerent frame of mind and gave out interviews airing her negative thoughts about the whole project in no uncertain terms.

Filmed entirely in and around New York City, *Butterfield 8* concerns the romantic life of a fashionable Manhattan beauty who's part model, part call girl—and all man-trap. Of her illicit amours, the one that finally destroys her is with a married socialite (Laurence Harvey). Their turbulent affair comes to a tragic end when our heroine, under the mistaken impression that he'll never divorce his wife (Dina Merrill) and marry her, loses control of her car while driving recklessly on a New England-bound parkway and crashes through a barricade to her death.

With Laurence Harvey

Trash or not, *Butterfield 8* received the benefit of Metro's behind-the-scenes production gloss and, strangely enough, Taylor's performance (under the circumstances of her discontent) is one of her best. Not only was the press favorably disposed toward her performance, but she was nominated for her third Academy Award. The competition for Best Actress included Greer Garson in *Sunrise at Campobello,* Deborah Kerr in *The Sundowners,* Shirley MacLaine in *The Apartment,* and Melina Mercouri in *Never On Sunday—* formidable contenders all. Comparing Taylor's Gloria Wandrous to her work in *Raintree County, Cat On a Hot Tin Roof,* and *Suddenly, Last Summer,* many reasoned that her award for *But-*

terfield 8 was more one of sympathy for her successful battle with pneumonia, coupled with a belated tribute to her past performances, than one of respect for this mediocre film.

The 1935 John O'Hara novel—a property MGM had long had "on the shelf"—had its original basis in the never-solved real-life case of a New York call girl who went under the exotic name of Starr Faithfull. In 1931, she disappeared from a·yacht, only to turn up as a corpse, washed in by the tide. Whether accident or foul play, the matter was never settled.

CRITICS' CORNER

"Under director Daniel Mann's guidance, it is an

With Laurence Harvey

With Eddie Fisher and Susan Oliver

extremely sexy and intimate film, but the intimacy is only skin deep, the sex only a dominating behavior pattern that dictates some strange, wild relationships and activities rarely rooted in logic.

"The picture's major asset is Miss Taylor, who makes what is becoming her annual bid for an Oscar. While the intensity and range of feeling that marked several of her more recent endeavors is slightly reduced in this effort, it is nonetheless a torrid, stinging overall portrayal with one or two brilliantly executed passages within. Harvey seems ill-at-ease and has a tendency to exaggerate facial reactions. Eddie Fisher cannot unbend and get any warmth into his role. Miss Merrill's portrayal is without animation or depth. There is better work from Mildred Dunnock as Miss Taylor's mother and Susan Oliver as Fisher's impatient girl friend. Betty Field is a standout as Miss Dunnock's friend, particularly in one or two acid exchanges with Miss Taylor."

"Tube," VARIETY

"Here, in *Butterfield 8,* we have the ancient hackneyed story of the tinseled but tarnished prostitute. By the odds, it should be a bomb. But a bomb it is not, let us tell you. At least it is not the

With Betty Field and Mildred Dunnock

[149]

With Laurence Harvey

sort of thing to set you to yawning or squirming, unless Elizabeth Taylor leaves you cold. She looks like a million dollars, in mink or negligee.

"The dialogue is rough. And the ending is absurd. But so is most of it, for that matter. It's the living it up that gets you in this film."

Bosley Crowther, THE NEW YORK TIMES

"*Butterfield 8* as a novel by John O'Hara was a crude but affecting tart's tragedy. As a film, it has been turned into a sleek and libidinous meller. Even in these conventional contexts, the classic theme of salvation by prostitution preserves a little of its ancient power. The power is blunted—though commerce is served—by a glossy production, slick direction, solid but stolid performances, and a script that reads as though it had been copied off a washroom wall."

TIME

With Kay Medford

With Laurence Harvey

"In *Butterfield 8* the object seems to have been to make some unpleasant people attractive. Dressmakers and interior decorators must have worked overtime on it, and, of course, Elizabeth Taylor, who has a crackling effect on the screen, would dress up a rag-picker's shack. But the effect of all this lush camouflage only makes things ambiguous and cancels out the hard, brittle definitions that the theme promises."

Paul V. Beckley, NEW YORK HERALD TRIBUNE

"MGM has packed into this free adaptation of John O'Hara's novel most of the ingredients considered essential for the new trend in 'frank, outspoken' romantic dramas: i.e., a few bold words, a touch of semi-nudity and some noisy, emotional love scenes. In this case, the mixture resolutely refuses to come to the boil, due mainly to an inadequate script and theatrical, styleless direction. None of the players is able to sustain interest in the unending stream of smart talk and literary wisecracks, and Elizabeth Taylor and Laurence Harvey, in particular, strive for an intensity which only leads to bathos."

"J.G.," MONTHLY FILM BULLETIN

"Miss Taylor obviously tries very hard to get a tragic quality into the girl—Lord, how she tries!—but not even acting can help this script."

Hollis Alpert, SATURDAY REVIEW

"John O'Hara's 1935 novel has been made into a powerful, dramatic and psychotic case history: a film of profound proportions, subtlety, depth, warmth and great sympathy. With Elizabeth Taylor in the leading role giving the finest performance of her career, *Butterfield 8* shines with an insight into character and an honesty in story development not frequently met with in Hollywood dramas that so often glamorize the free-wheeling girls-about-town who refuse to face what they are because they accept gifts, instead of money, for services too freely given."

Jesse Zunser, CUE

"It's a wretched thing, but I doubt whether it casts much of a pall on the work from which it has been wrenched.

"Elizabeth Taylor plays Gloria, and is very beautiful; Dina Merrill plays the wife, and is also very beautiful (but, like all rich, chaste wives in movies, is given nothing really interesting to say); and Laurence Harvey plays the bounder, and is radically miscast."

THE NEW YORKER

[151]

With Hume Cronyn

Cleopatra

A 20th Century-Fox Picture / 1963
In Todd-AO
Color by DeLuxe

CAST

Cleopatra: Elizabeth Taylor; *Mark Antony:* Richard Burton; *Julius Caesar:* Rex Harrison; *High Priestess:* Pamela Brown; *Flavius:* George Cole; *Sosigenes:* Hume Cronyn; *Apollodorus:* Cesare Danova; *Brutus:* Kenneth Haigh; *Octavian:* Roddy McDowall; *Rufio:* Martin Landau; *Agrippa:* Andrew Keir; *Germanicus:* Robert Stephens; *Eiras:* Francesca Annis; *Pothinos:* Gregoire Aslan; *Ramos:* Martin Benson; *Theodotos:* Herbert Berghof; *Phoebus:* John Cairney; *Lotos:* Jacqui Chan; *Charmian:* Isabelle Cooley; *Achilles:* John Doucette; *Canidius:* Andrew Faulds; *Cimber:* Michael Gwynn; *Cicero:* Michael Hordern; *Cassius:* John Hoyt; *Euphranor:* Marne Maitland; *Casca:* Carroll O'Connor; *Ptolemy:* Richard O'Sullivan; *Calpurnia:* Gwen Watford; *Decimus:* Douglas Wilmer; *Queen at Tarsus:* Marina Berti; *High Priest:* John Karlsen; *Caesarion (age four):* Loris Loddi; *Octavia:* Jean Marsh; *Marcellus:* Gin Mart; *Mithridates:* Furio Meniconi; *Caesarion (age twelve):* Kenneth Nash; *Caesarian (age seven):* Del Russell; *Valvus:* John Valva; *Archesilaus:* Laurence Naismith; *First Officer:* John Alderton; *Second Officer:* Peter Forster.

CREDITS

Director: Joseph L. Mankiewicz; *Producer:* Walter Wanger; *Screenwriters:* Joseph L. Mankiewicz, Ranald MacDougall, and Sidney Buchman; *Based upon Histories by:* Plutarch, Suetonius, and Ap-

[153]

pian, and *The Life and Times of Cleopatra* by C. M. Franzero; *Cinematographer:* Leon Shamroy; *Second Unit Photographers:* Claude Renoir and Pietro Portalupi; *Production Designer:* John De Cuir; *Art Directors:* Jack Martin Smith, Hilyard Brown, Herman Blumenthal, Elven Webb, Maurice Pelling, and Boris Juraga; *Set Decorators:* Walter M. Scott, Paul S. Fox, and Ray Moyer; *Special Photographic Effects:* L. B. Abbott and Emil Kosa, Jr.; *Choreographer:* Hermes Pan; *Musical Score:* Alex North; *Editor:* Dorothy Spencer; *Miss Taylor's Costumes:* Irene Sharaff; *Additional Costumes:* Vittorio Nino Novarese; *Miss Taylor's Hairstyles:* Vivienne Zavitz; *Running Time:* 243 minutes.

THE FILM

More than a decade after its overpublicized creation, the 1963 version of *Cleopatra* remains undoubtedly the longest (outside of India) and most expensive (reputedly close to $40 million) motion picture ever made.

Cleopatra was a role Elizabeth Taylor had coveted. One reason for her compliance with Metro's *Butterfield 8* was that she hoped to finish that role and be free to contract with Fox for *Cleopatra*. The legendary Egyptian queen, though frequently portrayed on screen, has seldom made either histrionic history or produced a celluloid classic. Among the most notable have been Theda Bara in 1917, Claudette Colbert in Cecil B. DeMille's 1934 version, and Vivien Leigh in an eye-filling 1945 offering that was Britain's most costly film ever.

Originally, Walter Wanger's production of *Cleopatra* began production under the direction of Rouben Mamoulian with Stephen Boyd and Peter Finch as, respectively, Mark Antony and Julius Caesar. When the film ran too far behind schedule, Mamoulian was replaced with Joseph L. Mankiewicz, who also assumed a major rewrite job on the script. But the film's greatest setback was Elizabeth Taylor's near-fatal illness, a long siege during which a tracheotomy was performed,

With Rex Harrison

With Isabelle Cooley and Francesca
Annis

saving her life but leaving a large scar at the base of her neck, visible in some of the film's production stills and in most of her subsequent movies.

During Taylor's lengthy health sabbatical, both Boyd and Finch had to withdraw from the film due to prior contractual commitments and were, of course, eventually replaced by Richard Burton and Rex Harrison. Although extensive sets had been constructed in Britain, Elizabeth's health precluded returning to film in so damp a climate, and production eventually resumed in Rome, with massive new sets swelling the budget beyond all expectations.

Although first released at a running time of 243 minutes, Darryl F. Zanuck saw to it that 21 minutes of footage were removed a few days later, during its New York engagement. (Critical condemnation had suggested that such a move might help, if only to a minor degree—and *Cleopatra*, for a time, provided a serious threat to the very future existence of 20th Century-Fox).

Perhaps out of intimidation or embarrassment, industry members saw fit to nominate *Cleopatra* as one of 1963's five best films. The Oscar went to Britain's *Tom Jones*. However, this mammoth movie did win a handful of technical awards for its art direction, costumes, and color photography.

Despite inferior notices, *Cleopatra* did attract customers to the box-office, partly out of curiosity deriving from the muckraking publicity emanating from the smouldering off-screen romance of

With Rex Harrison

its two then-married co-stars, Taylor and Burton.

CRITICS' CORNER

"Physically, *Cleopatra* is as magnificent as money and the tremendous Todd-AO screen can make it. Sad to say, however, the deep-revolving, witty Mankiewicz fails most where most he hoped to succeed. As drama and as cinema, *Cleopatra* is raddled with flaws. It lacks style both in image and in action. Never for an instant does it whirl along on wings of epic elan; generally it just bumps from scene to ponderous scene on the square wheels of exposition. Part of what is wrong went wrong in the cutting room, and for that Darryl Zanuck, boss of 20th Century-Fox, is possibly to blame. But much of what is wrong was wrong in the script, and for that Chief Scenarist Mankiewicz must wear the ears.

"As for Taylor, she does her dead-level best to portray the most woman in world's history. To

With Rex Harrison

look at, she is every inch 'a morsel for a monarch.' Indeed, her 50 gorgeous costumes are designed to suggest that she is a couple of morsels for a monarch. But the 'infinite variety' of the superb Egyptian is beyond her, and when she plays Cleopatra as a political animal she screeches like a ward heeler's wife at a block party.

"Harrison alone deserves the laurel. He makes a charming a surprisingly impressive Caesar."

TIME

"Certainly, if you want to devote the best part of four hours to looking at Elizabeth Taylor in all her draped and undraped physical splendor, surrounded by elaborate and exotic costumes and sets, all in the loveliest of colors, this is your movie.

"She is an entirely physical creature, no depth of emotion apparent in her kohl-laden eyes, no modulation in her voice that too often rises to fishwife levels. Out of royal regalia, en negligee or au naturel, she gives the impression that she is really carrying on in one of Miami Beach's more exotic resorts."

Judith Crist, NEW YORK HERALD TRIBUNE

"Richard Burton and Elizabeth Taylor, it must be admitted, remain very much Mr. Burton and Miss Taylor."

Penelope Houston, SIGHT AND SOUND

"*Cleopatra* has a few rewards. There is some splendid spectacle. Some of the dialogue by Joseph L. Mankiewicz is, to put it negatively, not heavy. But his script never develops an inner dynamism that propels it. Miss Taylor is a plump, young American matron in a number of Egyptian costumes and makeups. She needs do no more

With Richard Burton and Rex Harrison

With Richard Burton

than walk around the throne room to turn Alexandria into Beverly Hills. Except for the veracity of Harrison's performance, some of Burton's moments, and the solidity of Martin Landau's Rufio, the tedium is only occasionally lightened by the laughable vulgarity of the display."

Stanley Kauffmann, NEW REPUBLIC

"One of the great epic films of our day. These are not obvious actors in gewgaw costumes who march around in a fake world staked out by Cecil B. DeMille. These are plausible people, maturely conceived and turned loose in a realm of political intrigues, conflicts and thrusts for personal power. Elizabeth Taylor's Cleopatra is a woman of force and dignity, fired by a fierce ambition to conquer and rule the world. Caesar is no fustian tyrant; played stunningly by Rex Harrison, he is a statesman of manifest wisdom, shrewdness and magnanimity. Richard Burton is nonetheless exciting as the arrogant Antony. Unless you are one of those skeptics who are stubbornly predisposed to give *Cleopatra* the needle, I don't see how you can fail to find this a gener-

With Richard Burton

With Richard Burton

With Francesca Annis, Isabelle Cooley and Roddy McDowall

ally brilliant, moving and satisfying film."

Bosley Crowther, THE NEW YORK TIMES

"Director/co-author Mankiewicz and producer Walter Wanger have not extended the frontiers of cinema art, but they have completed under harrowing conditions a very respectable job of spectacle-making."

"Anby," VARIETY

"Rex Harrison does justice to some dry, donnish jokes as Caesar; Richard Burton plays Antony along sub-Olivier lines of alternately brooding and ranting masochism. Elizabeth Taylor, in the past an underrated actress, here proves herself vocally, emotionally and intellectually overparted to a disastrous degree. Her rages (the burning of the library at Alexandria, the news of Antony's marriage) are the merest petulance; her beauty and cunning shorn of mystery and complexity. But how can you take a Cleopatra seriously who plays with plastic barges in the bath?"

Peter John Dyer, MONTHLY FILM BULLETIN

"The film never rises above the level of the Italian Hercules and Maciste spectaculars, and for long periods lacks their pace and ebullience. Director Mankiewicz will be remembered for better films."

Peter Baker, FILMS AND FILMING

"Despite her great beauty, Miss Taylor simply does not possess the emotional range—in voice control or movement—to match consistently the professional perfection of Rex Harrison, superb as Caesar, Cleopatra's conquerer and lover, or Richard Burton as the tempestuous, passionate, and ultimately tragic Antony. Yet, Miss Taylor does manage, here and there, several effective scenes with both stars."

Jesse Zunser, CUE

"Mankiewicz, as writer or director, has no genuine flair for the action-crammed historic canvas; his gift, such as it is, is for the brisk comedy, which is of small avail here, and for witty repartee, which will not be squeezed from stones like Elizabeth Taylor."

John Simon, THE NEW LEADER

With Richard Burton

The V.I.P.s

A Metro-Goldwyn-Mayer Picture / 1963
In Panavision and Metrocolor

CAST

Frances Andros: Elizabeth Taylor; *Paul Andros:* Richard Burton; *Marc Champselle:* Louis Jourdan; *Gloria Gritti:* Elsa Martinelli; *The Duchess:* Margaret Rutherford; *Miss Mead:* Maggie Smith; *Les Mangam:* Rod Taylor; *Miriam Marshall:* Linda Christian; *Max Buda:* Orson Welles; *Coburn:* Robert Coote; *Sanders:* Richard Wattis; *Commander Millbank:* Dennis Price; *Joslin:* Ronald Fraser; *Mr. Damer:* Peter Illing; *Airport Director:* Michael Hordern; *Waiter:* Stringer Davis; *First Reporter:* Brook Williams; *Second Reporter:* Alan Howard; *Third Reporter:* Lewis Fiander; *Fourth Reporter:* Barry Steele; *Miss Potter:* Joan Benham; *Bar Steward:* Arthur Howard; *Doctor:* Peter Sallis; *Mrs. Damer:* Joyce Carey; *Porter:* Griffiths Davis; *Waitress:* Maggie McGrath; *Assistant to Airport Director:* Frank Williams; *Meteorological Man:* Angus Lennie; *Rolls Chauffeur:* Ray Austin; *Airport Announcers:* Rosemary Dorken and Pamela Buckley; *Hotel Receptionist:* Duncan Lewis; *Met. Official:* Richard Briers; *Young Reporter:* David Frost; *Dr. Schwutzbacher:* Martin Miller; *Airport Official:* Lance Percival; *Captain:* Terrence Alexander; *Air Hostess:* Jill Carson; *Hotel Representatives:* Richard Caldicott; *Lady Reporter:* Ann Castle; *Mr. Rivers (Hotel Manager):* Clifford Mollison; *Official:* Gordon Sterne; *Head Waiter:* Reginald Beckwith; *Barman:* John Blythe; *Visitors (Knebworth House):* Virginia Bedard and Cal McCord; *Air Hostess:* Moyra Fraser; *Jamaican Gentleman:* Clifton Jones.

CREDITS

Director: Anthony Asquith; *Producer:* Anatole de Grunwald; *Screenwriter:* Terence Rattigan; *Cinematographer:* Jack Hildyard; *Art Director:* William Kellner; *Set Decorator:* Pamela Cornell; *Musical Score:* Miklos Rozsa; *Editor:* Frank Clarke; *Miss Taylor's Clothes:* Hubert de Given-

With Richard Burton

chy; *Miss Martinelli's Clothes:* Pierre Cardin; *Wardrobe Supervisor:* Felix Evans; *Miss Taylor's Hairstyles:* Vivienne Walker Zavitz; *Running Time:* 119 minutes.

THE FILM

Elizabeth Taylor reports that *The V.I.P.s* developed as a vehicle for her and Richard Burton while filming added *Cleopatra* scenes in Paris. Burton was signed first; when she quipped, "Why don't I do it, too?" producer Anatole de Grunwald took her up on it.

Filmed and released in short order, to capitalize on the *Cleopatra* publicity, *The V.I.P.s* was an original Terence Rattigan script in the *Grand Hotel* tradition, intermixing the problem-beset lives of a motley group of airline passengers grounded at London Airport by a heavy fog. Much of the action focused on a romantic triangle involving Elizabeth, Richard, and Louis Jourdan as, respectively, pampered wife, millionaire husband, and playboy lover of the wife, at a crisis in their tangled lives. Although about to fly away with her lover, the wife, given time to reconsider her move, decides that her destitute husband's need for her is the greater, and they reconcile.

Released on the heels of the monumental, high-priced *Cleopatra,* and at a time when Burton and Taylor were still unwed traveling companions, *The V.I.P.s* cleaned up at the box office for MGM. It also won a Best Supporting Actress Oscar for Margaret Rutherford for her delightfully extraneous scene-stealing as, characteristically, an eccentric duchess bound for Florida.

Filmed in Britain, *The V.I.P.s* was known during production as *International Hotel,* with reference to the stop-over locale.

CRITICS' CORNER

"The top roles, as you hardly need be told, are enacted by Elizabeth Taylor and Richard Burton, the assisting cast is dotted with 'name' players, Miss Taylor features expensive furs and jewels, and the general mood is one of luxury. It all makes for slick and glossy entertainment, at times

With Louis Jourdan

perhaps a bit too slick in its workings, but constantly colorful."

Rose Pelswick, NEW YORK JOURNAL-AMERICAN

"In particular, it exploits the much-celebrated sufferings of its principal players, Elizabeth Taylor and Richard Burton. After Margaret Rutherford, Burton and Taylor hardly seem worth watching. But Rod Taylor holds his own pretty well, and Orson Welles does a magnificent take-off on Orson Welles."

TIME

"Unfortunately, while it is easy to predict that *The V.I.P.s*, for example, will undoubtedly do land-office business wherever it is shown, it is also disconcertingly simple to discern the mechanisms of casting, plotting and mounting that produce this kind of success. *The V.I.P.s* is overwhelmingly a safe film, but it is also an entertaining one. The talk is bright, the characters are sharply drawn, and the production is polished and handsome."

Arthur Knight, SATURDAY REVIEW

"Although Miss Taylor plays appropriately, with a strange sort of icy detachment—almost cruelty—toward both men, and is very lovely to look at, she does not generate much sympathy. She is mainly an instigator of uncertainty and anguish in both men. Mr. Burton is better as the husband, particularly in the early scenes when he is weathering the shock of discovering the perfidy of his wife."

Bosley Crowther, THE NEW YORK TIMES

"There's a lot to be said for *The V.I.P.s*, and most of all, that it combines celebrated actors playing in the grand manner in a lavishly produced combination of juicy drama, light comedy,

With Richard Burton

[164]

good caricature, and—despite characterization and dramatic flaws—a good show. Except for the incredible hamming of Mr. Welles, the cast is tops."

Jesse Zunser, CUE

"If you haven't your wits about you, you might, from time to time, mistake it for the solid gold Cadillac it resembles, courtesy of a couple of 24-carat performances by Margaret Rutherford and Maggie Smith. Mr. Burton's performance is graceful and unremittingly gloomy and Miss Taylor's is unremitting."

Judith Crist, NEW YORK HERALD TRIBUNE

"Maybe Miss Taylor needs a sabbatical, but there is a feeling of ordinariness about her thesping these days which is disconcerting. In *V.I.P.s* she looks attractive, of course, and shows some moments of fun, fire and emotion. But it never seems likely that two such different characters as the tycoon and the gigolo would care deeply enough to play tug-o-war over her. Burton, however, gives a top-league performance. Jourdan is also excellent and he has one scene with Burton which is a little masterpiece of dual virtuosity. Finally, Margaret Rutherford is again likely to find her-

With Richard Burton and Louis Jourdan

self arraigned on a charge of grand larceny for scene stealing. She is a sheer joy."

"Rich," VARIETY

"*The V.I.P.s* is a pretty little cinematic soufflé that melts in the mind, but its flavor is spicy and sweet. If it benefits at the box-office from the publicity attendant on another, rather more expensive film, it will have a certain rough justice on its side."

Brenda Davies, MONTHLY FILM BULLETIN

With Louis Jourdan and Richard Burton

The Sandpiper

A Filmways Picture
A Metro-Goldwyn-Mayer Release / 1965
In Panavision and Metrocolor

CAST

Laura Reynolds: Elizabeth Taylor; *Dr. Edward Hewitt:* Richard Burton; *Claire Hewitt:* Eva Marie Saint; *Cos Erickson:* Charles Bronson; *Ward Hendricks:* Robert Webber; *Larry Brant:* James Edwards; *Judge Thompson:* Torin Thatcher; *Walter Robinson:* Tom Drake; *Phil Sutcliff:* Doug Henderson; *Danny Reynolds:* Morgan Mason; *Troopers:* Dusty Cadis and John Hart; *Trustee:* Jan Arvan; *Trustee's Wife:* Mary Benoit; *Trustee:* Tom Curtis; *Architect:* Paul Genge; *First Celebrant:* Rex Holman; *Second Celebrant:* Kelton Garwood; *Third Celebrant:* Jimmy Murphy; *Fourth Celebrant:* Mel. Gallagher; *Poet Celebrant:* Ron Whelan; *Sixth Celebrant:* Diane Sayer; *Seventh Celebrant:* Joan Connors; *Eighth Celebrant:* Peggy Adams Laird; *Ninth Celebrant:* Shirley Bonne; *Voice:* Peter O'Toole.

CREDITS

Director: Vincente Minnelli; *Producer:* Martin Ransohoff; *Screenwriters:* Dalton Trumbo and Michael Wilson; *Original Story by:* Martin Ransohoff; *Adaptation:* Irene and Louis Kamp; *Cinematographer:* Milton Krasner; *Art Directors:* George W. Davis and Urie McCleary; *Wildlife Photographer:* Richard Borden; *Musical Score:* Johnny Mandel; *Song* "The Shadow of Your Smile" *by:* Johnny Mandel and Paul Francis Webster; *Editor:* David Bretherton; *Costumes:* Irene Sharaff; *Running Time:* 116 minutes.

THE FILM

The Sandpiper, Elizabeth Taylor's first movie with director Vincente Minnelli since *Father of the Bride* in 1950, was also her first film in two years, during which time Richard Burton filmed

Beckett, The Night of the Iguana, and a version of his rehearsal-clothes rendition of *Hamlet,* based on a Broadway revival. Taylor reports having received no movie offers during this period and that, when *The Sandpiper* was proffered them, they consequently grabbed it.

The Sandpiper drew audiences, with its triangular love story suitably enlivened with flashes of a half-nude Taylor, references to swinging lifestyles, and atmosphere heavy with sin and salvation. Elizabeth played a hedonistic artist (inhabiting an impossibly expensive beach house, considering the modesty of her output) who proves irresistible to an Episcopalian minister (Burton) who, with his loving wife (Eva Marie Saint), runs a private school for boys. Their affair is tumultuous and, after his wife learns of it by accident, the minister confesses everything to her, breaks off with his paramour, and leaves job and marriage for an uncertain future.

The Sandpiper went into production on location in the Big Sur area of the California coast. After two months, the company then moved to a Paris studio where, for tax reasons, the Burtons had arranged to complete the film. Opening at New York's Radio City Music Hall, *The Sandpiper* proceeded to break four all-time records at that showplace. The critics had little but derision for the movie, a fact that didn't deter the stars' considerable fans.

Observing Elizabeth's artistic growth in the fifteen years since they had last worked together,

With Richard Burton

director Minnelli is quoted as having said, "Her talent as an actress has developed almost beyond belief."

CRITICS' CORNER

"When star Burton first read the script, he remarked that 'it hits pretty close to home.' Director Vincente Minnelli exploits this possibility with unctuous professionalism, fielding his glamorous duo in a romance *à clef* that they appear to take seriously."

TIME

"That shabby old Hollywood custom of pretending to a great piety while flirting around with material that is actually suggestive and cheap has seldom been more adroitly practiced than in Martin Ransohoff's *The Sandpiper*. And because it has Elizabeth Taylor and Richard Burton in the leading roles, the indelicacy of its implications is just that much more intrusive and cheap."

Bosley Crowther, THE NEW YORK TIMES

"Advertised as an 'adult love story,' *The Sandpiper* is tricked out in the full panoply of pretension so dear to the heart of the Hollywood highbrow, including the blatantly symbolic sandpiper which is clumsily equated with Laura's 'free soul.' The idea of an attractive woman's hedonistic philosophy coming into headlong conflict with the religious inhibitions of a man who desires her, is hardly new but has proved quite workable in the past. This time, Messrs. Trumbo and Wilson, who are credited with the screenplay, could hardly have done better if they had been intent on sending the whole thing up.

"Of control and direction there is hardly a sign, but there are some stunning opening shots of sea and sky in the wildly photogenic Big Sur area, and a colorful beach picnic choreographed so as to remind one momentarily that the director's name is Minnelli."

Brenda Davies, MONTHLY FILM BULLETIN

"There have been complaints about Miss Taylor's plumpness. Elizabeth Taylor, a man's woman, is stacked like a woman, curves and all. What do they want, an actress built like a fourteen-year-old boy?"

Wanda Hale, DAILY NEWS

"The prevalence of voyeurism and the cash to be derived therefrom provide the only possible explanation for this two-hour travesty which may not be the most perfectly awful movie ever made, but which is right down there fighting for the title.

"Miss Taylor and Mr. Burton were paid

With Richard Burton, James Edwards and Rex Holman

With Richard Burton

With Richard Burton and Charles Bronson

$1,750,000 for performing in *The Sandpiper*. If I were you, I wouldn't settle for less for watching them."

Judith Crist, NEW YORK HERALD TRIBUNE

"This plush romantic drama is at once pretentious and compelling, outspoken and naïve, provocative and rather silly. It is easy to see why Miss Taylor was attracted to her role. She is usually at her best playing a cornered, hostile woman berating the men around her. She is playing here that kind of woman who is also a free spirit, thumbing her nose at the world. What more could she ask? Miss Taylor is the best she has been in some years, while Burton is somewhat colorless."

William Peper,
NEW YORK WORLD-TELEGRAM & SUN

"Listening to lines like 'I never knew what love was before' and 'I've lost all my sense of sin,' it was impossible to separate this unconvincing performance from what we knew about the performers. The whole absurd enterprise up there on the screen seemed to be a vast double-entendre. Burton the clergyman makes high-toned literary remarks to beatnik artist Taylor like 'I can't dispel you from my thoughts,' and then when he hates himself in the morning, she reassures him with, 'Don't you realize what happened between us is *good?*' 'Great Lovers' should not be seen, not be heard, only imagined."

Pauline Kael

"It is possible to get one's kicks merely out of watching Miss Taylor, who has grown so ample that it has become necessary to dress her almost exclusively in a variety of ambulatory tents. On the few occasions when she dares reveal her bosom (or part thereof), one breast (or part thereof) proves sufficient to traverse an entire wide screen frame—diagonally."

John Simon, THE NEW LEADER

With Richard Burton

With George Segal and Sandy Dennis

Who's Afraid of Virginia Woolf?

An Ernest Lehman Production
A Warner Brothers Picture / 1966

CAST

Martha: Elizabeth Taylor; *George:* Richard Burton; *Nick:* George Segal; *Honey:* Sandy Dennis.

CREDITS

Director: Mike Nichols; *Producer:* Ernest Lehman; *Screenwriter:* Ernest Lehman; *Based on the Play by:* Edward Albee; *Cinematographer:* Haskell Wexler; *Production Designer:* Richard Sylbert; *Set Decorator:* George James Hopkins; *Musical Score:* Alex North; *Editor:* Sam O'Steen; *Costumes:* Irene Sharaff; *Miss Taylor's Make-up:* Gordon Bau; *Mr. Burton's Make-up:* Ronnie Berkeley; *Supervising Hairstylist:* Jean Burt Reilly; *Running Time:* 130 minutes.

THE FILM

Edward Albee's award-winning 1962 play had been a theatrical sensation and proved a triumph for its stars, Uta Hagen and Arthur Hill. There were many who hoped that this pair would re-create these roles when the property was filmed. Bette Davis admits that Martha was one of the few film roles she ever really wanted but didn't get. Because of its strong and frank language, this long and powerful play seemed an unlikely subject for the movies. Or, it was thought, the script would have to be so greatly altered that the work would lose all its power.

In the final analysis, the film version of *Who's Afraid of Virginia Woolf?* remains quite faithful to Albee; its greatest concession is to the star-system, then still very much prevalent. Without the controversial casting of Elizabeth Taylor and Richard Burton—without public concern over how the 1966 screen would get Albee's salty,

irreverent dialogue past censorship bodies—*Virginia Woolf* might never have attracted its large audiences or even earned back its considerable cost (a whopping $500,000 alone to playwright Albee).

At first it seemed that the odds were against this property. Screenwriter Ernest Lehman was making his debut as a movie producer with his adaptation of the play; ex-comedian Mike Nichols, despite a string of long-running Broadway hits, had yet to direct a film. And beautiful, glamorous Elizabeth Taylor as a frumpy, foul-tongued, middle-aged bitch? Nor was his role as a waspish, introverted college professor the usual assignment for forceful Richard Burton.

Taylor was Lehman's offbeat choice for Martha—a wildly unexpected, much-derided casting that had its inception in an eye to the boxoffice and its rewards in an Oscar and critical plaudits. Elizabeth reports having been, at first, "terrified" of the part, but Richard talked her into it and was then later signed himself. Nichols was their choice to direct this cast of four, to which was added George Segal, veteran of a handful of roles

With George Segal

in movies of varied merit, and Sandy Dennis, a Broadway actress making her motion picture début.

Virginia Woolf is short on plot but long on pungent dialogue and incisive characters. It offers its tiny cast a veritable thespian field day. Before any filming started, Mike Nichols rehearsed his four actors for over three weeks in a Hollywood studio. With the benefit of a completely closed set, both in rehearsal and performance, this quintet located their problems, worked them out, and mastered their characterizations to a degree to which film actors seldom have access. By the time cameras began to roll, the Burtons believed they could have taken to the road, offering *Who's*

Afraid of Virginia Woolf? in one-night stands.

For the shrewish Martha (Albee supplies no surnames for these unhappy people), Elizabeth added padding to her own extra pounds, allowed herself to look haggard, flabby, and lined, and sported a salt-and-pepper wig that was more often than not quite disheveled. Because the role was such an abrupt change of pace for her, Taylor says, oddly enough it was not a difficult one. Having Martha to hide behind, she could easily shake off Elizabeth Taylor; she reports, "There was a freedom that I've never known before in a role. I felt much more experimental. When I got into my Martha suit, I forgot me."

At a reported $5,000,000 cost, *Who's Afraid*

With Richard Burton

With Richard Burton

of Virginia Woolf? has been called the most expensive black-and-white movie ever made. Admittedly, the Burtons and the play alone accounted for a healthy $2,500,000 of that. And Nichols allows that using actual campus locations in Northhampton, Massachusetts (where bad weather held up production for several weeks), may have been ill-advised in the long run, although he thinks the academic atmosphere was helpful to his cast. However, when Academy Award nominations were announced, all such gambles would seem to have paid off: *Virginia Woolf* came away with thirteen citations, including all four cast members, director Nichols, screenwriter Lehman, Haskell Wexler's photography, the art direction,

editing, sound recording, costume design, and Alex North's score. With its major competition the British historical drama *A Man for All Seasons, Virginia Woolf* nevertheless walked away with five Oscars, including both distaff performers, Wexler's camerawork, Irene Sharaff's well-chosen wardrobe, and the sets and décor. And this time, there was little talk about Taylor's well-deserved Oscar being a consolation prize for either previous performances or personal misfortune. In her first genuine "character role," Elizabeth was a smash hit. Indeed, the star's detractors would have one believe that Martha is a part she has never stopped playing.

With George Segal, Richard Burton and Sandy Dennis

With George Segal and Richard Burton

CRITICS' CORNER

"At first blush—the first of many—the four-character work seems to be a game of mixed doubles with bludgeons. The contestants are one middle-aged and one young faculty couple in a New England college town, who pass a drunken Walpurgis Night turning on each other and then on themselves with no holds barred, no expletives omitted. Finally, their violence spent and their living-room arena splattered with the ugly shards of their secrets, the players take leave of each other: bloodied, bowed, yet still alive and—possibly—exorcised of the illusions that possessed them.

"For some, it heralds the welcome downfall of screen censorship. For others, its release represents a complete crumbling of the dikes of decency. To make the cause even more celebrated, the film's endless verbal karate provides a glittering metaphor for the life that a gossip-gulping public likes to think such people as Elizabeth Taylor and Richard Burton live off-screen.

"Burton plays Pa Masochist to Miss Taylor's Ma Sade: a mediocre professor at a mediocre college married to the aging daughter of the school's president. They are probably the most bellicose and vituperative helpmates in the long history of Western drama. Burton's performance is a marvel of disciplined compassion. With the self-contained authority of a great actor, he plays the part as if no one in the world had ever heard of Richard Burton.

"His wife takes another and far less fortunate approach. Though her last scenes of lament for a lost fantasy child are exquisite, Miss Taylor treats the rest of her role as if it were a prank, not a person. She seems to be the thin lady playing fat for fun, the beauty playing ugly, the sweet-voiced spouse mimicking a snarling harridan. She has acted extremely well at times in the past, but this time her work is monotonous and disappointingly crude."

NEWSWEEK

"It is far-and-away the best Elizabeth Taylor–Richard Burton achievement to date. The picture does, however, establish a new high mark in the use of vulgar and profane terms.

"Miss Taylor's portrayal of the blowsy, vulgar, domineering wife is easily the finest performance of her career. Burton's deeply etched delineation of the harried history instructor is a work that actors dedicated to their profession can use for a textbook.

"George Segal plays the ambitious young biology professor with impressive conviction. Sandy Dennis, making her screen debut after a Broadway success in *Any Wednesday*, handles promisingly the least rewarding of the four principal roles."

William Weaver, MOTION PICTURE HERALD

"Edward Albee's *Who's Afraid of Virginia Woolf?*, the best American play of the last decade, and a violently candid one, has been brought to the screen without pussy-footing. This in itself makes it a notable event in our film history.

"As for the acting, Richard Burton was part of the star package with which this film began, but—a big but—Mr. Burton is also an actor. He has become a kind of specialist in sensitive self-disgust and he does it well. He is not in his person the George we might imagine, but he is utterly convincing as a man with a great lake of nausea in him, on which he sails with regret and compulsive amusement. On past evidence, Mr. Nichols had relatively little work to do with Mr. Burton. On past evidence, he had a good deal to do with Elizabeth Taylor. She has shown previously, in some roles, that she could respond to the right director and could at least flagellate herself into an emotional state (as in *Suddenly, Last Summer*). Here, with a director who knows how to get an actor's confidence and knows what to do with it after he gets it, she does the best work of her career, sustained and urgent. Of course, she has an initial advantage. Her acceptance of gray

hair and her use of profanity make her seem to be acting even (figuratively) before she begins. Under Mr. Nichols' hand, she gets vocal variety, never relapses out of her role, and she charges it with the utmost of her powers—which is an achievement for any actress, great or little.

"The film's advertisements say, 'No one under 18 will be admitted unless accompanied by his parent.' This may safeguard the children; the parents must take their chances."

Stanley Kauffmann, THE NEW YORK TIMES

"The naked power and oblique tenderness of Edward Albee's incisive, inhuman drama have been transformed from legit into a brilliant motion picture. Keen adaptation and handsome production, outstanding direction and four topflight performances score an artistic bullseye.

"Miss Taylor, who has proven she can act in response to sensitive direction, earned every penny of her reported million plus. Her characterization is at once sensual, spiteful, cynical, pitiable, loathsome, lustful and tender. Shrews—both male and

With Richard Burton, George Segal and Sandy Dennis

female—always attract initial attention, but the projection of three-dimensional reality requires talent which sustains the interest; the talent is here. Burton delivers a smash portrayal. He evokes sympathy during the public degradations to which his wife subjects him, and his outrage, as well as his deliberate vengeance, are totally believable."

"Murf," VARIETY

"An orgy of truth or consequences, *Virginia Woolf* at best is a baleful, brutally funny explosion of black humor. Edward Albee, America's current master of theatrical invective, uses it here for potshots and heavy artillery in a marital Armageddon.

"Broadway Director Mike Nichols, in his first movie job, can claim a sizable victory simply for the performance he has wrung from Elizabeth Taylor. Looking fat and fortyish under a smear of makeup, with her voice pitched well below the belt, Liz as Martha is loud, sexy, vulgar, pungent, and yet achieves moments of astonishing tenderness. Only during sustained eruptions does she lapse into monotony, or look like an actress play-acting animosity instead of feeling it."

TIME

"If Taylor does not match Burton, it is not for want of trying. Nichols has worked hard with her on her big scenes, and she is never less than competent. What she lacks is Burton's heroic calm, particularly in the all-too-rare quiet moments when she is supposed to be listening and reacting, moments that are the supreme tests of acting. It is at those moments that a sullen coarseness invades her dulled features, and Burton simply soars by contrast, with inscrutable ironies flickering across his beautifully ravaged face. Without Burton the film would have been an intolerably cold experience."

Andrew Sarris, THE VILLAGE VOICE

With Richard Burton

The Taming of the Shrew

A Co-Production of Royal Films International
and F.A.I. Productions (United States-Italian)
A Columbia Pictures Release / 1967
In Panavision and Technicolor

CAST

Katharina: Elizabeth Taylor; *Petruchio:* Richard Burton; *Grumio:* Cyril Cusack; *Baptista:* Michael Hordern; *Lucentio:* Michael York; *Bianca:* Natasha Pyne; *Hortensio:* Victor Spinetti; *Tranio:* Alfred Lynch; *Gremio:* Alan Webb; *Pedant:* Vernon Dobtcheff; *Biondello:* Roy Holder; *Priest:* Giancarlo Cobelli; *Curtis:* Gianni Magni; *Nathaniel:* Alberto Bonucci; *Gregory:* Lino Capolicchio; *Philip:* Roberto Antonelli; *Vincentio:* Mark Dignam; *Haberdasher:* Anthony Garner; *Tailor:* Ken Parry; *Widow:* Bice Valori.

CREDITS

Director: Franco Zeffirelli; *Executive Producer:* Richard McWhorter; *Producers:* Richard Burton, Elizabeth Taylor, and Franco Zeffirelli; *Screenwriters:* Paul Dehn, Suso Cecchi D'Amico, and Franco Zeffirelli; *Based on the Play by:* William Shakespeare; *Cinematographers:* Oswald Morris and Luciano Trasatti; *Production Designer:* John De Cuir; *Art Directors:* Giuseppe Mariani and Elven Webb; *Set Decorators:* Dario Simoni and Carlo Gervasi; *Special Effects:* Augie Lohman; *Musical Score:* Nino Rota; *Editors:* Peter Taylor and Carlo Fabianelli; *Costumes:* Irene Sharaff (Taylor and Burton) and Danilo Donatti; *Running Time:* 122 minutes.

THE FILM

Shakespeare's rambunctious comedy first reached

the screen in 1908 in a D. W. Griffith Biograph production and, while the following decade brought another pair of silent adaptations, it remained for Mary Pickford and her husband Douglas Fairbanks to offer their only co-starring appearance in the 1929 all-talking version. Immortalized by the credit line "with additional dialogue by Sam Taylor" (the film's director), this *Shrew* proved an ill-advised change of pace for Pickford, and the public avoided it. In the event that talkies should prove a passing fad, Doug and Mary also prepared a silent version—needlessly. In the intervening years, *Shrew* has reached the cinema only through the altered auspices of *Kiss Me Kate* (1953), from the Bard-derived Broadway musical.

Franco Zeffirelli's colorful, free-wheeling 1967 adaptation, from the screenplay devised in collaboration with Paul Dehn and Suso Cecchi D'Amico, takes many liberties with Shakespeare but, in the opinion of not a few, they are justified. What's more, they work to the director's advantage, for this filmed-in-Rome *Shrew* retains the original story's ribald merriment against an interpretation of fourteenth-century Padua rich with earthy Renaissance vitality.

Shakespeare's rowdy boy-gets-girl classic provided, for the Burtons, an interesting parallel to *Who's Afraid of Virginia Woolf?*, their previous film together. Popular with both the public and many critics, *The Taming of the Shrew* would prove their last successful joint effort for some time to come.

CRITICS' CORNER

"Zeffirelli has succeeded in mounting the liveliest screen incarnation of Shakespeare since Olivier's *Henry V*. For all its virtues, this particular taming is sometimes more shrewd than *Shrew*. The writers have edited Shakespeare's speeches, transposed lines, and improvised bits of business for the Burtons that never took place in the Globe's wooden O. Despite such wild tampering, most of the words and—more important—all of the spirit of the play have been maintained.

"In one of her better performances, Taylor makes Kate seem the ideal bawd of Avon—a creature of beauty with a voice shrieking howls and imprecations. Whenever Liz strains at the Elizabethan, the camera shifts to Burton, who catches the cadences of iambic pentameter with inborn ease.

"When a classic is treated as deathless, it dies; by being brash and breezy, Zeffirelli has breathed new life into an old text."

TIME

"Those to whom Shakespeare's words are sacred will know by now that Franco Zeffirelli is something of a blasphemer. They will not be surprised to find that with *The Taming of the Shrew* his role is that of impresario rather than director, for

With Bice Valori, Richard Burton, Alfred Lynch and Michael Hordern

With Richard Burton

what emerges is a boisterous, bowdlerized version of the play, a Renaissance *Kiss Me Kate,* or an animated reproduction of one of Hogarth's wilder engravings.

"Richard Burton's lusty, ribald Petruchio is only marred by his jerky laugh, which soon lapses into a mannerism. Elizabeth Taylor, it must be said, is no match for Shakespeare's words. But she certainly looks the part, which in this production is much more to the point."

David Wilson, MONTHLY FILM BULLETIN

"There was never very much doubt about the abilities of Burton; he was a trained actor in the English tradition and, while climbing into the million-dollar category as a movie star, still dutifully maintained his contact with the stage. There was more question about Miss Taylor, originally a product of MGM's star system and star-crossed in her love and marital life. Her movie performances during the past ten years have ranged from mediocre to very good, and I, for one, found her splendid in *Who's Afraid of Virginia Woolf?*—the equal of some of our more prestigious stage actresses and equipped as well with the kind of camera sensitivity that only laborious experience

With Richard Burton and Cyril Cusack

[181]

can bring. But Shakespeare is another kind of peak to climb, and the challenge to Miss Taylor must have been a big one. She had to contend with her husband at his absolute best in a role for which he is so extremely well suited. Well, not only has she managed it; she has come through the ordeal with honor. She has held nothing back in attacking the role with blazing fury, and in her final moments, when she is at last the tamed wife—adjusted to her situation, so to speak—she is magnificent. I don't know exactly why I felt proud of her, but I did."

Hollis Alpert, SATURDAY REVIEW

"It is a shaky and unpoetic contraption, little more than a vehicle for a couple of players to exhibit their talent for merriment and romping in excelsis—and, too often, in excess. Miss Taylor, for her part, seems to be trying to make up with characterization (let alone squeals) for her discomfort with the language."

Judith Crist,
NEW YORK WORLD JOURNAL TRIBUNE

"Having had at one another very roundly and in a serious vein in *Virginia Woolf,* the Burtons are now turned loose with slapsticks for a free-swinging hit-as-hit-can in this forthrightly campy entertainment. They are refereed by Franco Zeffirelli out of the corner of one winking eye. And if any

With Richard Burton

crusty customer doesn't like it—well, a pox on him!"

Bosley Crowther, THE NEW YORK TIMES

"This newest version is a boisterous, often over-stagey frolic which will strike many as a fair compromise for mass audiences between the original Shakespeare and, say, *Kiss Me Kate.* The two stars pack plenty of wallop, making their roles meaty and flamboyant, with a larger-than-life Burton playing for plenty of sly laughs in the uninhibited wife-beating lark. Miss Taylor tends to over-exploit an 'earthy' aspect in early footage, and her switch to the subdued attitude comes too abruptly, but against that she's a buxom delight when tamed."

"Rich," VARIETY

With Cyril Cusack and Richard Burton

With Richard Burton

Doctor Faustus

An Oxford University Screen Production
  in Association with
Nassau Films and Venfilms (Rome)
Released in the United States
  by Columbia Pictures / 1967
In Technicolor

CAST

Doctor Faustus: Richard Burton; *Helen of Troy:* Elizabeth Taylor; *Mephistopheles:* Andreas Teuber; *Empress:* Elizabeth O'Donovan; *Emperor:* Ian Marter; *Beelzebub:* Jeremy Eccles; *Lucifer:* David McIntosh; *Valdes:* Ram Chopra; *Cornelius:* Richard Carwardine; *Pope:* Adrian Benjamin; *First Scholar:* Richard Heffer; *Second Scholar:* Hugh Williams; *Third Scholar/Lechery:* Gwydion Thomas; *Cardinal/Pride:* Nicholas Loukes; *Evil Angel/Knight:* Richard Durden-Smith; *Wagner:* Patrick Barwise; *Attendant at Emperor's Court:* Jeremy Chandler; *Rector Magnificus:* Angus McIntosh; *First Professor/Avarice:* Ambrose Coghill; *Second Professor/Envy:* Anthony Kaufmann; *Third Professor:* Julian Wontner; *Fourth Professor:* Richard Harrison; *Fifth Professor:* Nevill Coghill; *Good Angel:* Michael Menaugh; *Boy-Turned-into-Hind:* John Sandbach; *Idiot:* Sebastian Walker; *Wrath:* R. Peverello; *Sloth:* Maria Aitken; *Idleness:* Valerie James; *Gluttony:* Bridget Coghill, Petronella Pulsford, and Susan Watson; *Dancers:* Jacqueline Harvey, Sheila Dawson, and Carolyn Bennitt; *Nun/Court Lady:* Jane Wilford.

CREDITS

Directors: Richard Burton and Nevill Coghill; *Producers:* Richard Burton and Richard McWhorter; *Screen Adaptation:* Nevill Coghill; *Based on the Play* "The Tragicall History of Doc-

tor Faustus" *by:* Christopher Marlowe; *Cinematographer:* Gabor Pogany; *Production Designer:* John De Cuir; *Art Director:* Boris Juraga; *Set Decorator:* Dario Simoni; *Musical Score:* Mario Nascimbene; *Choreographer:* Jacqueline Harvey; *Editor:* John Shirley; *Costumes:* Peter Hall; *Running Time:* 93 minutes.

THE FILM

Doctor Faustus, perhaps the Burtons' least commercial motion picture undertaking, stemmed from a stage production of early 1966, for which

Burton returned to his alma mater. Under the direction of his former tutor, Professor Nevill Coghill, the actor joined the Oxford University Dramatic Society in a production of Marlowe's classic which, aside from Elizabeth Taylor in the silent role of Helen of Troy, was composed entirely of students. Any and all profits from this play and its subsequent film version were donated to the dramatic society.

Burton has reported that raising money for this movie version, as well as for his previous *The Taming of the Shrew,* was not easy, because it was based on a classic that many a prospective investor considered noncommercial. However, due to *Shrew*'s success, *Faustus* met with more investor-interest than it might otherwise have done, although its United States distributor, Columbia Pictures, did not release the property until early in 1968, well over a year after its completion.

Filmed at the De Laurentiis Studios in Rome and Britain's Shepperton Studios, *Doctor Faustus* met with a nearly universal drubbing from the press and finally broke the Burtons' until-then-infallible Midas touch at American boxoffices. A failure of awesome proportions, it undoubtedly did much to dissuade either Richard or Elizabeth from attempting another scholarly classic on the screen. Previous to this film, detailing the torments of that famed scholar who sold his soul to the devil in exchange for youth and pleasure, Burton had only directed briefly for the screen: when Franco Zeffirelli was forced to depart *The Taming of the Shrew* to honor a commitment to Samuel Barber's *Antony and Cleopatra* for the Metropolitan Opera, Burton shot the last four days of "relatively unimportant footage," following carefully laid-out instructions by Zeffirelli.

At a press conference held in New York in conjunction with the American premiere of *Faustus,* Burton spoke of directing his wife in a film adaptation of Shakespeare's *Macbeth,* opposite either Laurence Olivier or Paul Scofield. To date, unfortunately, no such project has come to fruition.

CRITICS' CORNER

"Lots of grads bring their wives back to the old

With unidentified player

school and ham it up for home movies—but this is ridiculous. Richard Burton is charging admission.

"Visually, the Burton *Faustus* is a darkling carnival of skeletons, candles, caves and necromancy, tricked out with such cinematic hocus-pocus as action shots montaged into a skull's eye socket and heartbeats lab-dubbed onto the sound track. There is even a bit of borrowing here too: a film clip of the magnificent charge of the French knights of Agincourt from Olivier's *Henry V* inexplicably turns up, and it is easily the best thing in the movie. The worst is Elizabeth Taylor, who has a series of walk-ons mostly meant to exemplify lust. Her makeup varies from Greek statuesque to a head-to-toe spray job of aluminum paint. When she welcomes Burton to an eternity of damnation, her eyeballs and teeth are dripping pink in what seems to be a hellish combination of conjunctivitis and trench mouth. Mercifully mute throughout, she merely moves in and out of camera range, breasting the waves of candle smoke, dry-ice vapor and vulgarity that swirl through the sets."

TIME

"Of all the classic works available for celluloid incarnation, Christopher Marlowe's sixteenth-century morality play is one of the stranger choices. Rigorously medieval in viewpoint, it has little to say to modern man—and even less in this transcription.

"And, finally, for what must surely be the costliest walk-on in film history, Burton has expanded Marlowe's wordless Helen of Troy (played, of course, by Elizabeth Taylor) to embrace *all* the temptations of the flesh that beset Faustus. Mephistopheles has but to whisper a word and Miss Taylor materializes with a fresh costume and a more outlandish makeup, the embodiment of fleshly delights."

Arthur Knight, SATURDAY REVIEW

"*Faustus* has degenerated into the story of a man who has sold his soul for Elizabeth Taylor, and you can draw whatever parallel with that that you would like to draw. But *Doctor Faustus* is hardly recognizable in what we might politely call a very high camp version of a classic."

Judith Crist, NBC-TV TODAY SHOW

With Richard Burton

"*Doctor Faustus* is of an awfulness that bends the mind. The Burtons are clearly having a lovely time; at moments one has the feeling that *Faustus* was shot mainly as a home movie for them to enjoy at home."

Renata Adler, THE NEW YORK TIMES

"Probably one of the most desperately non-commercial enterprises in motion picture history, this version of *Doctor Faustus* is a curio unlikely to recover its negative cost. Richard Burton is, as yet, too inexperienced as a director to translate it with confidence to celluloid. And, though there are some suitably somber and flickering episodes (with evocative lensing by Gabor Pogany), the rhythm and momentum necessary to carry one along with the plot are entirely lacking. What remains is an oddity that may have some archive appeal, for at least it records a performance by Burton that gives an insight into his prowess in classical roles, even more than his Petruchio in *The Taming of the Shrew.* One surprise is the general adequacy of the Oxford amateurs, with a good performance in any terms from Andreas Teuber as Mephistopheles."

"Otta," VARIETY

With Julie Harris

Reflections in a Golden Eye

A John Huston–Ray Stark Production
Released by Warner Brothers–Seven Arts / 1967
In Panavision and Technicolor

CAST

Leonora Penderton: Elizabeth Taylor; *Major Weldon Penderton:* Marlon Brando; *Lieutenant Colonel Morris Langdon:* Brian Keith; *Alison Langdon:* Julie Harris; *Anacleto:* Zorro David; *Stables Sergeant:* Gordon Mitchell; *Captain Weincheck:* Irvin Dugan; *Susie:* Fay Sparks; and introducing as *Private Williams:* Robert Forster.

CREDITS

Director: John Huston; *Producer:* Ray Stark; *Screenwriters:* Chapman Mortimer and Gladys Hill; *Based on the Novel by:* Carson McCullers; *Cinematographer:* Aldo Tonti; *Production Designer:* Stephen Grimes; *Art Director:* Bruno Avesani; *Set Decorator:* William Kiernan; *Musical Score:* Toshiro Mayuzumi; *Editor:* Russell Lloyd; *Costumes:* Dorothy Jeakins; *Hairstyles for Miss Taylor:* Alexandre of Paris; *Running Time:* 109 minutes.

THE FILM

Carson McCullers's 1941 novella about a collection of bizarre perversions on a Southern army post was, obviously, far too heady subject matter for the screen until the relaxed censorship restrictions of the late 1960s, and the past Hollywood successes of various Tennessee Williams works, paved the way. Even so, the collective downbeat neuroses of the various leading characters of *Reflections in a Golden Eye* necessitated assembling a combination of stars and director that might assure audience interest.

Originally Elizabeth Taylor found the story intriguing, especially as a vehicle to reunite her with a previous co-star, Montgomery Clift. That actor's unfortunate death at forty-five, two months before production was to begin, presented problems, for the role of a repressed, homosexual Army major, married to a contemptuous, adulterous wife, was not one to interest many a leading movie actor in 1966; Richard Burton refused to play the part, and so did Lee Marvin. Taylor then sought out Marlon Brando at a time when he happened to be not only available but also interested.

A not-unusual Taylor requirement was that the film be made in Rome, and the majority of *Reflections* was shot at the De Laurentiis studios, as well as using Roman locations that might resemble the environs of a Georgia army post. Just prior to the start of production in Rome, director John Huston filmed locations with much of his cast at Long Island's Mitchell Air Field. Although the Italian studio-work is excellent and hard to define as such, the 1940s Southern-army-post milieu seems elusive, and the resultant motion picture clearly lacks any definite sense of time and place.

Few of the movie's central characters succeed in eliciting any audience sympathy, despite some interesting performances and direction. Elizabeth Taylor plays the amoral wife of Brando's prissy, repressed major, a self-absorbed fetishist whose only outside love object appears to be a covert attraction to a moody, withdrawn soldier (Robert Forster), whose own odd proclivities take the form of naked horseback rides in the forest and nocturnal vigils at the bedside of the major's wife. Next door to the major is an equally abnormal household: his commanding officer (Brian Keith), whose neurotic wife (Julie Harris) prefers to sit up nights communing with an effete houseboy (Zorro David) who shares her penchant for the arts and a fantasy existence, while her husband dallies with the major's sexy wife.

By the film's climax, Harris has died in a sanitarium, thus shaking Keith's affair with Taylor. And in the violent finale Brando, discovering Forster quietly watching his estranged wife's sleeping form, erupts into a jealous fury and kills the soldier with his revolver. At the fade-out, director Huston swings his camera wildly back and forth from Forster's lifeless form to Brando's horrified face to Taylor's wild screams, finally closing on the Carson McCullers quotation with which the film had also begun: "There is a fort in the South where a few years ago a murder was committed."

Hardly a critic had any kind words for *Reflections in a Golden Eye*, although there was scattered praise for a few of the performers. Of even more interest, however, was the unusual color process attending the film's initial release, a

With Brian Keith and Marlon Brando

result of Huston experiments with desaturated Technicolor that left an effect of washed-out sepia tones, accompanied by a golden glow that was occasionally relieved by shades of pink and red introduced to emphasize certain specific objects for an intended effect. But, when the public did not appear particularly interested in seeing this downbeat melodrama, despite the supposed drawing power of the Taylor and Brando names, Warner Brothers junked these special-toned prints and released the film, for subsequent engagements, in full Technicolor. Although far more popular than *Doctor Faustus*, *Reflections in a Golden Eye* was no blockbuster, although it has managed to gather its partisans in the time since its 1967 release.

CRITICS' CORNER

"The recently demised Carson McCullers' novel *Reflections in a Golden Eye*, has been turned into a pretentious melodrama by director John Huston and producer Ray Stark. Urban audiences already are accustomed to sturdier, more direct treatments, and rural audiences could possibly miss the point completely.

"Stars Elizabeth Taylor and Marlon Brando alternate in mannered thesping. Brando struts about and mugs as the stuffy officer, whose Dixie dialect is often incoherent. Miss Taylor, again tongue-clucking and shrewish in the *Virginia Woolf* groove, is appropriately unaware of her husband's torment. Her dialect also obscures some vital plot points. The most outstanding and satisfying performance is that of Brian Keith. This versatile actor is superb as the rationalizing and insensitive middle-class hypocrite."

"Murf," VARIETY

"*Reflections in a Golden Eye* has one possible virtue: it will send you right back to Carson McCullers' book (hopefully to read it), because one can't imagine that her perceptive novel had nothing more to offer that nutty people and pseudo pornography.

"Brando barely opens his eyes throughout the entire film, but Miss Taylor is very good as the trollopy young woman and Brian Keith and Julie Harris are excellent in their thankless roles. But the film is simply an embarrassment for all concerned."

Judith Crist, THE NBC-TV TODAY SHOW

With Marlon Brando and unidentified players

With Robert Forster

"John Huston's adaptation of the Carson McCullers novel sinks into boredom very fast. Part of the problem certainly lies with the original book. The McCullers brand of Southern decadence lacks the Mr. Showmanship flamboyance of Tennessee Williams, and the tepid, Major-loves-Private plot might have happened just as easily at Fort Ord."

Margot S. Kernan, FILM QUARTERLY

"The film obviously could never be everybody's cup of tea, despite the presence of Elizabeth Taylor, who is really very good, and Marlon Brando, who gives one of his most tiresomely perverse and self-conscious performances as her mixed-up husband. The film is anyway nearly stolen by Julie Harris, effortlessly believable as the half-mad neighbour, and by Zorro David, a New York hairdresser making his acting debut as the epicene houseboy."

John Russell Taylor SIGHT AND SOUND

"Director John Huston spills the novel's poetry on the way to the screen, leaving only its gothic

With Brian Keith

On the Set with Marlon Brando

husk and a gallery of grotesques. As a cracked Southern-belle, Julie Harris is the only member of the cast who reflects the distinctive McCullers quality of loneliness and terror.

All that remains praiseworthy is the film's extraordinary photographic technique. Seemingly shot in black and white, the picture is actually severely muted Technicolor. Thus from time to time, faded reds and golds seep through the images to give them an eerie, trance-like quality."

TIME

"*Reflections in a Golden Eye* is a stupefying mish-mash of Southern clichés. As directed by John Huston and photographed in a sepia monotone—through which burst with maddening irrelevance mauve blouses, carpetings and shoulder patches—the film seems a grappling with sordid realism by people who have lost all touch with reality.

"As for Elizabeth Taylor, *Reflections* demonstrates by inversion the contributions of a strong director. Her virulent scenes in *Virginia Woolf* revealed her full capabilities; but when she shrieks 'You son of a bitch!' at Brando in this one, she might still be playing *National Velvet*."

Arthur Knight, SATURDAY REVIEW

"It takes no stretch of the imagination to see that *Reflections in a Golden Eye* might have been a risible disaster; but the film works because Huston plays absolutely straight by the novel, so that even scenes that ought to have looked grotesque on the screen seem to have their natural place in the film's order of things.

"Elizabeth Taylor (noisily effective as the major's wife), Brian Keith and Julie Harris are all good; and if one has initial doubts about Marlon Brando's clipped mannerisms, as the character develops they seem to be perfectly in keeping with his remoteness."

David Wilson, MONTHLY FILM BULLETIN

"Despite everything that is laboriously wrong with *Reflections*, the visual style—like paintings made from photographs—is interesting, and the director, John Huston, and the actors were able to do some extraordinary things with Carson McCullers' conceptions.

"Elizabeth Taylor is charming as a silly, sensual Southern 'lady'—a relief from the movies in which Burton ostentatiously plays down to her and she valiantly tries to act up to him and they're both awful."

Pauline Kael, THE NEW YORKER

"Elizabeth Taylor is erratic, showing genuine arrogance and cruelty in some scenes, but too often letting her bitchy housewife be merely postured and shrill."

Bosley Crowther, THE NEW YORK TIMES

With Richard Burton

The Comedians

A joint effort of
Maximilian Prods. (Bermuda) and Trianon
    Prods. (Paris) for
Metro-Goldwyn-Mayer / 1967
In Panavision and Metrocolor

CAST

Brown: Richard Burton; *Martha Pineda:* Elizabeth Taylor; *Jones:* Alec Guinness; *Ambassador Pineda:* Peter Ustinov; *Smith:* Paul Ford; *Mrs. Smith:* Lillian Gish; *Concasseur:* Raymond St. Jacques; *Michel:* Zaeks Mokae; *Petit Pierre:* Roscoe Lee Browne; *Joseph:* Douta Seck; *Cesar:* Albia Peters; *Mrs. Philipot:* Gloria Foster; *Angelito:* Robin Langford; *Henry Philipot:* Georg Stanford Brown; *Dr. Magiot:* James Earl Jones; *Marie-Thérèse:* Cicely Tyson.

CREDITS

Director/Producer: Peter Glenville; *Screenwriter:* Graham Greene, *Based on his Novel; Cinematographer:* Henri Decae; *Art Director:* François de Lamothe; *Set Decorator:* Robert Christides; *Musical Score:* Laurence Rosenthal; *Editor:* Françoise Javet; *Miss Taylor's Gowns:* Tiziani of Rome; *Miss Taylor's Hairstyles:* Alexandre of Paris; *Running Time:* 160 minutes.

THE FILM

Graham Greene's explosive novel about political turmoil amid the Haitian dictatorship of "Papa Doc" Duvalier, could hardly have been filmed on that Caribbean island. However, the appropriate settings and atmosphere were astonishingly well caught by producer-director Peter Glenville, who combined locations in Dahomey, West Africa, with exteriors in the South of France and interiors inside a Paris studio. Had they filmed any closer to the actual locales of Greene's story, cast and crew might not have survived to tell of it, for immediately on the heels of the movie's release late in 1967, it set off a storm of protest from the Haitian ambassador, whose official statement

With Peter Ustinov

called *The Comedians* "an inflammatory libel against Haiti, publicly released to mislead the American people." The protest further countered that "Haiti is one of the most beautiful, peaceful and safest countries in the Caribbean." In retaliation, both Graham Greene and Peter Glenville swore to knowledge of the film's accuracy in depicting terror and oppression prevalent in Haiti as recently as two years earlier.

This lengthy, often powerful study of a small group of people caught up in "Papa Doc's" reign of fear is quite a shocker, not only in certain of its terror scenes, but also in its implications. Elizabeth Taylor's role, as the German-born wife of Peter Ustinov's burly ambassador, and a lady given to adulterous bouts with Richard Burton's cynical hotel-owner, gives the story its novelettish touches. And, since Taylor's attempts at a German accent sound more like a *French* dialect, this character frequently rings quite false, although, needless to say, she is extremely decorative.

With Richard Burton and Georg Stanford Brown

CRITICS' CORNER

"By far the most agitating aspect of the film Peter Glenville has made from Graham Greene's novel, *The Comedians,* is the sinister image it presents of a rigid reign of terror in a Caribbean country under a black dictatorship—and thus, by a quick association out of our own recent experiences, an image of the fearful implications of burgeoning 'black power.'

"The tired and disgusted hotel owner is a character with many antecedents. And even though he is played with fine acerbity and bristling boredom by Richard Burton, he's a fellow we've all endured many times. Likewise, the lady is another familiar and predictable type. Elizabeth Taylor simply plays her so cruelly and confidently that she appears more ferocious than usual, especially in the kissing scenes. The husband is the customary cuckold as played politely by Peter Ustinov. And Alec Guinness comes on bright and breezy as the British boaster who turns out to be a fraud. Newer, yet conventional additions to this punctiliously uncommitted clutch of white people in a black man's country, are Lillian Gish and Paul Ford as a pair of visiting American do-gooders. All together, these characters contribute

With Richard Burton

only a moderately interesting account of apathy and personal self-indulgence in the midst of a nation undergoing terrible trial."

Bosley Crowther, THE NEW YORK TIMES

"No sooner does the plot begin to move than we are brought to a dead halt by the Burtons' cinematic amours and maulings, which are becoming not only boring but slightly less esthetic (the years are taking their toll, as they do on all sex symbols, especially from the chin-line down); even when it does move beyond performance, it bogs down in Peter Glenville's pedestrian direction. A pity—because if *The Comedians* ever got going, it might have gone somewhere."

Judith Crist, THE NBC-TV TODAY SHOW

"Except for the ending of the film, Greene has written a screenplay that is extremely faithful to his novel, including all the central incidents. The dialogue is crisp and literate, as one would expect. At two hours and forty minutes the picture is too long, but it holds the attention of the spectator most of the way."

Richard Gertner, MOTION PICTURE HERALD

"Peter Glenville's direction, with its ponderous stylistic trick of starting each sequence by focus-

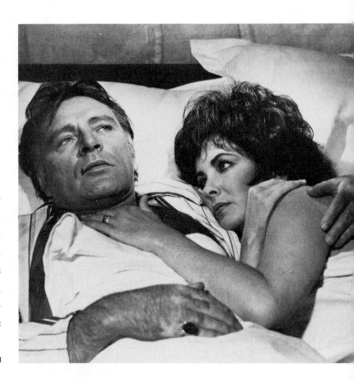

ing on some irrelevant detail before panning down to the real centre of interest, does nothing to alleviate the general air of sogginess; nor do Burton and Taylor, as they moon glumly, plumply and passionlessly through their romantic routine. As long as Lillian Gish and Paul Ford are around as a splendidly archetypal pair of innocents abroad, the film retains some semblance of life. But after they depart, there remains only Peter Ustinov, determinedly subdued as the cuckolded ambassador, and Alec Guinness, bringing exactly the right touch of jaunty ambivalence to his part though ultimately defeated by his blatantly rigged final scene. It isn't much in a *very* long-winded film."

Tom Milne, MONTHLY FILM BULLETIN

With Alec Guinness

"Elizabeth Taylor is every man's dream wife—beautiful, talented, and working. Since she earns at least a million dollars for every film she appears in, and has played in four in the last twelve months, she is also the kind of girl that any man can afford. The studios feel that they can afford her, too. She is one of the few stars—many say the *only* star—who is regarded as a true gilt-edged investment. Her presence in a picture is a sure guarantee that audiences will turn out in sufficient quantity to offset even the staggering costs of a *Cleopatra*. Miss Taylor's two latest efforts, *The*

Comedians and *Reflections in a Golden Eye,* seem almost specifically designed to test the loyalty of her public, each in its own way. *The Comedians,* skillfully adapted by Graham Greene from his own recent novel, is a thoughtful, thought-provoking work in which the star appears disadvantaged by the necessity to maintain the semblance of a German accent. On the other hand, the troublesome accent apart, she has a role that seems comfortably within her grasp at all times."

Arthur Knight, SATURDAY REVIEW

With Richard Burton, James Earl Jones, Alec Guinness and Peter Ustinov

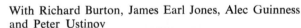

With Richard Burton

Boom!

A John Heyman Production
for Universal Pictures / 1968
In Panavision and Technicolor

CAST

Flora ("Sissy") Goforth: Elizabeth Taylor; *Chris Flanders:* Richard Burton; *The Witch of Capri:* Noël Coward; *Blackie:* Joanna Shimkus; *Rudy* Michael Dunn; *Dr. Lullo:* Romolo Valli; *Etti:* Fernando Piazza; *Simonetta:* Veronica Wells; *Manicurist:* Claudye Ettori; *Journalist:* Howard Taylor; *Photographer:* Gens Bloch; *Villager:* Franco Pesce.

CREDITS

Director: Joseph Losey; *Producers:* John Heyman and Norman Priggen; *Screenwriter* Tennessee Williams; *Based on His Short Story* "Man Bring This Up the Road" *and His Play* "The Milk Train Doesn't Stop Here Anymore"; *Cinematographer:* Douglas Slocombe; *Production Designer:* Richard MacDonald; *Musical Score:* John Barry; *Editor:* Reginald Beck; *Gowns:* Tiziani of Rome;

Hairstyles: Alexandre of Paris; *Running Time:* 110 minutes.

THE FILM

On the stage, Tennessee Williams's *The Milk Train Doesn't Stop Here Anymore* has had two incarnations, neither one a great success: in 1963, Hermione Baddeley created the flamboyant role of "Sissy" Goforth, the much-married, now-widowed millionairess, whose last exotic summer is consumed with an effort to dictate her memoirs before she expires—a Mediterranean summer disturbingly interrupted by the appearance of a handsome and enigmatic young poet, known to play companion to wealthy women as they near death. Although nowhere near the least of Williams's works—it's never less than interesting— *Milk Train,* the play, exemplified the playwright's

With Noël Coward

well-known talents for writing great parts for women. When that production ended after sixty-nine performances, Williams considerably revised the work and witnessed a disastrous Broadway revival a year later with Tallulah Bankhead pulling out all the stops in what turned out to be her farewell to Broadway.

On the screen, *Milk Train* is still a failure, although not an uninteresting one. Few playgoers would have imagined it as a vehicle for the Burtons. Instead, were a movie "name" required for the bizarre, colorful Flora Goforth, producers John Heyman and Norman Priggen could have done well to engage, say, Bette Davis and possibly Robert Redford. With that sort of casting,

the Williams original would not have been betrayed as it was by making it a campy vehicle for a far-too-young-and-beautiful Elizabeth Taylor and a somewhat-over-the-hill-for-his-role Richard Burton. Equally bizarre (though, obviously pandering to the more-liberal cinema of the late 1960s) was Williams's changing the waspish Witch of Capri role (so well created on Broadway by Mildred Dunnock) to a bitchy male, in the person of Noël Coward.

The film's director, Joseph Losey, has reported that considering the script's "difficult" subject matter and lack of past-Broadway-hit status to support him, he was hard put to find a star suitably aged for the role *and* one who would

With Joanna Shimkus, Fernando Piazza, Richard Burton and Michael Dunn

insure box-office success for *Boom!* One exception, of course, was Elizabeth Taylor, who had not yet suffered the loss of the drawing power she later showed with the dismal reception accorded George Stevens's 1970 *The Only Game in Town.*

During production, this film had trouble settling on a title, and was variously known as *Goforth* and *The Milk Train Doesn't Stop Here Anymore,* before Universal Pictures settled on the cryptic *Boom!,* a puzzling reference to the rhythmic pounding of the surf at the cliffs below the terraces of Mrs. Goforth's island retreat.

Though miscast, Taylor makes a dynamic effort at bringing this Tallulah Bankhead-like lady to blazing life. But what one remembers best about the film is the physical look of the work, especially production designer Richard MacDonald's pink-and-white, modernistic, sprawling villa, an edifice constructed on the rocks of Sardinia, where much of *Boom!* was filmed. Against the vivid blues of Mediterranean sky and sea, the sets and Elizabeth Taylor's flamboyant wardrobe are almost enough to distract one from the misguided, heavily symbolic script. A failure *Boom!* most definitely was—and is—but in the hands of cinematographer Douglas Slocombe, it's a visually splendid one.

A casting note of minor interest: Elizabeth's brother, Howard Taylor, for a lark, plays the bit role of a journalist in *Boom!.* Although not an actor, he had also taken a minor part in his sister's first big success, *National Velvet.* Thus this was in a sense a professional reunion. For Taylor and Burton, this was their eighth film as a team and for a time their last, as each would now be making several movies without the other.

CRITICS' CORNER

"For directors with visual flair, Williams' *confined* material is a bonanza. Case in point: Joseph Losey's underrated *Boom!,* yet another—in fact, the slackest and fuzziest—version of the standard Williams fable: aging woman, a once-renowned actress and celebrated fag-hag (Williams admits

With Noël Coward

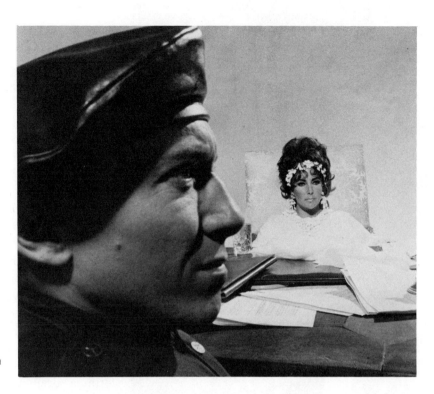

With Michael Dunn

to basing the character on Tallulah Bankhead), is courted by a mystical young man, an angel of death masquerading as an angel of mercy.

"The film went haywire in casting a voluptuous Elizabeth Taylor as the dying Sissy Goforth and sagging Richard Burton as the strapping ministrant. Their dance of death—a Williams blend of death and desire, sex as salvation and as putrefaction—is played against one of Williams' lushest settings, a pink villa overlooking the Mediterranean. Losey brings this house to life in a way a stage never could, and his aptly sensuous pans and dollies, his detailed interest in decor, enhance (despite the miscasting) one of Williams' most fragile ideas, a story he admits he never got quite right."

Foster Hirsch, CINEMA

"Elizabeth Taylor, twenty years too young and thirty acting eons away from the role, simply isn't dying, cry out for codeine, gulp away at whiskey and pills and cough up red-ink blots on Kleenex though she does at given moments. Bitch she may be—and a remark about defecation and all to her servants is not the least of her verbal sallies—but never more radiant and healthy and vital has she appeared on screen. This rather cuts the ground out from under poor Richard, who looks more like a bank clerk on campy holiday, kimono and all, than a poet. And to complete the camp atmosphere, the so-called 'witch' of Capri, portrayed on stage by Mildred Dunnock and then Ruth Ford, has been transvestized into Noël Coward, who seems to be sitting by having a giggle at the lovely Miss Taylor's coping with alternate doses of rhetoric and mortality. Anyway, we hope they all had a ball in sunny Sardinia but Noël, dear Noël, you really should have wiped that smirk off on camera."

Judith Crist, NEW YORK

"Lacking Margaret Leighton, Losey had to make do with Elizabeth Taylor in a role that required only the simplest Swansonish bravura, and did not receive even that. But although Taylor sounds as throatily shrill as ever, she looks better than she has for a long time. Losey, unlike Nichols in *Virginia Woolf,* opted for glamorous fantasy rather than grubby realism with a subject that was fantastic to begin with, the Albee play being only somewhat less so than Williams. If Taylor is utterly inadequate in her part as the lusty, much-married and much-widowed Mrs. Goforth, Burton seems at first entrance utterly miscast as the morbid gigolo masquerading as the Angel of Death, but his final Booming exit line caps what

turns out to be the most brilliant performance of his career, a performance no less brilliant for its extraordinarily generous and sensitive rapport with his wife's limited talents."

Andrew Sarris, THE VILLAGE VOICE

"Elizabeth Taylor's delineation is off the mark: instead of an earthy dame, hypochondriac and hyper-emotional, who survived six wealthy husbands, she plays it like she has just lost the first, who would appear to have taken her away from a truck-stop job. The wealth is shown in too *nouveau riche* a manner. The gowns, jewels and sets only emphasize the point. Richard Burton is far more believable. The rather pointless verbal meanderings of worthlessness eventually impel the eye to the sets, the excellent work of production designer Richard MacDonald. Joseph Losey's direction achieves some dynamic results, but like modern wonder drugs it merely prolongs the terminal dramatic cancer."

"Murf," VARIETY

With Richard Burton

With Mia Farrow

Secret Ceremony

A Universal/World Film Services, Ltd./Paul M.
 Heller Production
Released by Universal Pictures / 1968
In Technicolor

CAST

Leonora: Elizabeth Taylor; *Cenci:* Mia Farrow;
Albert: Robert Mitchum; *Aunt Hilda:* Pamela
Brown; *Aunt Hanna:* Peggy Ashcroft; and in
extra footage added for the TV version, *Dr.
Walter Stevens:* Michael Strong; *Sir Alex Gordon:* Robert Douglas.

CREDITS

Director: Joseph Losey; *Producers:* John Heyman and Norman Priggen; *Screenwriter:* George
Tabori; *Based on a Short Story by:* Marco Denevi; *Cinematographer:* Gerald Fisher; *Production
Designer:* Richard MacDonald; *Art Director:*
John Clark; *Set Decorator:* Jill Oxley; *Musical
Score:* Richard Rodney Bennett; *Editor:* Reginald Beck; *Miss Taylor's Wardrobe:* Marc Bohan
and Christian Dior; *Costumes:* Susan Yelland;
Miss Taylor's Hairstyles: Alexandre of Paris;
Running Time: 109 minutes.

THE FILM

Again, Elizabeth Taylor was teamed with director
Joseph Losey in another Heyman-Priggen co-production. And yet again, her considerable drawing-power was required to help "sell" a bizarre, non-commercial, and puzzling script. Of additional
help at the boxoffice were Mia Farrow (her blonde
hair hidden under a long black wig) and Robert
Mitchum, though his role was little more than a
cameo, about which he has been quoted as saying, "They did some weird things with that script.
They were in trouble when I got there, and I
don't think I improved the situation any!"

Secret Ceremony's plot, such as it is, almost

With Mia Farrow

defies description: in London, a fading, middle-aged prostitute is picked up by a wistful young girl who resembles the woman's dead child. The girl brings the whore to her home, a large, shuttered townhouse with luxurious trappings. The woman is persuaded to stay on there and play "mother" to this love-starved child, an orphan who passes the newcomer off as her late mother's sister. Into this strange household eventually comes the girl's stepfather, a bearded sensualist who, the child claims, has raped her. Later, the man tells the woman that his stepdaughter is a sexual psychotic who has tried to seduce *him*. Eventually, after much ambiguity of emotional and sexual involvements among its offbeat trio, the child rejects her fantasy "mother" and commits suicide. When "mother" and stepfather meet again over the girl's coffin, the mystery woman stabs him with a knife.

On television, Universal and the National Broadcasting Company were united in deciding that this was much too heady stuff to pass the censorship standards of the living-room medium—to say nothing of confusing the armchair movie-watcher even more than the film's theater audiences may have been confused. Consequently, *Secret Ceremony* was considerably doctored for TV. Miss Taylor, it was decided, must not be thought of as any kind of a streetwalker! Instead, the narrative explained that she was an aging wig model, no less, employed by a London department store. Further worried about the film's ambiguities, especially after the necessary scissoring of sex and violence for the "tube," Universal's executives added footage filmed with Robert Douglas and Michael Strong (not filmed by Losey) portraying, respectively, an attorney and a psychiatrist, whose conversations might serve to explain such newly added plot devices as Miss Taylor's (off-screen) arrest for Mitchum's murder, and a few other pat storyline conclusions not necessarily contained in George Tabori's original screenplay. Also, an out-take of Taylor's confession to a priest was reinserted, with the voice-over of her confession carrying into a subsequent scene. Among the deletions for TV were seminude bathing and massaging scenes that suggested a Lesbian relationship between Farrow and Taylor and implications of Mitchum's being a child-molester.

Any connection between the *Secret Ceremony* seen in theaters and the version available on television is thus quite remote and should be viewed accordingly.

CRITICS' CORNER

"The search for style can have sorry results, as *Secret Ceremony* so woefully demonstrates. Joseph Losey, who has been effective on other occasions, here wanders in a miasma of what I guess must be called atmosphere. He has taken a witless girl, a matronly prostitute, and a lecherous professor and has them hint drearily of madness, rape, incest and incurable disease. Losey evidently has a fondness for unhealthy houses in which unspeakable events occur. But this house (though it is a real house he found) lacks reality, and so do the people. The execrable dialogue written by George Tabori only adds to the prevailing ennui, and if the principal players come out badly, this is no reflection on them. Mr. Losey may have felt there was an opportunity for stylish display in the flabby material, and, if so, he miscalculated."

Hollis Alpert, SATURDAY REVIEW

"A haunting, powerful drama, *Secret Ceremony* unfolds like the anguished hallucination of a schizophrenic mind. It is unsavory and often an irritating picture. But it leaves a strong impact."

Mandel Herbstman, THE FILM DAILY

"Moody, leisurely developed and handsomely produced, Joseph Losey's *Secret Ceremony* is a macabre tale of mistaken identity, psychological and sexual needs, ultimate suicide and murder. The performances are generally good—Mia Farrow's via an emphasis on facial expressions, Elizabeth Taylor's via a salutary toning down of her shrieking-for-speaking tendencies, and Robert Mitchum's casual, stolid projection. Peggy Ashcroft and Pamela Brown are excellent as Miss Farrow's aunts, who periodically visit her to loot the house of knickknacks for their antique shop."

"Murf," VARIETY

"*Secret Ceremony* is truly terrible, but I don't

With Mia Farrow

With Peggy Ashcroft and Pamela Brown

With Mia Farrow

know how to fight a bowl of fudge without getting stuck in the goo."

Pauline Kael, THE NEW YORKER

"In many ways, notably in its insidious illumination of the fascination of madness, *Secret Ceremony* reminds one of *Lilith,* but the style is entirely Losey's own, a return to the crystalline ellipses of *Accident* after the opulent undulations of *Boom!,* and with superb, unexpectedly funny characterizations by the entire cast."

Tom Milne, MONTHLY FILM BULLETIN

"Mr. Losey has certainly displayed Miss Taylor in a remarkably interesting fashion, giving her face a depth of character and a variety it has hith-

erto lacked, while still preserving her remarkable beauty. He also exploits to a fare-thee-well Mia Farrow's hitherto unrealized (or unexplored) depths as an almost painfully sensitive actress and, perhaps the year's major accomplishment, he has made Robert Mitchum open his eyes from time to time, albeit during a relatively minor role."

Judith Crist, NEW YORK

"What's it all about really? Difficult to guess, through the jerks and plunges of all the cast save Mia Farrow, who manages to be touching and perverse and human, and the heavy-handed doses of religion and allegory that Losey dishes out."

"E.C.," FILM QUARTERLY

With Robert Mitchum

With Mia Farrow

"In many of his previous films, Losey has shown skill at conjuring up corruption and terror. Here he is undone by his scenarist, George Tabori, who attempts a ghostly esthetic melodrama in the style of Henry James. Tabori provides all of the mannerisms of the master, but brings none of his talent to the task. Nor is Losey much aided by his actors. Farrow continues to radiate a fragile elegance and a shrewd sense of character and timing. But she alone cannot make a movie. Confined to a few brief scenes, Robert Mitchum is little more than a cameo of a goat. The bloated, bejeweled Elizabeth Taylor seems less a depleted call girl than a prosperous madam. But alternately snooty or snarling, she does underline the message of her role there is nothing more pretentious than swank posing as class. Unfortunately, that is the message of the film as well."

TIME

"The distintegration of Elizabeth Taylor has been a very sad thing to stand by helplessly and watch, but something ghastly has happened over the course of her last four or five films. She has be-come a hideous parody of herself—a fat, sloppy, yelling, screeching banshee, turning awkwardly into a kind of American Magnani. The screen produces so few natural works of art that to see them untended and used with disrespect is rather like chewing gum in the Louvre. I have always reacted to her beauty and talent in much the same way as the late James Agee, who once remarked, after seeing *National Velvet*, that he was so blinded by her personal magnetism he hardly felt qualified to arrive at any sensible assessment of her work. Working from a new axiom that an artist who is his own worst, enemy deserves no sympathy, I am no longer intimidated after flinching through *Secret Ceremony*.

"Joseph Losey, without the added benefit of his usual Harold Pinter screenplays to check his extravagances at the door, seems to have temporarily gone to seed as a director. What they've all tried to do is make a Gothic tale of role reversal, but all they've come up with is a masterpiece of confusion."

Rex Reed, HOLIDAY

With Warren Beatty

The Only Game In Town

A George Stevens–Fred Kohlmar Production
for 20th Century-Fox / 1970
In DeLuxe Color

CAST

Fran Walker: Elizabeth Taylor; *Joe Grady:* Warren Beatty; *Thomas J. Lockwood:* Charles Braswell; *Tony:* Hank Henry.

CREDITS

Director: George Stevens; *Producer:* Fred Kohlmar; *Screenwriter:* Frank D. Gilroy, *Based on His Broadway Play; Cinematographer:* Henri Decae; *Art Directors:* Herman Blumenthal and Auguste Capelier; *Set Decorators:* Walter M. Scott and Jerry Wunderlich; *Musical Score:* Maurice Jarre; *Editors:* John W. Holmes, William Sands, and Pat Shade; *Costumes:* Mia Fonssagrives and Vicki Tiel; *Miss Taylor's Hairstyles:* Alexandre of Paris; *Running Time:* 113 minutes.

THE FILM

A fourteen-performance Broadway failure in 1968, *The Only Game in Town,* Frank D. Gil-roy's three-character play, reached the screen courtesy of the playwright's own adaptation in much the same form as originally performed, with the addition of only one other character, a bar-owner. The story still concentrates on the no-strings Las Vegas love affair of a stranded chorus girl and a piano player whose big problem is a compulsion to gamble away his earnings. On the stage, Tammy Grimes and Barry Nelson played the lovers enacted on screen by Elizabeth Taylor and Warren Beatty—an unexpected and surprisingly compatible teaming of controversial personalities.

Originally signed for the Beatty role was Frank Sinatra, who had to bow out when the shooting schedule was put back, resulting in a curious casting-switch, in age as well as type and style of leading man. Because of Taylor's characteristic desire to be near Richard Burton while he

With Charles Braswell

worked opposite Rex Harrison in the film version of *Staircase,* producer Fred Kohlmar and director George Stevens were forced to construct the Las Vegas settings in Paris studios, while second-unit photographers took care of the atmospheric backgrounds back in the States.

George Stevens, under whose direction Elizabeth Taylor had given two of her best performances in *A Place in the Sun* and *Giant,* was returning to motion pictures after a five-year hiatus caused by the disastrous reception accorded his ambitious life of Christ, *The Greatest Story Ever Told.* Unfortunately, the combined critical and audience reception for *The Only Game in Town* proved not only that Stevens' once-magic touch was no longer in line with the changing taste of a fickle public, but also that Elizabeth Taylor, after one too many a cinematic bomb, had completely lost her power as a box-office star—one who was once worth any sum one had to pay her, for the sake of the film's success. Not even Warren Beatty's immense popularity in *Bonnie and Clyde,* three years earlier, could save this new film. Unfortunately, audiences thus missed seeing Taylor

and Beatty handling a combination of light comedy and engaging romance in an uneven style that, nevertheless, revealed some of their best work.

CRITICS' CORNER

"*The Only Game in Town* is a rather mixed blessing. Elizabeth Taylor and Warren Beatty star as two Vegas drifters who find love with each other; their performances are generally very good, Miss Taylor in particular delivering one of her best characterizations. Perhaps director George Stevens is the guiding hand under which she flowers best. At times, her personal wardrobe belies her chorus-girl profession, emphasized when she denies that longtime boyfriend Charles Braswell, a married Frisco square who visits her on occasion, is paying any of the freight. However, Miss Taylor looks in great shape, and the clothes will provide some femme appeal though it erases some plot credibility."

"Murf," VARIETY

"Beatty is so very good as a run-of-the-mill piano

player waiting to bolt Vegas when in the money that the film is worth seeing for his performance alone. Miss Taylor, while not as skillful, is still colorfully convincing as a lonely hoofer in love with a married man but falling for Beatty."

William Wolf, CUE

"The Only Game in Town is very much a George Stevens film in its slow, almost too casual pace, in its reliance on closeups, in its careful, deliberate establishment of character rather than action, and especially in its sense of intimacy. Under Stevens' guidance, Elizabeth Taylor and Warren Beatty make us *care* very much about what happens to these two losers. The final sequence in which Joe discards the camouflaging jokes, admits his love, and tries to convince Fran that marriage is the only game in town, that an abused heart would, in the long run, be better than an unused heart, is so beautifully done that it can be termed nothing less than a triumph for the actors. Joe Grady is certainly the best acting that Beatty has ever done and Miss Taylor, looking prettier than she has in her recent films, achieves a very affecting vulnerability."

THE INDEPENDENT FILM JOURNAL

"George Stevens' attentiveness to the actors might have shown to some advantage if the script weren't so transparent; there's nothing behind the dialogue, no sense of the texture of people's lives. It's a movie that should never have been made, because everyone will see through it. After the initial pleasure of finding Elizabeth Taylor looking prettier than she has looked in years, and watching Warren Beatty's attractively relaxed style, it turns into a sluggish star vehicle of the old, bad days."

Pauline Kael, THE NEW YORKER

"As played by Miss Taylor, Fran is so top-heavy in bouffant hair styles by Alexandre of Paris, and badly proportioned minidresses by Mia Fonssagrives, that she has the non-dancing silhouette of an apple balanced atop a pair of toothpicks. Miss Taylor's face is still one of the great scenic attractions of our time, but the performance is awfully royal. Beatty, who can be an interesting actor, is required to deliver breezy, bad comedy lines that have the effect of making him look and act like George Hamilton."

Vincent Canby, THE NEW YORK TIMES

With Warren Beatty

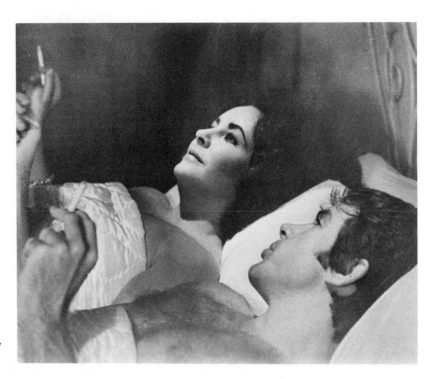

With Warren Beatty

"Hovering with expert balance between sophistication and sentimentality, Frank D. Gilroy's adaptation of his stage play gives some delightful words to Elizabeth Taylor and Warren Beatty, who speak them with evident appreciation. The timing of lines is impeccable, the shifts from humor to tenderness could scarcely be managed better, and this is about as much as we should expect of a movie adapted from the theatre. Miss Taylor's entire response to the unaccustomed genre of light comedy is a pleasure to witness, and the interplay between her and Beatty is delightful. George Stevens does unobtrusive wonders in his direction of what is mainly a two-handed show. Occasionally, the action moves beyond the chorus girl's apartment and into the night-glow of Las Vegas and the crush and tension of the casino, but mostly the thing is a series of conversation pieces. The more credit, then, to all concerned for bringing such joy to the task and for maintaining the precise emotional control."

Gordon Gow, FILMS AND FILMING

With Warren Beatty

Under Milk Wood

A Timon Production
Released in Britain by
    The Rank Organisation / 1971
United States Distributor:
    Altura Films International (1973)
In Technicolor

CAST

First Voice: Richard Burton; *Rosie Probert:* Elizabeth Taylor; *Captain Cat:* Peter O'Toole; *Myfanwy Price:* Glynis Johns; *Mrs. Pugh:* Vivien Merchant; *Mrs. Ogmore-Pritchard:* Sian Phillips; *Mog Edwards:* Victor Spinetti; *Second Voice:* Ryan Davies; *Gossamer Beynon:* Angharad Rees; *Mr. Waldo:* Ray Smith; *Sinbad Sailors:* Michael Forrest; *Polly Garter:* Ann Beach; *Mr. Cherry Owen:* Glynn Edwards; *Mrs. Cherry Owen:* Bridget Turner; *Mr. Pugh:* Talfryn Thomas; *Mr. Willy Nilly:* Wim Wylton; *Mrs. Willy Nilly:* Bronwen Williams; *Lily Smalls:* Meg Wynn Owen; *Butcher Beynon:* Hubert Rees; *Mrs. Beynon:* Mary Jones; *Rev. Eli Jenkins:* Aubrey Richards; *Evans the Death:* Mark Jones; *Mr. Ogmore:* Dillwyn Owen; *Mr. Pritchard:* Richard Davies; *Nogood Boyo:* David Jason; *Lord Cut Glass:* Davydd Havard; *Utah Watkins:* David Davies; *Mrs. Utah Watkins:* Maudie Edwards; *Ocky Milkman:* Griffith Davies; *Bessie Bighead:* Peggyann Clifford; *Dai Bread:* Dudley Jones; *Mrs. Dai Bread One:* Dorothea Phillips; *Mrs. Dai Bread Two:* Ruth Madoc; *P. C. Attila Rees:* David Harries; *Mary Ann Sailors:* Rachel Thomas; *Waldo Wife One:* Andree Gaydon; *Second Woman/Waldo Wife Two:* Eira Griffiths; *First Neighbor/Waldo Wife Three:* Margaret Courtenay; *First Woman/Waldo Wife Four:* Rhoda Lewis; *Waldo Wife Five:* Pamela Miles; *Jack Black:* John Rees; *Mrs. Rose Cottage:* Jill Britton; *Mae Rose Cottage:* Susan Penhaligon; *Inspector:* Edmond Thomas; *Organ Morgan:* Richard Parry; *Mrs. Organ Morgan:* Dilys Price; *Gwennie:* Olwen Rees; *Mother:* Iris Jones; *First Fisherman:* Gordon Styles; *Second Fisherman:* Brian Osbourne; *First Drowned Sailor:* Shane Shelton; *Second Drowned Sailor:* Paul Grist; *Third Drowned Sailor:* Bryn Jones; *Fourth Drowned Sailor:* John Rainer; *Fifth Drowned Sailor:* Bryn Williams; *Villagers in "Sailors Arms":* Aldwyn Francis, Ifor Owen, Dudley

Owen, and Gladys Wykeham-Edwards; *Gomer Owen:* Ieuan Rhys Williams; *Old Man:* T. H. Evans; *Second Neighbor:* Gwyneth Owen; *Third Neighbor:* Lucy Griffiths; *Fourth Neighbor:* Angela Brinkworth.

CREDITS

Director: Andrew Sinclair; *Producers:* Hugh French and Jules Buck; *Screenwriter:* Andrew Sinclair; *Based on the Radio Play by:* Dylan Thomas; *Cinematographer:* Bob Huke; *Art Director:* Geoffrey Tozer; *Musical Score:* Brian Gascoigne; *Editor:* Willy Kemplen; *Running Time:* 90 minutes.

THE FILM

Dylan Thomas's lengthy, poetic radio play had frequently been performed in staged readings or even on occasion in an attempt at full play form. But few seriously considered making a motion picture of this episodic series of vignettes dramatizing life in a Welsh village until writer-director Andrew Sinclair tackled the problem. In Sinclair's words, *"Under Milk Wood* was one of the more impossible films to make, and I doubt that I will ever put that sort of thing together again."

Originally, Dylan Thomas had written this play for himself and Richard Burton, and the latter had long wanted to do the First Voice. Sinclair had once been a fellow drama student of Peter O'Toole, and with the knowledge that O'Toole had once played Captain Cat in his student days, Sinclair offered the actor his screenplay and got an acceptance from him. With O'Toole heading his cast, Sinclair had no trouble getting Richard Burton for the narrating First Voice, and with Burton came Elizabeth Taylor for the cameo role of Rosie Probert, the town trollop. With this powerful trio of big-name stars, financing was obtained for *Under Milk Wood,*

Richard Burton

With Peter O'Toole

despite the noncommercial nature of the project, and shooting was accomplished within forty days on location in the Gwaun Valley of Wales, with many of the local residents taking part in the filming.

The resultant film was an uneven critical success, but not a popular one. Because of the brevity of her role, Elizabeth asked producer Jules Buck to remove her name from star billing on the movie, since she thought it unfair to Burton and O'Toole, considering the length of *their* footage. She did not get her wish; Buck refused on the grounds that her contract called for such billing as she now received. All three of the film's stars worked for small fees but large percentages. In financial terms, of course, the loss was theirs. On the other hand, they made possible the realization of an admirable production that cast no shadow on anyone's career.

CRITICS' CORNER

"The winning film of the moment is *Under Milk Wood,* Andrew Sinclair's beautiful screen adaptation of the Dylan Thomas play, a triumph of visualization of the verbal visions and vignettes the poet created.

"No question but that Burton was born to recite Thomas's luxuriant and flowing poetic realities and lusciously lilting prose; his voice washes over the screen, penetrates to the very heart of each matter explored.

"The only outsider seems to be Miss Taylor, all movie-star with the blue eye-shadow and surplus hair—but in the arms of the young Captain Cat, and perhaps in his dreams, she becomes possible.

"*Under Milk Wood* is all our dreams, engulfing and refreshing. I don't know what 'special sell' a great and lovely work, translated with inspiration to the screen, needs. I have seen the film three times; I shall see it at least as many times more, for with each viewing there has been a new detail of sight and sound, a fresh nuance and an underplayed wordplay to bring a further enrichment to a work whose richness can be reveled in again and again."

Judith Crist, NEW YORK

With Peter O'Toole

"Thomas, of course, originally wrote *Under Milk Wood* as a radio play for the BBC in 1945, and, though he himself subsequently adapted it for the stage and it has now belatedly turned up as a movie, the work stubbornly remains a radio play. *Under Milk Wood* is, in short, written for the ear and not for the eye, and it is cheapened and debased when used by Sinclair as the voice-over narration for something akin to a Fitzpatrick travelogue of a Welsh village.

"As an unseen voice, Burton is first-rate; a Welshman himself, of course, he gives a brilliant reading of Thomas's densely imaged lines. But, unfortunately, Burton is also seen in the movie as a stranger to Llareggub trudging dumbly about the village with a seedy companion at his side and looking mainly hung over and bored. Elizabeth Taylor appears briefly in the picture, too, as a dead whore of fond memory named Rosie Probert. But with her heavy blue eye make-up, modish hair-do and tentlike gown, Mrs. Burton looks as though she belongs in the audience at the Academy Awards, rather than in a grave in Llareggub."

Thomas Meehan, SATURDAY REVIEW

"The movie of *Under Milk Wood* offers a beautiful reading of the Dylan Thomas material, with illustrations, and fundamentally it doesn't try to be anything else, but the work was already complete in its original form, as a radio play—a play for voices. Though the movie doesn't really add to it, I enjoyed sitting back and listening.

"Sinclair isn't unctuously faithful, and his imagery generally avoid the obvious forms of redundancy—he's intelligently faithful. But this still leaves him with a wild effusion on the track while a modest, sometimes undernourished set of visual images passes before us. However, Sinclair brings the material emotionally close. In a sense, *Under Milk Wood* is a people's poem—a celebration of the originality and eccentricity in 'ordinary' life— and the movie is a very warm experience. You feel the affection of the cast and you share in it."

Pauline Kael, THE NEW YORKER

With Margaret Leighton

Zee & Co. *(X Y & Zee)*

A Zee Film
A Kastner-Ladd-Kanter Production
Released by Columbia Pictures / 1972
In Color

CAST

Zee Blakeley: Elizabeth Taylor; *Robert Blakeley:* Michael Caine; *Stella:* Susannah York; *Gladys:* Margaret Leighton; *Gordon:* John Standing; *Rita:* Mary Larkin; *Gavin:* Michael Cashman; *Head Waiter:* Gino Melvazzi; *Oscar:* Julian West; *Shaun:* Hilary West.

CREDITS

Director: Brian G. Hutton; *Executive Producer:* Elliott Kastner; *Producers:* Jay Kanter and Alan Ladd, Jr.; *Screenwriter:* Edna O'Brien; *Cinematographer:* Billy Williams; *Art Director:* Peter Mullins; *Set Decorator:* Arthur Taksen; *Musical* *Score:* Stanley Myers; *Songs:* "Going in Circles" by Ted Myers and Jaiananda; "Whirlwind" and "Coat of Many Colours" by Rick Wakeman and Dave Lambert, *Played by* Iroko; "Revolution" and "Granny's Got a Painted Leg," *Played by* The Roy Young Band; "Gladys' Party" by John Mayer; *Editor:* Jim Clark; *Costumes:* Beatrice Dawson; *Hairstyles:* Allen McKeown; *Running Time:* 110 minutes.

THE FILM

Zee & Co. is a British film better known by its American title, *X Y & Zee.* An original screenplay by Irish novelist Edna O'Brien, who specializes in triangular romantic dramas of an explicit nature *(Three Into Two Won't Go)*, *Zee* centers on a childless but quite volatile marital relationship (Elizabeth Taylor, Michael Caine) that appears to thrive on cruel role-playing, below-the-belt sparring matches, and occasional spates of adultery. Zee and Robert Blakeley are members of swinging London's Bohemian upper crust, whose unique love-hate union seems headed for its ultimate destruction when he falls genuinely in love with Stella, a beautiful young widow (Susannah York). Zee makes an unsuccessful but messy attempt at suicide, and then plays her trump card—a mention Stella had once made of a schoolgirl crush she'd had on a nun. At the story's close, husband discovers wife and girlfriend in bed together, and the film ends in a freeze-frame,

leaving its audience totally up-in-the-air as to the plot's resolution.

It is interesting to note that Edna O'Brien's screenplay, which was published in Britain under the movie's original title, takes the story a step beyond the implications of the film's freeze-frame ending. In the screen version, director Brian Hutton implies that Zee has won Robert back from his mistress, whereas Miss O'Brien intended her three-way battle of the sexes to end in a draw—a sexual threesome: "The last we see are their three bodies—arms, heads, torsos, all meeting for a consummation."

For Elizabeth Taylor, *Zee* offered a tour-de-force the like of which she hadn't had since *Who's Afraid of Virginia Woolf?*, and she met the challenge in a manner few critics could ignore, whether they admired her performance or de-

With Susannah York and Michael Caine

plored it. In one bathroom scene, although nudity was required of her, Elizabeth arranged (as she had done before in *Reflections in a Golden Eye*) to have the scene so photographed that a stand-in of more modest proportions played the scene in her stead.

CRITICS' CORNER

"Elizabeth Taylor, who is rapidly turning into a latter-day Marie Dressler, manages to keep *Zee & Co.* more or less afloat through its opening scenes by gleefully flaying practically everyone in sight with a non-stop stream of truculent bitchery. The trouble is that apart from a pronounced sexual hysteria, she is given no character to work on, and since neither she nor the other two members of the tormented triangle ever develop beyond the cartoon poses they adopt at the beginning (shrewish wife, patient husband, soulful mistress), the film gradually sinks into a quagmire of repetition from which the only way out is through melodrama—the suicide attempt, the drunken party and, most ludicrous of all, the final Lesbian twist."

Tom Milne, MONTHLY FILM BULLETIN

With Michael Caine

"There are few actresses who can sustain the strident and sarcastic barrage of invective and double entendre of which Miss Taylor is capable; the script is near the mark when it suggests that she would make a first-rate fishwife."

Joseph Gelmis, NEWSDAY

"The film is coarse, noisy and, finally, stupid, like people at a nearby table who won't shut up."

With Susannah York

With Michael Caine

raccoon, seemed ridiculous and—well, monstrous. But as the picture went on, I found myself missing her whenever she wasn't onscreen, and I'm forced to conclude that, monstrous though she is, her jangling performance is what gives this movie its energy. She has grown into the raucous-demanding-woman role she faked in *Who's Afraid of Virginia Woolf?* When she goes too far, she's like the blowziest scarlet woman in a Mexican movie, but she's still funny. She wears her hair like upholstery, to balance the upholstery of flesh. The weight she has put on in these last years has not made her gracefully voluptuous; she's too hard-boiled to be Rubenesque. The weight seems to have brought out this coarseness, and now she basks in vulgarity. She uses it as a form of assault in *X Y & Zee,* and I don't think she's ever been as strong a star personality.

"Elizabeth Taylor has changed before our eyes from the fragile child with a woman's face to the fabled beauty to this great bawd. This one has a script that enabled Elizabeth Taylor to come out. The aging beauty has discovered in herself a gutsy, unrestrained spirit that knocks two very fine performers right off the screen—and, for the first time that I can recall, she appears to be having a roaring good time on camera."

Pauline Kael, THE NEW YORKER

"Miss Taylor is not a very interesting actress, but she need not seem as bad as she does here. Mr. Hutton allows her to play Zee as if she were the ghost of whores past, present and future, clanking her jewelry, her headbands, her earrings and her feelings behind her like someone out to haunt a funhouse. It is an unfortunately ridiculous performance."

Vincent Canby, THE NEW YORK TIMES

"At the beginning of *X Y & Zee,* Elizabeth Taylor, peering out of blue lamé eyeshadow like a

"*X Y & Zee* is a loud, boozy celebration of the fact that no matter what Elizabeth Taylor says or does, she's a movie star. The movie in this case is

With John Standing

no masterpiece, but audiences are having fun at it because it unzips along at a nice, vulgar clip. It's soft-core pornography, sort of like John O'Hara's later novels, and Miss Taylor plops herself down in the middle of it as a bitchy wife. *X Y & Zee* is a superior screenplay, but that doesn't help the movie very much because the focus of attention is always Elizabeth Taylor. We don't get a sense of three actors relating with one another, but of two skilled actors supporting a star whose charisma is apparently ageless. Elizabeth Taylor remains glamorous no matter what she does to herself, and she's especially effective when she plays against the glamor by taking semi-sluttish roles. *X Y & Zee* follows such films as *Virginia Woolf, Secret Ceremony, Reflections in a Golden Eye* and *The Only Game in Town,* and in all of them Elizabeth plays a zaftig, slightly sloppy, enduringly sexy middle-aged broad. She's great at it. This time she drapes herself with loud jewelry, wears a lot of makeup, zips herself into a wardrobe that looks designed by Frederick's of Hollywood and has a lot of great suitcase-packing scenes. *X Y & Zee* is her show, and the audience loves it when she spits out a Clark Gable imitation with a twist: 'Frankly, my dear, I don't give a she-it.' "

Roger Ebert, CHICAGO SUN-TIMES

"Elizabeth Taylor, who won't let go of *Virginia Woolf* no matter what, screams and carries on ad nauseam as the prime attraction of a film whose distinction is that its characters are uniformly repulsive, its style totally vulgar, its situations incredible, its dialogue moronic and its redeeming social values nil."

Judith Crist, NEW YORK

"It comes across as a mixture of Albee and Gilliatt, a sort of 'Who's Afraid of Bloody Sunday.' Elizabeth Taylor, on the right occasion, can be a startlingly good actress; here she is simply startling, relishing her excessiveness all the way. Still, it's an entertaining if overdone turn, one of those fireworks displays that can be mistaken for bravura performing. Michael Caine, who gets better with each film, looks as if he had a great time matching his co-star with temper tantrums and profanity. Susannah York is stuck with being the not-so-straight man in the proceedings. It is not her fault that a previous film assignment *(The Killing of Sister George)* tends to make *X Y & Zee's* concluding moments even more foolish than they are. In the supporting role of Gladys, London's reigning partygiver who's got the goods on all of her guests, Margaret Leighton is made up to look an aging, spaced-out Dory Previn. The distinguished actress, wearing a see-through hostess gown, is violently amusing and in her own special way is as hysterical and spectacular as anything else in the film."

THE INDEPENDENT FILM JOURNAL

With Michael Caine

With Beau Bridges

Hammersmith Is Out

A J. Cornelius Crean Films Inc. Production
Distributed by Cinerama Releasing Corporation
1972
In Du Art Color

CAST

Jimmie Jean Jackson: Elizabeth Taylor; *Hammersmith:* Richard Burton; *Billy Breedlove:* Beau Bridges; *Doctor:* Peter Ustinov; *General Sam Pembroke:* Leon Ames; *Dr. Krodt:* Leon Askin; *Henry Joe:* John Schuck; *Guido Scatucci:* George Raft; *Oldham:* Anthony Holland; *Princess:* Marjorie Eaton; *Kiddo:* Lisa Jak; *Miss Quim:* Linda Gaye Scott; *Fat Man:* Mel Berger; *Pete Rutter:* Brook Williams; *Cleopatra:* Carl Donn; *Duke:* Jose Espinoza.

CREDITS

Director: Peter Ustinov; *Producer:* Alex Lucas; *Screenwriter:* Stanford Whitmore; *Cinematographer:* Richard H. Kline; *Set Decorator:* Robert Benton; *Musical Score:* Dominic Frontiere; *Songs:* "For Openers," "Requiem," and "When Your Dreams Were Worth Remembering" by Dominic Frontiere and Sally Stevens; *Editor:* David Blewitt; *Miss Taylor's Costumes:* Edith Head; *Wigs:* Alexandre of Paris; *Hairdresser:* Claudye Bozzacchi; *Running Time:* 108 minutes.

THE FILM

This modern variation on the Faust legend marked the ninth teaming of Taylor and Burton, although her romantic vis-à-vis in the film is actually Beau Bridges. An independent production from the start, *Hammersmith Is Out* was financed by J. Cornelius Crean, a self-made West Coast millionaire (house trailers) who managed to interest Peter Ustinov in doing the script both as director and actor, impersonating the German doctor whose institution houses Hammersmith, a criminal mastermind and the counterpart of Mephistopheles. Ustinov cast his film as he wished:

Burton for Hammersmith; Elizabeth Taylor as Jimmie Jean Jackson, the voluptuous blonde waitress who slings hash in a Southern roadside diner; and the up-and-coming Beau Bridges as the film's nose-picking nonhero, Billy Breedlove, a sloppy, offbeat Faust, who picks up the waitress, promises her fine things and whisks her off on a series of outlandish adventures.

To accommodate the Burtons on this not-too-commercial enterprise, Ustinov settled on Cuernavaca, Mexico, as the center of filming, not far from Puerto Vallarta, where Elizabeth and Richard had maintained a home since 1963, when he had filmed *The Night of the Iguana* there. Ustinov has termed *Hammersmith* "a crime picture with humor" and claims that the story fascinated him because "it represents so much that is wrong with modern society."

A virtual labor of love, *Hammersmith Is Out* was made for little gain by the Burtons, who received expenses and a sizable chunk of future profits, such as there might be. Filmed in 1971, the movie had production problems involving a falling-out between backer Crean and his producer, Alex Lucas. There followed nearly a year in which the picture was edited and reedited, scored and rescored.

Several magazines ran stories of *Hammersmith* in production, since anything involving the Burtons was newsworthy. But the film took a long

With Beau Bridges

[223]

time to reach theaters in the spring of 1972, courtesy of Crean himself, who soon found that film distribution was not something for a newcomer to dabble in. After stirring moderate interest in a few key cities where it played, *Hammersmith* disappeared, surfacing again that autumn under the more experienced auspices of the Cinerama Releasing Organization. By then, the film had unexpectedly picked up a Best Actress award for Elizabeth Taylor's performance at that year's Berlin Film Festival, a factor which helped draw audiences, though the film was no box-office winner. However, Cinerama knew that the foreign box-office rights would make up for any domestic losses, as the Taylor and Burton names had elsewhere retained much of the value that a poor choice of vehicles had dimmed Stateside.

Few American film critics cared for *Hammersmith Is Out,* although Ustinov and the Burtons were loyal in championing their investment. Said Elizabeth later, "Maybe it's a mistake to have fun on a picture, from the way the critics acted."

CRITICS' CORNER

"The audience that saw and liked the Burtons in *Boom!* may appreciate what goes on in *Hammersmith Is Out,* but it isn't likely that they'll understand this one either. What is, apparently, an exercise in spoofery on the part of Elizabeth Taylor, Richard Burton and the even more energetic Peter Ustinov, starts as a variation on the Faust legend, but almost immediately turns into a belabored antic that eventually breaks down into a dependence on sight gags and shock appeal.

"Only Miss Taylor is given plenty of opportunity for exposure—moving from a waitress in a hashhouse through the various stages of Bridges' success as the tool of the Mephistophelian Hammersmith until she and the devil conspire against the unfortunate youth. She looks terrific throughout and almost makes sense of the ridiculous figure.

"The entire film was financed by California mobile-home manufacturer J. Cornelius Crean. Perhaps he'd be best advised to stick to trailers and forget about features."

"Robe," VARIETY

"Hammersmith Is Out is another of those heavy-handed 'the criminally insane are running the

With Richard Burton

With Beau Bridges

With John Schuck and Beau Bridges

world' parables that almost comes off—but not quite, in spite of Elizabeth Taylor and Richard Burton giving their best performances of recent years; Beau Bridges proving himself a very good character actor indeed, and Peter Ustinov doubling, with his usual suavity and worldly wit, as actor and director. But alas, the four actors,

creating truly dimensional characters, are indeed in search of an author, let alone a screenplay."

Judith Crist, NEW YORK

"*Hammersmith Is Out* is both too elaborate and not quite witty enough to be especially convincing as contemporary morality comedy. However, just when the patience is at the point of exhaustion, when one might leave the theater with a clear conscience, the film comes to fitful life.

"Both Bridges and Miss Taylor display a certain vulgar, ratty charm that is often funny. Not so funny are Burton and Ustinov, but this may be simply a matter of ordinary material that has not been improved by direction or editing. Most of the laughs actually are the result of the blunt use of four-letter words."

Vincent Canby, THE NEW YORK TIMES

"Acting is above average with Burton in a subdued, deadly role. Miss Taylor does well as the waitress, her beauty, though matured, still with her. Beau Bridges manages not to be overshadowed by the two. The cast is good, but the film isn't."

Ann Guarino, NEW YORK DAILY NEWS

"*Hammersmith Is Out* is intended to be a free-wheeling comedy and while it's a format that would normally relish chaos, the treatment it receives is leaden. Richard Burton goes through his role with a grim, unblinking stare, looking like a stoned Frankenstein. Elizabeth Taylor, whose characterization here is described as having 'great lungs but kinda dumb,' has a few amusing moments, wears dozens of wigs, and screeches a lot, in a vocal pattern that ranges from Deep Southern to baby talk. When she goes for an afternoon swim, she reveals an almost Amazonian figure. Beau Bridges is tiresome as the nose-picking Billy Breedlove, and Peter Ustinov, who directed the movie with total disregard for pacing or camera composition, hams up his role of the German asylum keeper who sees sexuality in automobiles. There is very little sense or humor in this film, and producer J. Cornelius Crean will probably find it difficult to convince moviegoers otherwise."

THE INDEPENDENT FILM JOURNAL

With Richard Burton

Divorce; his / Divorce; hers

A Co-Production of
General Continental Productions
    and Harlech Television
for The ABC Television Network / 1973
In Color

CAST

Martin Reynolds: Richard Burton; *Jane Reynolds:* Elizabeth Taylor; *Diana Proctor:* Carrie Nye; *Donald Trenton:* Barry Foster; *Turi Livecchi:* Gabriele Ferzetti; *Franca:* Daniela Surina; *Minister:* Thomas Baptiste; *McIntyre:* Ronald Radd; *Kaduna:* Rudolph Walker; *Tommy:* Mark Colleano; *Peggy:* Rosalyn Landor; *Judith:* Eva Griffith; *Gina:* Marietta Schupp.

CREDITS

Director: Waris Hussein; *Executive Producer:* John Heyman; *Producers:* Terence Baker and Gareth Wigan; *Screenwriter:* John Hopkins; *Cinematographers:* Ernst Wild and Gabor Pogany; *Production Designer:* Roy Stannard; *Musical Score:* Stanley Myers; *Editor:* John Bloom; *Miss Taylor's Costumes:* Edith Head; *Miss Taylor's Hair Styled by:* Alexandre of Paris; *Running Time:* 180 minutes.

With Richard Burton

THE FILM

In the spring of 1972, it was announced that the Burtons would star in a pair of ninety-minute motion pictures to be filmed for ABC's Movie of the Week TV series. Planned were two separate dramas designed to probe the disintegration of a marriage, one part of which would present the husband's point of view, and the other the wife's, with each to have a minor role in the *other's* portion.

Elizabeth and Richard portray a sophisticated couple whose eighteen-year marriage is splitting apart because of mutual indifference, enforced separations, turbulent quarrels, and adultery. Presented in two parts, televised on neighboring nights, their story becomes, via British TV writer

With Richard Burton

With Richard Burton

John Hopkins's script, a complex tangle of flashbacks and flash-forwards mixing a confused play structure with dialogue that verged from the commonplace to the risible ("Beat me black and blue," pleads the wife in one scene, after the husband has struck her, "but please don't leave me.")

Filmed in Rome and Bavaria, the production cost a mint and went considerably over its original shooting schedule. Reports from those involved indicated that much of the trouble derived from the Burtons' unfamiliarity with the customary methods of filming TV movies, as well as their absolute refusal to make any adjustments to modest budgets and fast-filming itineraries.

CRITICS' CORNER

"When you're a Liz Taylor–Richard Burton watcher, just about anything goes. As long as the beauteous Liz's hair is styled by Alexandre of Paris, she's dripping in jewels by Kenneth Lane and she's wearing Edith Head designs, who could ask for anything more, unless it's the resonant voice of Burton on the glamorous scene? This, at least, had always been our attitude about the Burtons, until we suffered through an abominable two-part movie, *Divorce; his/Divorce; hers.* This mawkish drama about a crumbling marriage has to be the worst thing we've seen on television in years. And that goes for daytime soap operas, too! The two-parter is actually a one-parter repeated. We were led to believe that we'd get different insights from *Divorce; his* that weren't there in *Divorce; hers,* and vice versa. Not so. So twice we're asked to agonize with a married couple, very much in love and with three children but still unable to keep their marriage going.

"Liz Taylor, if nothing else, looks fantastic! But what dreadful lines to deliver, and what dreadful scenes to fight one's way through, and all played and replayed in flashbacks and instant replays. To Burton's credit, he gets the most anybody could out of his role."

Kay Gardella, NEW YORK DAILY NEWS

"This two-part soupbone made it official: Liz and Dick Burton are the corniest act in show business since the Cherry Sisters.

"*Divorce,* etc., billed as their 'first dramatic appearance on TV,' was the ultimate. Rarely has the medium achieved such parity between the ethics and morality of performance and script in the program and the blurbs. Posh sets and a lot of sado-masochistic dialog, about breaking bones and kissing them well and such, did nothing to lift boredom and dismay. The same goes for virtually all supporting performances (that posh scenery took a fierce chewing from virtually all the helpmeets).

"Miss Taylor wallowed in suds to a point where the many close-ups between her ample bazooms failed even in distracting from the nonsense. Burton was wooden-legged and wooden-lipped, and seemed to grow stiffer as the two-night fiasco crept on its petty pace.

"Only the teachings of democratic behavior prevent the spelling out here of the punishment in mind for scripter John Hopkins."

"Bill," VARIETY

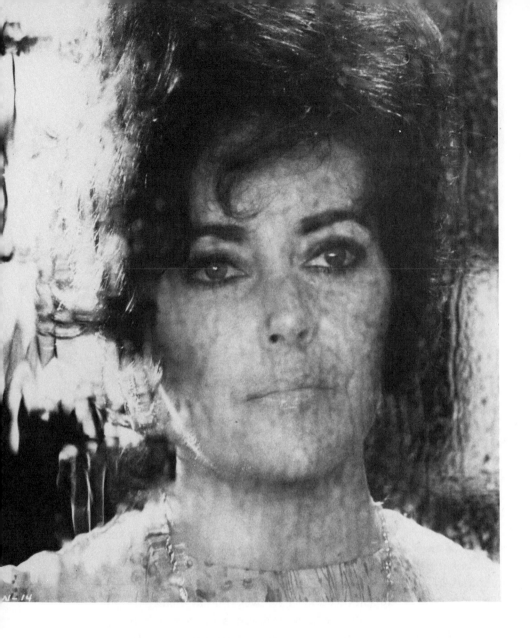

Night Watch

A Joseph E. Levine and
    Burt Productions Presentation
An Avco Embassy Release / 1973
In Technicolor

CAST

Ellen Wheeler: Elizabeth Taylor; *John Wheeler:* Laurence Harvey; *Sarah Cooke:* Billie Whitelaw; *Appleby:* Robert Lang; *Tony:* Tony Britton; *Inspector Walker:* Bill Dean; *Sergeant Norris:* Michael Danvers-Walker; *Dolores:* Rosario Serrano; *Secretary:* Pauline Jameson.

CREDITS

Director: Brian G. Hutton; *Producers:* Martin Poll, George W. George, and Barnard S. Straus; *Screenwriter:* Tony Williamson; *Based on the Play by:* Lucille Fletcher; *Additional Dialogue:* Evan Jones; *Cinematographer:* Billy Williams; *Art Director:* Peter Murton; *Set Dresser:* Peter

With Laurence Harvey

James; *Musical Score:* John Cameron; *Title Song:* "The Night Has Many Eyes" by George Barrie and Sammy Cahn; *Editor:* John Jympson; *Miss Taylor's Costumes:* Valentino; *Miss Taylor's Personal Hairdressers:* Michael John and Claudye Bozzachi; *Running Time:* 99 minutes.

THE FILM

This adaptation of the Lucille *(Sorry, Wrong Number)* Fletcher mystery thriller, which had enjoyed a modest Broadway run starring Joan Hackett and Len Cariou, marked a distinct change of pace for Elizabeth Taylor, who had never before played in this genre. It also marked a reunion for her and Laurence Harvey, who had remained good friends since *Butterfield 8,* some twelve years earlier. In the midst of shooting *Night Watch,* production had to be suspended while Harvey underwent an emergency operation, during which some twenty feet of his intestines were reportedly removed.

In a *New York Post* interview with Tom Topor contingent with the film's release, Harvey spoke of his co-star with uncharacteristic praise: "She is the most talented screen actress in the world today. Professionalism without equal.

There's much of that girl that isn't seen by the world, which is a pity. Funny, bright as a button, tough, unafraid—she did *Night Watch* for nothing; we all did. All the money is deferred percentages. We're thinking of doing another one. I hope we can work it out." Three months later, Laurence Harvey was dead of cancer.

The plot of *Night Watch* is tangled and tricky. In a way, it's a return to the psychological melodramas so popular in the 1940s: a lovely wife sees—or thinks she sees—a murder in the deserted house across the courtyard. Her husband humors her, suggesting rest and a doctor. Her girlfriend is equally solicitous. The wife also has mental flashbacks to the violent death of her first husband, an adulterer killed in an auto accident with his paramour. Does our heroine see what she thinks she sees? Is she mad? Is her husband up to something sinister? Is he in league with her girlfriend? Who is the mysterious neighbor next door who digs in the garden at midnight amid heavy electrical storms?

A lot of *Night Watch* is not what it seems, and director Brian G. Hutton, who guided Elizabeth through her tempestuous role in *Zee & Co.,* plays up the red herrings and admittedly cheats

[231]

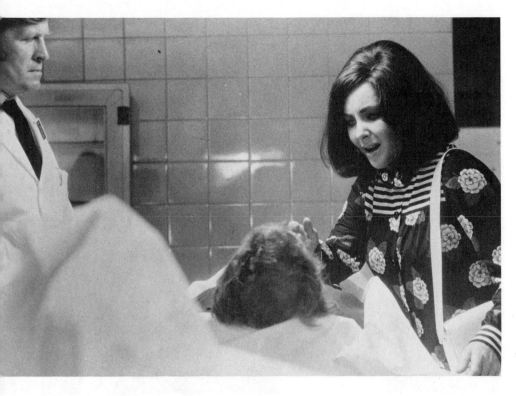

With unidentified players

on his audience, though the film's ending is best not explained here, in the interests of its inevitable exposure to TV viewers.

CRITICS' CORNER

"Elizabeth Taylor, and about time, has got herself a good picture, and a whodunit at that. Seldom, at least recently, has a mystery carpet-pulling been so effective, especially after a familiar suspense set-up that seems to be carelessly shedding red herrings.

"Miss Taylor churns up a fine, understandable lather of nerves, Mr. Harvey is properly sleek, Miss Whitelaw makes a peppery parrot, and Mr. Lang is neat. The deliciously cunning postscript may make you feel like a perfect fool. Once in a while it's fun."

Howard Thompson, THE NEW YORK TIMES

"Plots like this are a dime a dozen, and neither Harvey nor Taylor do much to rescue it from itself."

Archer Winsten, NEW YORK POST

"What's amazing about this film is that it's so *bad*. In fact it almost defies description. The direction at times (particularly towards the end) has the appearance of a pastiche of the worst of Hammer's Gothic productions. The bodies and blood soon become indulgent, and the perpetual thunder and lightning seems absolutely ludicrous—where is it set? Transylvania? The art of cinema suspense is suggestion. Perhaps Hutton should try taking a look at some of Hitchcock's better works before he attempts to chill our spines again."

Alexander Stuart, FILMS AND FILMING

"This is one of those gimmick thrillers, the effectiveness of which depends on performance and direction. I didn't much care for the Broadway play, but that at least had some style, plus the acting of Joan Hackett. The film action has moved from New York's Murray Hill to England; the suspense elements are perverted into visual horror of the worst sort; the lead is played by Elizabeth Taylor with nary a nuance; and the direction by Brian G. Hutton is cloddishly heavy. The trouble is that there is little of the sense of atmosphere, time, place and character that helps create a truly fine thriller.'"

William Wolf, CUE

"*Night Watch* has all the trappings of a Joan Crawford vehicle of the Forties, with numerous

With Billie Whitelaw

elegant dresses for Miss Taylor, an appropriately unbecoming wardrobe for Billie Whitelaw, and a set which is an art director's dream. None of this—combined as it is with a thumping score, constant jump-cuts and an almost continuous thunder storm—can compensate, however, for the banality of the script and its almost total lack of characterisation. The cast perform with immaculate professionalism and Brian Hutton directs with vigour, presumably in the hope of making the material work by administering a shock every few minutes. Sadly, it is all to no avail, and neither the extremely bloody murders at the climax nor the 'immoral' ending are likely to arouse an audience long lost to boredom."

Brenda Davies, MONTHLY FILM BULLETIN

With Laurence Harvey

Barbara (Before)

Ash Wednesday

A Sagittarius Production
A Paramount Pictures Release / 1973
In Technicolor

CAST

Barbara Sawyer: Elizabeth Taylor; *Mark Sawyer:* Henry Fonda; *Erich:* Helmut Berger; *David Carrington:* Keith Baxter; *Doctor Lambert:* Maurice Teynac; *Kate:* Margaret Blye; *German Woman:* Monique Van Vooren; *Bridge Player:* Henning Schlüeter; *Mario:* Dino Mele; *Mandy:* Kathy Van Lypps; *Nurse Ilse:* Dina Sassoli; *Paolo:* Carlo Puri; *Comte D'Arnoud:* Andrea Esterhazy; *Simone:* Jill Pratt; *Silvana del Campo:* Irina Wassilchikoff; *Viet Hartung:* Muki Windisch-Graetz; *Helga:* Nadia Stancioff; *Prince von Essen:* Rodolfo Lodi; *Gregory de Rive:* Raymond Vignale; *Tony Gutierrez:* Jose de Vega; *Samantha:* Samantha Starr.

[234]

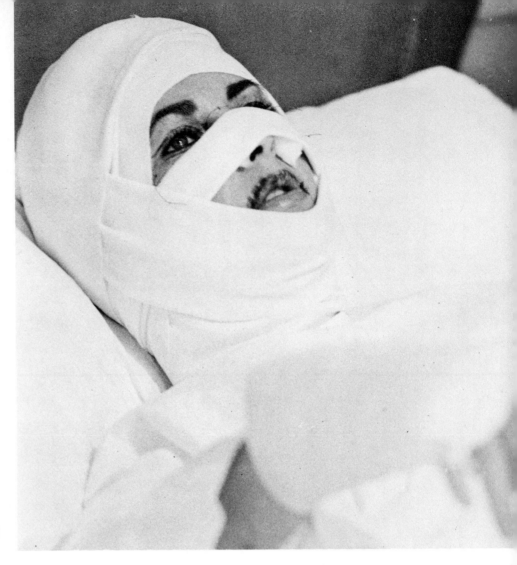

Barbara (During)

CREDITS

Director: Larry Peerce; *Producer:* Dominick Dunne; *Screenwriter:* Jean-Claude Tramont; *Cinematographer:* Ennio Guarnieri; *Art Director:* Philip Abramson; *Musical Score:* Maurice Jarre; *Editor:* Marion Rothman; *Miss Taylor's Costumes:* Edith Head; *Miss Taylor's Mardi Gras Costume:* Valentino; *Miss Taylor's Make-up:* Alberto De Rossi; *Hairstylists:* Giancarlo Novelli and Mirella De Rossi; *Technical Advisor on Plastic Surgery:* Dr. Rodolphe Troques; *Running Time:* 99 minutes.

THE FILM

This stylish, glossy soap opera about a middle-aged, well-to-do matron's efforts to save her disintegrating thirty-year marriage by taking off for a European face-and-body lift, revealed a slimmer and more subdued Elizabeth Taylor than audiences had seen in years. To create the illusion of the actress as an overweight, heavily wrinkled woman of fifty-five, two hours in make-up preparation was required of her each day. "Playing an old bag doesn't bother me in the least," she later reported. "But that damn latex makeup drove me crazy. I thought I was out of the woods when those scenes were over, but then I had to have postsurgical makeup . . . scars, stitches, and black and blue marks."

Somewhat controversial were those early scenes detailing the operating-room processes involved in lifting a woman's face, breasts, thighs, buttocks—and even hands. Decidedly not for the squeamish, their realism derived from a clever integration of studio scenes with details of actual operations performed in the suburban Paris hospital of Dr. Rodolphe Troques, who served as *Ash Wednesday*'s technical advisor. After the film's completion, Dr. Troques had only praise for Elizabeth Taylor's performance: "She never

Barbara (After)

had to be coached and yet, in the picture, she behaved exactly like the average patient I operate on."

Ash Wednesday was filmed entirely on location, chiefly at Lake Como, north of Milan, and in Cortina d'Ampezzo, the famed posh ski resort nestled in the Dolomites. Although there is little non-Taylor footage in the movie, director Larry Peerce was forced to "shoot around" her when she was quarantined for a week with German measles.

Henry Fonda's role is little more than a cameo in the film, coming on the scene as he does long after the audience has learned that he no longer loves his wife and intends to divorce her for a younger woman with whom he has been involved. More impressive in other supporting parts were Margaret Blye as Taylor's visiting, approving daughter (after the surgery scenes), Keith Baxter as the much-face-lifted fashion photographer who befriends her in the hospital, and Helmut Berger as a callous playboy who makes the woman feel loved again—if only for a night.

Although originally planned for release in February, 1974, *Ash Wednesday* was rushed into release during November, 1973, presumably to benefit from publicity attendant on the break-up of the Taylor-Burton marriage (it was patched up a month later).

CRITICS' CORNER

"It's more about the metamorphosis of Elizabeth Taylor than anything else, and as one of her most active detractors in recent years, I can only say it's a genuine pleasure to welcome her back like a lost Rembrandt. She's gone through so many bad directors and so many rotten scripts in the past few years, looking like one of the Cockettes, that it's a thrill to watch her come to her senses. Gone is the screeching voice and the truckdriver's

[236]

With Keith Baxter

it instead of the usual hacks she overrules with her flair for bad taste, and Larry Peerce fills the shoes with powerful persuasion. The first thing he did was fire that miserable hairdresser whose designs for Taylor's head have for years made her hair look like a rat's nest glued in place with ceiling wax. Next, he washed off all the purple makeup and threw out the trashy clothes that made her look like a Miami Beach rummage sale in *Hammersmith Is Out* and *X Y & Zee*. And he even got a performance. In *Ash Wednesday,* she's subtle, sensitive, glowing with freshness and beauty, fifty pounds lighter in weight; her hair is coiffed simply, her clothes ravishing, her makeup a symphony of perfection. For those who grew up in love with Elizabeth Taylor (I assume we are legion), this movie is pure magic. She is once again the kind of star marquees light up for.

"*Ash Wednesday* is the kind of slick entertainment that rises above its clichés and defies ordinary nit-picking."

Rex Reed, NEW YORK DAILY NEWS

slump. Gone are the costumes that looked like Halloween pumpkins. It's the first time she's given anything approximating a real performance in years. It's the first time she's even combed her hair in years. And it's the first time she hasn't been a bad parody of Bette Davis in *Beyond the Forest*.

"*Ash Wednesday* gives her a new career as well as a new face. It took a strong director to do

"Is there life after plastic surgery? Everything about the film is fashioned for those who enjoy watching emotional turmoil in opulent surroundings. As the core is the plight of women struggling to live up to an image thrust upon them, but the film only exploits the problem for its own soap-operatic ends. Peerce endows his picture with a sleek, showy look, and Miss Taylor, indeed beautiful here, even acts well, within expectations of this genre. I know there are audiences who will

With Helmut Berger

With Henry Fonda

revel in her torment. For me, the film sags beyond the power of surgery."

William Wolf, CUE

"It would have us believe that such pursuits of youth are doomed to failure, yet it treats the reconstructed Barbara (who is, after all, Elizabeth Taylor, one of the world's great beauties) less as a woman to be understood than as an artifact to be admired. Mostly the film is interested in what Barbara is going to wear next. This is not a male chauvinist's conception of a woman, but her hairdresser's, full of envy, awe and superficial compassion."

Vincent Canby, THE NEW YORK TIMES

"Beauty is only skin deep—because a boring, insipid matron, from Grosse Pointe or any old place, is a boring insipid matron whether she looks 55 or 35, and so both Miss Taylor and we are right back where we were before we had to endure that nauseating surgery and all that pseudosmart *dolce vita* in all that chic Italian scenery."

Judith Crist, NEW YORK

"Taylor, fashionably gowned and bejewelled, carries the film almost single-handedly, surrounded as she is by largely two-dimensional characters. Berger's presence is spare, while Keith Baxter does well as a compassionate fashion photographer who provides guidance for Taylor and exposition for the audience. Taylor's performance also is very good after discounting the before-and-after visuals, which sometimes evoke unduly excessive huzzahs for 'acting' that really belong to the makeup crew. But relative to many of her recent roles, this is one of the strongest and most effective in some time. Her beauty remains sensational."

"Murf," VARIETY

"*Ash Wednesday* places Elizabeth Taylor in that most vulnerable position of the Face Lift. And she undergoes it with an astonishing realism which is both personal and surgical. Ladies who flinch at blood, and flesh, and the skin cut back, will close their eyes at some of the sequences. The psychological barriers, and the bruised face as it gradually comes back to normal, are handled most believably."

Archer Winsten, NEW YORK POST

With Henry Fonda

That's Entertainment!

A Metro-Goldwyn-Mayer Picture
A United Artists Release / 1974
In Metrocolor

NARRATORS

Fred Astaire, Bing Crosby, Gene Kelly, Peter Lawford, Liza Minnelli, Donald O'Connor, Debbie Reynolds, Mickey Rooney, Frank Sinatra, James Stewart, Elizabeth Taylor.

CREDITS

Director-Producer-Writer: Jack Haley, Jr.; *Executive Producer:* Daniel Melnick; *Cinematographers:* Gene Polito, Ernest Laszlo, Russell Metty, Ennio Guarnieri, and Allan Green; *Opticals:* Robert Hoag and Jim Liles; *Editors:* Bud Friedgen and David E. Blewitt; *Film Librarian:* Mort Feinstein; *Music Supervision:* Jesse Kaye and Henry Mancini; *Sound:* Hal Watkins, Aaron Rochin, Lyle Burbridge, Harry W. Tetrick, and William L. McCaughey; *Assistant Directors:* Richard Bremerkamp, David Silver, and Claude Binyon, Jr., *Running Time:* 132 minutes.

THE FILM

Three years in preparation, this tremendously popular feature-length documentary salute to MGM musicals contains a wealth of color and black-and-white footage from that studio's motion pictures, from the 1929 *Broadway Melody* to 1958's *Gigi,* both Oscar winners. Although the original answer-print ran to an unwieldly six hours, *That's Entertainment* was edited to a mere two hours and twelve minutes before its release. Appearing in a brief sequence filmed in Rome, Elizabeth Taylor is among the eleven still-living Metro stars delivering the narration that helps bridge and illuminate the multitude of film clips. She also appears in musical moments from two of her 1940s movies—delivering in a reedy soprano a number called "The Melody of Spring" from *Cynthia* (1947), with S. Z. Sakall at the piano; and, in a dubbed voice, offering an insinuating rendition of "Love Is Where You Find It," to the misery of her screen brother, Scotty Beckett, from *A Date with Judy* (1948).

CRITICS' CORNER

"While many ponder the future of Metro-Goldwyn-Mayer, nobody can deny that it has one hell of a past. The 50-year-old company is celebrating the anniversary with *That's Entertainment!,* an outstanding, stunning, sentimental, exciting, colorful, enjoyable, spirit-lifting, tuneful, youthful, invigorating, zesty, respectful, heart-warming, awesome, cheerful, dazzling, and richly satisfying feature documentary commemorating its filmusi-

cals. Jack Haley Jr. wrote, produced and directed the sensational panorama, which should appeal to nostalgia fans of any age."

"Murf," VARIETY

"Ars Gratia Artis indeed. . . . Today there's a pang in watching that lion roar above MGM's motto, to see the ravaged sets of the studio whose existence was imperiled for a while (although movie production has resumed). This isn't nostalgia, it's history."

Nora Sayre, THE NEW YORK TIMES

"Jack Haley Jr. has written witty, stimulating narration that bridges the eras and styles of the various MGM musicals and ties the various sections of the movie together in a bright, contemporary package. And the musical numbers—snappy and elegant as ever, taken from the original Technicolor negatives and not from faded release prints of the old movies that you get on TV—have been selected and edited in such a way that the whole film seems a miracle of modern technology.

"Elizabeth Taylor descends a staircase with the arc lights and boom mikes of today making way for her entrance as she tells with misty sweetness of the 18 years she spent at MGM, enraptured by the great presences around her."

Rex Reed, NEW YORK SUNDAY NEWS

As the schizophrenic Lise

Identikit (*The Driver's Seat*)

A Rizzoli Film / 1974
An Avco Embassy Pictures Corp. Release / 1974
In Technicolor

CAST

Lise: Elizabeth Taylor; *Richard:* Ian Bannen; *Carlo:* Guido Mannari; *Mrs. Fiedke:* Mona Washbourne; *Bill:* Maxence Mailfort. Mario Ceroli; *Musical Score:* Franco Mannino; *Costumes:* Gabriella Pescucci; *Running Time:* 105 minutes.

CREDITS

Director: Giuseppe Patroni Griffi; *Producer:* Franco Rossellini; *Screenwriters:* Raffaele La Capria and Giuseppe Patroni Griffi; *Based on Muriel Spark's novella,* "The Driver's Seat"; *Cinematographer:* Vittorio Storaro; *Art Director:*

THE FILM

Filmed in Rome and Munich during the summer and fall of 1973, *Identikit* (or *The Driver's Seat,* as it is called in English-speaking countries) represents Elizabeth Taylor's first appearance in a totally foreign production, with no American

With Maxence Mailfort

monies involved. Based on the 1970 novella by Muriel Spark, who wrote *The Prime of Miss Jean Brodie,* this film had its gala world premiere May 20, 1974 in Monte Carlo, as a benefit for the Monaco Red Cross. As such, it featured a personal appearance by Taylor, had Prince Rainier and Princess Grace as hosts, and detracted so much attention from the then-in-progress Cannes Film Festival that the whole event became a *cause célèbre*.

Since its premiere, *Identikit* has been little seen by the public. At the start of 1975, it was announced that Avco Embassy had acquired U.S. and Canadian rights to the film, and it

With Guido Mannari

was shown in a limited number of American theaters packaged with Sophia Loren's *Jury of One*. Perhaps its theme, that of a mentally disturbed woman's determined search for someone to kill her (the Monte Carlo audience was, reportedly, "shocked and stunned" by the movie), was considered too uncommercial, requiring a careful advertising campaign. Artist-author-filmmaker Andy Warhol makes a special guest appearance.

CRITICS' CORNER

"The story is told with many flashes of slightly surrealistic implications, while Miss Taylor just walks through it all (or occasionally writhes on a

With Guido Mannari

bed) in the most old-fashioned of surrealistic styles. Throughout she wears a tent-like striped dress, but does expose her nice legs and ample bosom. Otherwise, it will still be her temper tantrums that could make the film interesting to die-hard Taylor fans."

"Kell.," VARIETY

"The Driver's Seat is a strange, morbid, but intensely fascinating psychological study of a woman going mad that provides Elizabeth Taylor with her most colorful and demanding role in years. She meets the challenge with imperial efficiency. From the opening scene, when she flies into a fury in a dress shop, there are evidences along the way that here is a tortured character on the verge of something terrifying.

But the film is cleverly structured, alternating glimpses of her daily activities with police interrogations of the people she meets in her bizarre encounters, so you don't really know if you are watching flashbacks or flash-forwards until the final denouement. The film drives to its horrifying finale washed in white light, as though to accent her madness and, in her hideous clashing colors, with her hair in wild disarray, carrying a tacky plastic shopping bag, Elizabeth Taylor allows the camera to search out her darting flight into insanity with penetrating self-assurance, giving her most imaginative performance in years. With dark blue circles around her eyes and her raspberry-tinted sunglasses, she has a ball and so does the audience."

Rex Reed, NEW YORK SUNDAY NEWS

With Ian Bannen

As Light.

The Blue Bird

A 20th Century-Fox Picture / 1976
In DeLuxe Color

CAST

Mother/Maternal Love/Witch/Light: Elizabeth Taylor; *Night:* Jane Fonda; *Luxury:* Ava Gardner; *Cat:* Cicely Tyson; *Father Time:* Robert Morley; *Oak:* Harry Andrews; *Tyltyl:* Todd Lookinland; *Mytyl:* Patsy Kensit; *Grandfather:* Will Geer; *Grandmother:* Mona Washbourne; *Dog:* George Cole; *Bread:* Richard Pearson; *The Blue Bird:* Nadejda Pavlova; *Sugar:* George Vitzin; *Milk:* Margareta Terechova; *Fat Laughter:* Oleg Popov; *Father:* Leonid Nevedomsky; *Water:* Valentina Ganilaee Ganibalova; *Fire:* Yevgeny Scherbakov; *Sick Girl:* Pheona McLellan.

CREDITS

Director: George Cukor; *Executive Producer:* Edward Lewis; *Producer:* Paul Maslansky; *Screenwriters:* Hugh Whitemore, Alfred Hayes and Alexei Kapler; *Based on the novel by:* Maurice Maeterlinck; *Cinematographers:* Freddie Young and Ionas Gritzus; *Production Designer:* Brian Wildsmith; *Art Director:* Valery Urkevich; *Set Decorators:* Yevgeny Starikovitch, Edward Isaev and Tamara Polyanskaya; *Music composed and conducted by:* Irwin Kostal; *Lyrics by* Tony Harrison; *Ballet music composed by* Andrei Petrov; *Editors:* Ernest Walter, Tatyana Shapiro and Stanford C. Allen; *Running Time:* 100 minutes.

THE FILM

Maurice Maeterlinck's 1908 children's classic first reached the screen in a 1910 British film that starred Pauline Gilmer and Olive Walter as the selfish little brother and sister who find the bird of happiness, courtesy of a helpful fairy. American filmmakers tackled the story in 1918, when Paramount/Artcraft released an adaptation directed by Maurice Tourneur that cast Robin Macdougall and Tula Belle as the adventurous children. Twenty years later, Fox produced a Technicolor remake to showcase its fast-maturing child star, Shirley Temple, that lost money because it had cost so much to make.

Fox's 1976 remake, the first major Soviet-American co-production in film history, was at first slated to be, according to executive producer Edward Lewis, "the most expensive musical ever made" (the "musical" idea was later abandoned). Filming began in Leningrad in January of 1975, and didn't shut down until some seven difficult months had passed, during which veteran director George Cukor did his diplomatic best to get Maeterlinck's fantasy onto film, often under extremely taxing circumstances. Among the production drawbacks: the language barrier, different moviemaking techniques, less sophisticated Russian equipment and food that proved detrimental to most Western stomachs—necessitating daily importations from London. For a time during production, Elizabeth

Taylor was in a London hospital suffering not only back problems but also a series of ills contracted during her initial filming stay in Leningrad. In *The Blue Bird,* she essayed four different roles, which required her presence throughout most of the long shooting schedule, and afterwards, director Cukor had only kind words for her: "Elizabeth Taylor has been very ill, but a darling. She is a total professional. She has been no trouble at all." But *The Blue Bird* itself continued to spell nothing *but* trouble for 20th Century-Fox, and its spring 1976 release brought nothing but negative reviews. Nor did the public respond with enthusiasm; soon after its release, it disappeared altogether. The movie has yet to appear on videocassette.

CRITICS' CORNER

"Mr. Cukor, a director of wit and immense verve . . . seems to have had less chance to direct in this case than to act as the good-will ambassador who got his actors on and off the sets on time."

Vincent Canby, THE NEW YORK TIMES

"Elizabeth Taylor appears in four of the larger roles. To tell the truth, she seems slightly uncomfortable in all of them. A few of the other big names fare better. *The Blue Bird* is a fairy tale that eludes a child's appreciation while it batters into semi-consciousness any adult who is determined to follow it to the bitter end."

Archer Winsten, NEW YORK POST

"*The Blue Bird* is so soporific and dull it looks like the work of an embalmer, or like a 1950s movie in suspended animation. As the first major Soviet-American co-production and something of a pioneer effort, it was filmed under the most trying conditions, but that does not really excuse its general ineptitude. Showing gritty determination if nothing else, Elizabeth Taylor plays four different roles: the children's mother and the hard-working wife of a poor woodcutter (the sight of Taylor slaving away in a peasant hut was a little difficult to take). She then transfers herself into a cackling witch (a seemingly impossible assignment) and, as Maternal Love and Light, she looks her beautiful self again, but speaks in such hushed, reverent tones one can barely hear her."

Kathleen Carroll, DAILY NEWS

With Todd Lookinland and Patsy Kensit.

With Kirk Douglas.

Victory at Entebbe

A David L. Wolper Production for the
ABC Television Network / 1976
In Color

CAST

German Tourist: Helmut Berger; *Yakov Shlomo:* Theodore Bikel; *Chana Vilnofsky:* Linda Blair; *Hershel Vilnofsky:* Kirk Douglas; *Col. Yonatan "Yonni" Netanyahu:* Richard Dreyfuss; *Mordecai Gur:* Stefan Gierasch; *Benyamin Wise:* David Groh; *President Idi Amin:* Julius Harris; *Mrs. Wise:* Helen Hayes; *Yitzhak Rabin:* Anthony Hopkins; *Shimon Peres:* Burt Lancaster; *Capt. Dukas:* Christian Marquand; *Edra Vilnofsky:* Elizabeth Taylor; *Nomi Haroun:* Jessica Walter; *Gen. Dan Shomron:* Harris Yulin; *Natan Haroun:* Allan Miller; *German Woman:* Bibi Besch; *Aaron Olav:* David Sheiner; *Moshe Meyer:* Severn Darden.

CREDITS

Director: Marvin J. Chomsky; *Executive Producer:* David L. Wolper; *Producer:* Robert Guenette; *Screenwriter:* Ernest Kinoy; *Cinematographer:* James Kilgore; *Production Designer:* Edward Stephenson; *Music:* Charles Fox; *Editors:* Jim McElroy and Mike Gavaldon; *Supervising Editor:* David Saxon; *Running Time:* 152 minutes.

THE FILM

This was the first to reach the home screen of a pair of network-TV movies re-creating the events of July 4, 1976, when Israel staged a lightning raid on the airport at Entebbe, Uganda. Their mission: the rescue of a planeload of hostages held by Palestinian terrorists. Taylor and Kirk Douglas are a fictitious concentration camp-surviving couple trying to bring pressure on Israeli officials on behalf of their daughter, Linda Blair, one of the hostages. To facilitate its early airing, ABC's version was videotaped and later converted to film and shown theatrically outside of the U.S. Godfrey Cambridge was originally cast as Idi Amin, but his untimely death necessitated recasting the part with Julius Harris. The rival NBC version, *Raid on Entebbe,* was shown three weeks later, and, like its predecessor, used an array of familiar names to attract viewers. The critics seemed more impressed with the NBC TV-movie, as well as the 1977 theatrical film *Operation Thunderbolt.* However, Ernest Kinoy received an Emmy nomination for *Victory at Entebbe*'s teleplay.

CRITICS' CORNER

"As suspected, *Victory at Entebbe,* which was not made available for pre-reviewing, turned out to be a long-winded, boring outing, filled with cliches, stereotypes and dialogue so unbelievable that we were climbing walls by the end. Obviously, this Robert Guenette production was rushed onto the screen; even the airport at Entebbe looked like papier mâché. Anthony Hopkins as Prime Minister Rabin was good, and the Julius Harris portrait of Uganda's President Idi Amin hysterically funny. Otherwise the film was a disaster."

Kay Gardella, NEW YORK DAILY NEWS

"Variable; very exciting when concerned with the details of the raid, more routine when concerned with the hostages and their stories, and embroidered with some needless sequences, such as the one shared by Kirk Douglas and Elizabeth Taylor.

F. Maurice Speed, FILM REVIEW

With Anthony Hopkins and Kirk Douglas.

With Len Cariou.

A Little Night Music

A Sascha Wien-Elliott Kastner Production
A Roger Corman Presentation for
New World Pictures/1977
In Eastmancolor

CAST

Desiree Armfeldt: Elizabeth Taylor; *Charlotte Mittelheim:* Diana Rigg; *Frederick Egerman:* Len Cariou; *Anne Egerman:* Lesley-Anne Down; *Mme. Armfeldt:* Hermione Gingold; *Carl-Magnus Mittelheim:* Laurence Guittard; *Erich Egerman:* Christopher Guard; *Fredericka Armfeldt:* Chloe Franks; *Kurt:* Heinz Maracek; *Petra:* Lesley Dunlop; *Conductor:* Jonathan Tunick: *Franz:* Hubert Tscheppe; *Band Conductor:* Rudolf Schrympf; *Mayor:* Franz Schussler; *Mayoress:* Johanna Schussler.

CREDITS

Director: Harold Prince; *Executive Producer:* Heinz Lazek; *Producer:* Elliott Kastner; *Screenwriter:* Hugh Wheeler; *Based on* the stage musical; *Music and Lyrics:* Stephen Sondheim; *Suggested by* the Ingmar Bergman film *Sommarnattens Leende (Smiles of a Summer Night); Cinematographer:* Arthur Ibbetson; *Production Designer:* Laci von Ronay; *Art Directors:* Herta Pischinger and Thomas Riccabona; *Music scored and supervised by:* Jonathan Tunick; *Costumes:* Florence Klotz; *Choreographer:* Patricia Birch; *Editor:* John Jympson; *Running Time:* 124 minutes.

THE FILM

Ingmar Bergman's 1955 *Smiles of a Summer Night* gave that Swedish director of tragic love stories and Nordic mysticism an uncharacteristic excursion into the sort of sly sex farce more customarily associated with the French. Its American release inspired librettist Hugh Wheeler and composer-lyricist Stephen Sondheim to devise a delightful stage operetta from the material which they called *A Little Night Music,* that charmed both critics and audiences in 1973 and enjoyed a healthy engagement on Broadway and in London. Harold Prince, who staged the hit show, had proven his cinematic deftness with the black comedy *Something for Everyone,* which was filmed in Bavaria in 1970 with Angela Lansbury and Michael York. But his efforts at repeating the feat, mounting a motion picture version of *A Little Night Music* there, seemed to fail on every count. Adding Elizabeth Taylor's star-name to a cast that included leading men from the Broadway original (Len Cariou and Laurence Guittard) didn't help; where Glynis Johns' wistful rendition of the show's big hit number "Send in the Clowns" had moved audiences, Taylor's efforts seemed little more than effortful. And, although some numbers (Hermione Gingold's "Liaisons" for one) appear to have been filmed but then edited out at the last minute, the movie did retain such tuneful Sondheim creations as "Every Day a Little Death," "The Glamorous Life," "Now," "Love Takes Time," "Soon," "Later," "You Must Meet My Wife" and "A Weekend in the Country." Nevertheless, something was very much missing in this film; unlike its stage predecessor, it came and went very quickly, scarcely attracting any kind of audience at all. Even the original soundtrack recording from the film has become a cult item of sorts among Taylor's fans.

CRITICS' CORNER

"*A Little Night Music* is one of the first in a growing number of English-speaking features being made abroad with German tax-shelter aid and Austrian production help. Uneven and sometimes slow, pic has good looks and the name of Elizabeth Taylor for possible playoff use. She is somewhat posey, but does sing agreeably. Director Prince has been too cautious, and has failed to give the film sufficient visual flair and movement."

"Mosk." VARIETY

"The Broadway show, like the Bergman film, is a wickedly lyric rondel, a romantic, turn-of-the-century masquerade about three mismatched couples who, in the course of a limpid summer night, on a magnificent country estate, more or less stumble into perfect happiness. They are a beautiful, worldly actress of certain years (Elizabeth Taylor), her lover, a foolish hussar (Laurence Guittard), the hussar's jealous wife (Diana Rigg), the wife's school friend (Lesley-Anne Down), whose much older husband (Len Cariou) loves the actress and whose stepson (Christopher Guard) loves his stepmother. Having elected to transform the Sondheim show into a film, Mr. Prince appears to have made every decision that could sabotage the music and the lyrics. He has cast the film with people who don't sing very well and then staged almost every number in such a way that we can't respond to the lyrics. It is, of course, possible to hear the songs, but in this movie it seems like work. 'Send in the Clowns' will survive Miss Taylor's game way with a lyric, but *A Little Night Music* shouldn't be a matter of survival. It should be ebullient and fun. It isn't. It often seems to be mean-tempered."

Vincent Canby, THE NEW YORK TIMES

"Although the movie is framed as a formal stage presentation for an opening and closing chorus, the film treatment itself is a peculiarly static one, the operetta structure lost in an absence of style, the fragile dreamlike mood of romantic nostalgia dissipated by the literalization of the camera and the super-elegance of the turn-of-the-century Viennese settings. The casting of Elizabeth Taylor as the edging-over-the-hill Desiree—obviously the box-office draw for this $7.5 million extravaganza—is surface viable, even though the camera is only intermittently kind to her particular plump maturity. One can even accept her recitative-like singing, given the plum of 'Send in the Clowns.' But Taylor is unfortunately surrounded by stylish performers and is left to her own prosaic talents, with an overwhelming opulence of bosom too often a total distraction."

Judith Crist, NEW YORK POST

With Joseph Bottoms.

Return Engagement

A Presentation of The Production Company
for the NBC Television Network/1978
In Color

CAST

Dr. Emily Loomis: Elizabeth Taylor; *Stewart Anderman:* Joseph Bottoms; *Florence:* Allyn Ann McLerie; *George Riley:* Peter Donat; *Mr. Keith:* James Ray; *Janice:* Susan Buckner; *Audrey:* Alston Ahern; *Victor:* Robin Strand; *First Girl:* Melanie Henderson; *Second Girl:* Jennifer Myers; *Third Girl:* Wendy Sommerstein; *Waiter:* Don Stark.

CREDITS

Director: Joseph Hardy; *Producers:* Franklin R. Levy and Mike Wise; *Screenwriter:* James Prideaux; *Music:* Arthur B. Rubinstein; *Costumes:* Edith Head; *Running Time:* 74 minutes.

THE FILM

Elizabeth Taylor's first dramatic performance for TV's long-running "Hallmark Hall of Fame" cast her in the unlikely role of a professor of ancient history at a small California college who reluctantly agrees to rent a room in her house to one of her new students (Joseph Bottoms). Both happen to be loners—she with a secret past—and although each initially grates on the other's nerves, they eventually realize the rapport to help one another emerge from their shells.

CRITICS' CORNER

"First, we're asked to believe Elizabeth Taylor as an intellectual poring over the works of Aristotle. Then, we're expected to believe she's also lonely. Enter another wounded soul—Joseph Bottoms as a student loner who rents a room in Liz's organdy-enshrouded house. He watches old Carmen Miranda movies with the TV volume turned up too loud, wakes her up at 3 A.M. for a cup of coffee, and it's hate at first sight. Until, that is, the boarder discovers her secret past: beneath that stern and crusty exterior beats the heart of a tap-dancer. Liz, you see, was once part of a husband-wife song-and-dance team that played the *Ed Sullivan Show.* Twice. Naturally, she gets bamboozled into resuscitating one of her old dance routines for the campus varsity show with her young boarder playing Fred Astaire to her Ginger Rogers, and naturally she falls in love with him, and naturally there are tears and guilt and homilies dispensed before the final fadeout. The big number, which is a campus sensation, leaves the faculty cheering, when in fact it is so genuinely awful it reduced me to a state of stupefaction. Neither Taylor nor Bottoms can sing or move with an ounce of coordination, and the whole thing has the bizarre effect of looking like a mating dance between Jughead and Kate Smith. Still, it's fun to watch Elizabeth Taylor romp through this idiotic creampuff like the old trouper she is. One thing is certain. Taylor has guts. She wears a lot of weskits, vests, cardigans and men's shirt tails, carefully designed by Edith Head to conceal her shape. No matter how inane the material becomes, she rises above it and in the process manages miraculously to make it work. *Return Engagement* is not one of television's finest hours, but it beats most of the junk they're serving at the movies."

Rex Reed, DAILY NEWS

"By now, it is merely ridiculous to point out that Miss Taylor is fat—not just plump but fat. Careful costuming and lighting, with heavy shading for the left side of her face, can only provide minimum camouflage. Below her still beautiful face, the actress teeters on the edge of being matronly. Her dancing is perfunctory, her singing worse. Yet, she is marvelously appealing. There is an admirable element of sassy determination, of what used to be called gumption, in her performance."

John J. O'Connor, THE NEW YORK TIMES

"Elizabeth Taylor carried the film stalwartly, managing to invest her lonely character with much thoughtfulness and the suggestion of the vibrant lady the teacher once was; there was a confidence and resourcefulness evident that came across to very commending results. Bottoms was effective, if somewhat inconsequential, mainly because his role wasn't as dimensional or as accessible to audience empathy. Joseph Hardy's direction was articulate and precise. Mike Wise and Franklin R. Levy produced this significant entry that had a quality too rare in TV circles: taste."

Earl Davis, THE HOLLYWOOD REPORTER

With Joseph Bottoms.

As Lola Comante.

Winter Kills

A Leonard J. Goldberg-Robert Sterling Production
Released by Embassy Pictures/1979
In Color

CAST

Nick Kegan: Jeff Bridges; *Pa Kegan:* John Huston; *John Cerruti:* Anthony Perkins; *Z.K. Dawson:* Sterling Hayden; *Joe Diamond:* Eli Wallach; *Emma Kegan:* Dorothy Malone; *Frank Mayo:* Tomas Milian; *Yvette Malone:* Belinda Bauer; *Gameboy Baker:* Ralph Meeker; *Keith:* Toshiro Mifune; *Keifitz:* Richard Boone; *Lola Comante:* Elizabeth Taylor; *Captain:* Donald Moffat; *Miles:* David Spielberg; *Capt. Heller:* Brad Dexter; *Doctor:* Peter Brandon; *Ray:* Michael Thoma; *Capt. Heller Two:* Ed Madsen; *Irving Mentor:* Irving Selbert; *Jeffreys:* Chris Soldo; *Arthur Fletcher:* Joe Spinell.

CREDITS

Director-Screenwriter: William Richert; *Executive Producers:* Leonard J. Goldberg and Robert Sterling; *Producer:* Fred Caruso; *Based on the novel by:* Richard Condon; *Cinematographer:* Vilmos Zsigmond; *Production Designer:* Robert Boyle; *Art Director:* Norman Newberry; *Set Decorator:* Arthur Seph Parker; *Musical Score:* Maurice Jarre; *Costumes:* Robert De Mora; *Editor:* David Bretherton. *Running Time:* 97 minutes.

THE FILM

William Richert's star-crossed film, based on the Richard Condon novel about a Presidential assassination plot resembling the Kennedy tragedy, is a black comedy-melodrama that has become something of a cult favorite. Shortly before its completion, the $6.5 million production had its financial rug pulled out from under it by backers who had lost faith (unfounded rumors attribute financial restraints to pressure from the Kennedy clan). Eventually, after much struggle, Richert found investors sufficient to complete the picture, and eventually it was picked up for distribution by Avco Embassy. But its 1979 release had little impact, and the film soon disappeared from cinema screens—later to surface in a 1983 revival that offered a new musical score, some re-editing and a revised ending. Finally, the movie found its most appreciative audience on videocassette.

Elizabeth Taylor's brief cameo performance got her a fur coat. But part of the agreement was that neither her name nor her image could be used to publicize the film; nor would she receive any billing. All of which makes this motion picture's importance in *The Films of Elizabeth Taylor* somewhat on a par with 1960's *Scent of Mystery*. And to cap the situation, *Variety* reported in 1978 that Taylor was the only member of the film's cast to have been fully paid.

CRITICS' CORNER

"Seeing the completed version of the financially troubled *Winter Kills,* one wonders how they ever raised the money to finish the film. The ingredients are there for a strong, albeit controversial political thriller, but it's all been pretty well botched up by writer-director William Richert. Elizabeth Taylor's much publicized but unbilled silent cameo appearance is that of a former movie star who served as a procuress for the late President."

Ron Pennington, THE HOLLYWOOD REPORTER

"I'm still not exactly sure who did what to whom, but it all has something to do with Elizabeth Taylor. Who makes an uncredited, non-speaking cameo appearance. And mouths only one word, not a very nice one. And plays the President's procuress. And is by no means the most far-fetched creature this movie has to offer."

Janet Maslin, THE NEW YORK TIMES

"Elizabeth Taylor has a wordless cameo as a procuress for the late President, but contractual provisions prevent her name from being used in connection with *Winter Kills.* The rest of the cast should have been so lucky."

"Poll.", VARIETY

With Kim Novak, Rock Hudson, Geraldine Chaplin and Tony Curtis.

The Mirror Crack'd

An EMI Films Presentation Released by
Associated Film Distribution/1980
In Technicolor

CAST

Miss Marple: Angela Lansbury; *Cherry:* Wendy Morgan; *Mrs. Bantry:* Margaret Courtenay; *Bates the Butler:* Charles Gray; *Heather Babcock:* Maureen Bennett; *Miss Giles:* Carolyn Pickles; *The Major:* Eric Dodson; *Vicar:* Charles Lloyd-Pack; *Dr. Haydock:* Richard Pearson; *Mayor:* Thick Wilson; *Mayoress:* Pat Nye; *Scoutmaster:* Peter Woodthorpe; *Ella Zielinsky:* Geraldine Chaplin; *Marty N. Fenn:* Tony Curtis; *Inspector Craddock:* Edward Fox; *Jason Rudd:* Rock Hudson; *Lola Brewster:* Kim Novak; *Marina Rudd:* Elizabeth Taylor; *Margot Bence:* Marella Oppenheim; *Sir Derek Ridgeley:* Anthony Steel; *Lady Amanda Ridgeley:* Dinah Sheridan; *Kate Ridgeley:* Oriana Grieve; *Charles Foxwell:* Kenneth Fortescue; *Lady Foxcroft:* Hildegard Neil; *Peter Montrose:* Allan Cuthbertson; *DaSilva:* George Silver; *Barnsby:* John Bennett; *Inspector Gates:* Nigel Stock.

CREDITS

Director: Guy Hamilton; *Producers:* John Brabourne and Richard Goodwin; *Screenwriters:* Jonathan Hales and Barry Sandler; *Based on the novel "The Mirror Crack'd From Side to Side" by:* Agatha Christie; *Cinematographer:* Christopher Challis; *Production Designer:* Michael Stringer; *Art Director:* John Roberts; *Musical Score:* John Cameron; *Costumes:* Phyllis Dalton; *Editor:* Richard Marden; *Running Time:* 105 minutes.

THE FILM

Mystery-novel queen Agatha Christie's celebrated Miss Marple character has been played by a number of actresses on stage, screen and television. Because of her own delightfully eccentric personality, the late Margaret Rutherford was a memorable Marple in a series of four British films of the early '60s. Helen Hayes has played that same character several times in TV-movies, but no one has yet come as close to the Christie original as Joan Hickson, the British character actress who began portraying Miss Marple in a series of British television adaptations of the Christie mysteries in 1984, when she was 78. After Hickson, Angela Lansbury most nearly approached the mark in *The Mirror Crack'd*, a Christie-Marple adaptation that derived most of its interest from its milieu (an English village of the '50s) and from its array of "guest stars," most of whose careers had peaked in that decade. For Lansbury, it paved the way to her very successful TV series *Murder, She Wrote*, which cast her as a sort of *American* Marple.

In *The Mirror Crack'd*, Lansbury's Miss Marple is largely disabled by a sprained ankle, and thus solves this rather genteel multiple-murder case "by remote," as it were—largely with the more agile aid of Edward Fox's Inspector Craddock character. Otherwise, the movie's vitality depends on the intriguing situation of an American film company working on location to shoot their version of *Mary, Queen of Scots*, with Tony Curtis as the tough-talking producer, Rock Hudson as the director married to one comeback-making star (Elizabeth Taylor), while she uneasily plays opposite an equally faded rival (Kim Novak), at the same time the director is carrying on secretly with his secretary (Geraldine Chaplin). That murder should visit this hotbed of moviemaking rivalries is a given.

Asked how he managed to line up so many big movie names from '50s Hollywood, director Guy Hamilton told an interviewer: Well, I just asked them. They read the script and said they'd love to. They saw how juicy the roles were."

CRITICS' CORNER

"That *The Mirror Crack'd* never builds up much momentum has less to do with Guy Hamilton's direction and the performances than with the screenplay by Jonathan Hales and Barry Sandler, which promises more sophistication than it ever delivers. Both Miss Taylor and Miss Novak, as

Marina Rudd as Mary, Queen of Scots.

larger-than-life silver-screen rivals of a certain age, get all wound up for some fancy, high-toned tongue-lashings, but the material isn't up to their power. It's too bad because each of them has the toughness and the wit to carry it off with some splendor."

Vincent Canby, THE NEW YORK TIMES

"She may no longer be the fairest of them all, but Elizabeth Taylor has become adept at spoofing her Hollywood glamour-girl image. Indeed, it is such fun watching Taylor bat her violet eyes at the camera and deliver her tart lines as an aging movie star trying for a career comeback that the other actors, possibly because they didn't have the benefit of Taylor's personal make-up artist, look completely pale and insignificant next to her. Only Kim Novak, who throws all her considerable curves into her role as a rival movie star, holds her own with Taylor, and their catty exchanges are about all that saves *The Mirror Crack'd* from putting the audience to sleep."

Kathleen Carroll, DAILY NEWS

" . . . is a nostalgic throwback to the genteel British murder mystery pix of the 1950s. The central part really is Elizabeth Taylor's. Taylor comes away with her most genuinely affecting dramatic performance in years as a film star attempting a comeback following an extended nervous breakdown. Taylor has an uproarious good time (and so will the audience) as she trades bitchy insults with Kim Novak, wife of producer Tony Curtis, who insists on grossly miscasting Novak as Queen Elizabeth I opposite Taylor's Mary, Queen of Scots. Proving themselves very good sports, Taylor and Novak pelt each other with hilarious zingers about their physical appearances and screen images."

"Mac.", VARIETY

With Samuel Belzberg following the taping of her narration.

Genocide

An Arnold Schwartzman Production
A Simon Wiesenthal Center Release/1981

CREDITS

Producer-Director: Arnold Schwartzman; *Screen-writers:* Schwartzman, Martin Gilbert and Rabbi Marvin Hier; *Location Cinematographers:* David and Peter Shillingford; *Editors:* Roy Watts, Robert Jenkis and Richard Zukaitis; *Musical Score:* Elmer Bernstein; Historical Consultant: Efraim Zuroff; *Animation Design and Direction:* Pat Gavin; *Narrators:* Elizabeth Taylor and Orson Welles; *Introduction by:* Simon Wiesenthal; *Running Time:* 90 minutes.

THE FILM

Like most non-fiction features of recent years, this 1981 Academy Award-winning Best Documentary Feature has had far bigger audience "saturation" from its PBS television showings than from theatrical distribution. A powerful history lesson for us all, it traces the roots of Jewish persecution in Europe, culminating in the unspeakable extermination of millions by the Nazis. As the renowned Nazi-hunter Simon Wiesenthal declares in his cautionary introduction to the film, "The Holocaust...Believe me, it can happen again."

CRITICS' CORNER

"The film is at its best when it dispenses with its razzle-dazzle techniques, slows its breathless pacing and lets the facts speak searingly for themselves. When *Genocide* moves on to the Holocaust itself, it becomes as chilling and forceful as its makers wished it to be. Miss Taylor, whose narration is particularly simple and affecting, reads letters from victims of the Nazis, farewells to friends and loved ones, and horrifying accounts by first-hand observers."

Janet Maslin, THE NEW YORK TIMES

"Alongside the strictly historical material, *Genocide* gains its greatest force as a film via Elizabeth Taylor's emotional voice-over of personal testimony by witnesses to the Holocaust terrors. A moving performance by Taylor conveys in human terms what a sober rendering of mere facts and figures cannot."

"Lor.", VARIETY

With Carol Burnett.

Between Friends
(Nobody Makes Me Cry)

A Presentation of HBO Premiere Films on the
Home Box Office cable system / 1983
In Color

CAST

Deborah Shapiro: Elizabeth Taylor; *Mary Catherine Castelli:* Carol Burnett; *Francie Castelli:* Barbara Bush; *Sam Tucker:* Henry Ramer; *Malcolm Hollan:* Bruce Gray; *Dr. Seth Simpson:* Charles Shamata; *Lolly James:* Lally Cadeau; *Essie:* Vera Cudjoe; *Martin:* Stephen Young; *Michael:* Michael J. Reynolds; *Carolyn:* Patricia Idlette; *Limel:* Jim Morris; *Mrs. Ingram:* Jeri Craden; *Heather:* Shelach MacKerd; *Young Customers:* Clare Barclay and Nancy Kerr; *Woman at Party:* Maida Rogerson; *Realty Office Customer:* Jim Bearden; *Man at Party:* David Clement.

CREDITS

Director: Lou Antonio; *Executive Producers:* Robert Cooper and Marian Rees; *Writer-Producers:* Shelley List and Jonathan Estrin; *Based on* List's novel "Nobody Makes Me Cry"; *Cinematographer:* Francois Protat; *Art Director:* Lindsey Goddard; *Musical Score:* James Horner; *Editor:* Gary Griffen; *Running Time:* 100 minutes.

THE FILM

Shot on location in Toronto, this second TV-movie filmed especially for Home Box Office teamed superstars Elizabeth Taylor and Carol Burnett as divorcees who form an unlikely friendship. Taylor is looking for a man who can keep her in luxurious style; Burnett's a real-estate agent merely looking for a man. The Shelley List-Jonathan Estrin script had been written with Taylor and Burnett in mind, and once one actress agreed to participate in the project, it was an easy matter to sign the other, as well. During the six weeks of Canadian production, the two became close friends. As Burnett later told an interviewer: "I don't know what there was, but I spent six weeks laughing. I felt like I was 11 years old. She (Taylor) is a very funny person."

CRITICS' CORNER

"A juicy story of a pair of middle-aged divorcees made juicier by the teaming of Carol Burnett and Elizabeth Taylor. Frank and forthright—and predictable—their relationship, marked by bits of comedy and low-keyed melodrama, is given complete credibility by Burnett, at her dramatic best, and by Taylor, at her most open and honest level. The two provide a class act."

Judith Crist, TV GUIDE

"Neither Taylor nor Burnett has what you might call a red-hot Hollywood film career at the moment. But they've found just the right vehicle for their wit, their wisdom, their maturity, and their talents in *Between Friends.* They are both marvelous, and as different as they are in personality, looks, temperament and background, they go together on film like Lum and Abner, or Mamie and Dwight. Elizabeth Taylor may have been clobbered for her stage acting in *Private Lives,* but it's obvious from this that she's a first-rate screen performer. Some of her reactions to people and situations are dazzlingly inventive. Funny, lost, glamorous, drunk, or cussing like a lumberjack, Liz is funny, gentle, wonderfully natural. Carol is sturdy, reliable and letter-perfect as the strong, durable friend who is always there to pick up the pieces. The writing, by Shelley List and Jonathan Estrin, and Lou Antonio's perceptive direction provide both actresses with their juiciest, showiest, and most three-dimensional roles in years."

Rex Reed, NEW YORK POST

On the set with director Lou Antonio and Carol Burnett.

With Jane Alexander.

Malice in Wonderland
(The Rumor Mill)

An ITC Production for the
CBS Television Network / 1985
In Color

CAST

Louella Parsons: Elizabeth Taylor; *Hedda Hopper:* Jane Alexander; *Louis B. Mayer:* Richard Dysart; *Dema Harshbarger:* Joyce Van Patten; *Dr. Harry "Docky" Martin:* Jon Cypher; *Harriet Parsons:* Leslie Ackerman; *Ida Koverman:* Bonnie Bartlett; *William Hopper:* Thomas Byrd; *Andy Kenderson:* Joel Colodner; *Iceman:* Rick Lenz; *Dot:* Mary McCusker; *Tommy Gallep:* John Pleshette; *Orson Welles:* Eric Purcell; *Joseph Cotten:* Tim Robbins; *Howard Strickling:* Mark L. Taylor; *Ann:* Nancy Travis; *June:* B.J. Ward; *Sam Goldwyn:* Vernon Weddle; *Joel:* Allen Williams; *Collins:* Theodore Wilson; *Jack Warner:* Jason Wingreen; *Ellen:* Helen Baron; *Hotel Clerk:* Thomas Bellin; *Carole Lombard:* Denise Crosby; *Heiner:* Robert Darnell; *Betty:* Christine Dickinson; *Young Bill Hopper:* Douglas Emerson; *Mrs. Washburn:* Edith Fields; *Mrs. Clayton:* Lyla Graham; *Dema's Secretary:* Anne Haney; *Starlet:* Mindi Iden; *Elizabeth Arden:* Amelia Laurenson; *Hal:* Galen Thompson; *Mike Romanoff:* Jan Triska; *Albert:* Keith Walker; *Clark Gable:* Gary Wayne; *Journalists:* Noni White and Leigh Kavanaugh.

CREDITS

Director: Gus Trikonis; *Executive Producer:* Judith A. Polone; *Producer:* Jay Benson; *Screenwriters:* Jacqueline M. Feather and David Seidler; *Based on the book* "Hedda and Louella" *by* George Eels; *Cinematographer:* Philip Lathrop; *Art Director:* John D. Jeffries; *Musical Score:* Charles Bernstein; *Miss Taylor's Costumes:* Nolan Miller; *Other Costumes:* Mina Mittleman; *Editors:* Allan Jacobs and Rebecca Ross; *Running Time:* 94 minutes.

THE FILM

Based on George Eels factual dual-biography, this TV-movie purports to tell the story of the legendary, once-formidable Hollywood gossip queens Louella Parsons and Hedda Hopper, who ruled the American movie capital with wills of iron during much of its so-called golden era. At the close of the year's TV season, *Malice in Wonderland* garnered an Emmy award for Philip Lathrop's cinematography; Jane Alexander won a nomination for her portrayal of Hedda.

With Richard Dysart and Theodore Wilson.

CRITICS' CORNER

"It's unquestionable that without the magnetism of Liz Taylor, this film probably would not have made it onto the network's prime-time schedule during the all-important May [TV] sweeps. And, while Louella never looked so good—she was somewhat dowdy—Liz gives a 60-karat performance as bright, multi-faceted and effectively cutting as that much-talked-about sparkler that Richard Burton once gave her. While she no longer has that giant gem, she proves here that she does possess a gift for comedy and caricature. In support, talented Jane Alexander is sufficiently nasty and gives her Hopper characterization depth by supplying the gossip with a heart—though it doesn't prevent her from scratching at the competition of uncooperative performers.

Laurel Gross, NEW YORK POST

"Louella Parsons and Hedda Hopper, once the gossiping terrors of Hollywood, are being given the screen biographies they deserve. Less than an inch deep, *Malice in Wonderland* is as silly as any of their newspaper columns. The casting is suitably unreal. "Lolly" Parsons, a pudgy and somewhat dumpy woman, is played by Elizabeth Taylor, the "new" Elizabeth Taylor who has lost weight and is looking very glamorous again. And Hedda Hopper, a rather goofy type partial to outrageous hats, is portrayed by Jane Alexander, an actress of unconcealable intelligence. Both Miss Taylor and Miss Alexander tackle their parts with verve and, in the process, have a good deal of infectious fun. Miss Taylor clearly gets a great deal of pleasure from her nifty impersonation of the whining Lolly, and Miss Alexander is marvelous at making Hedda something more than dotty."

John J. O'Connor, THE NEW YORK TIMES

"Together, Taylor and Alexander keep this lightly treated, and somewhat slightly plotted, comedy-drama buzzing with vicious intent, and crackling with personality conflict. They make an absorbing pair of invidious 'best enemies' in this stylishly executed production."

Gail Williams, THE HOLLYWOOD REPORTER

With Robert Wagner.

There Must Be a Pony

An R.J. Production in association with
Columbia Pictures Television for the
ABC Television Network/1986
In Color

CAST

Marguerite Sydney: Elizabeth Taylor; *Ben Nichols:* Robert Wagner; *Merwin Trellis:* James Coco; *Lee Hertzig:* William Windom; *David Hollis:* Edward Winter; *Jay Savage:* Ken Olin; *Chief Investigator Roy Clymer:* Dick O'Neill; *Josh Sydney:* Chad Lowe; *Himself (unbilled):* Mickey Rooney; *Detective:* Richard Bright; *Ron Miller:* Richard Minchenberg; *Chris:* Robby Weaver; *Woman at Airport:* Helen J. Siff; *Scott:* Charles Stratton.

CREDITS

Director: Joseph Sargent; *Executive Producer:* Robert Wagner; *Producer:* Howard Jeffrey; *Screenwriter:* Mart Crowley; *Based on the novel by:* James Kirkwood; *Cinematographer:* Gayne Rescher; *Production Designer:* James J. Agazzi; *Art Director:* Ross Bellah; *Musical Score:* Billy Goldenberg; *Miss Taylor's Costumes:* Nolan Miller; *Editor:* Jack Harnish; *Running Time:* 100 minutes.

THE FILM

Novelist James Kirkwood's book and play (which toured in the Sixties with Myrna Loy but never reached Broadway) reportedly derived from a hushed-up scandal that had once involved him (as a child) and his movie-star mother, Lila Lee, with the mysterious death of one of her lovers. As adapted for TV by Mart Crowley (*The Boys in the Band*), *There Must Be a Pony* casts Elizabeth Taylor as a once-famous Hollywood star aiming for a comeback on television after a sojourn in a mental hospital. In so doing, she threatens to destroy her relationships with her current lover, businessman Robert Wagner and her sensitive, teen-aged son, Chad Lowe.

CRITICS' CORNER

"Right at the beginning of *There Must Be a Pony*, Elizabeth Taylor has a scene where a pushy fan runs up to her and says, 'You're Joan Collins, aren't you?' Smiling sweetly through her clenched teeth, the star says, 'Yes, I am,' and proceeds to scribble a forged autograph. It is a treasured moment for avid collectors of Elizabeth Taylor memorabilia, and there are many more to come in this strange little movie. She triumphs, even as the production sinks."

John J. O'Connor, THE NEW YORK TIMES

"Taylor acts up a fury, the sort of performance that plays with the public's perceptions tied to the life of La Liz, rather than Ms. Marguerite Sydney. Yet *Pony*'s presentation of the cultural maelstrom that is Elizabeth Taylor creates an undeniable on-screen vortex. She's on and you watch. Period. (She looks fab, svelte and sexy.) *There Must Be a Pony* is a fable about a myth, a painting of a photograph whose resonance derives from its stars' garish notoriety. Is it real or is it make-believe real? Inquiring minds want to know."

Miles Beller, THE HOLLYWOOD REPORTER

"It would seem like a perfect vehicle for Taylor's talents. She gets to emote a-plenty in this dramatic plot, which develops into tragedy, set against a Hollywood backdrop. But dressed in tacky outfits by Nolan Miller—the *Dynasty* designer—Taylor is a lone star marooned in a soap opera that hopelessly wants to be taken seriously. The fault seems to lie in the writing and direction. It's as if a couple of pages of script are missing in different places. You feel like one of those disciples of Method acting, constantly asking questions like 'What's this character's motivation, and what's supposed to be happening here?' As for Taylor, she brings her 'mad-actress' role out of her theatrical trunk like an old costume that still fits remarkably well. But where is the acting depth we've seen in *Butterfield 8* or *Who's Afraid of Virginia Woolf?*"

Laurel Gross, NEW YORK POST

With George Hamilton.

Poker Alice

A Harvey Matofsky Production in association
with New World Television for the
CBS Television Network/1987
In Color

CAST

Alice Moffett: Elizabeth Taylor; *Jeremy Collins:*
Tom Skerritt; *Cousin John:* George Hamilton;
Sears: Richard Mulligan; *Amos:* David Wayne;
Mad Mary: Susan Tyrrell; *McCarthy:* Pat Corley;
Baker: Paul Drake; *Miss Tuttwiler:* Annabella
Price; *Baby Doe;* Merrya Small; *Gilmore:* Gary
Bisig; *Big Irma:* Liz Torres; *Marshall:* Gary
Grubbs; *Frank Hartwell:* John Bennett Perry;
Harris: Ed Adams; *Steward:* Sid Dawson; *Carlyle:*
Jack Dunlop; *Gray:* Maarten Goslins; *Mason:*
William M. Hannah; *Carter:* Henry Max Kendrick;

Pellum: Stephen Jace Kent; *Saloon Girl:* Gloria
Manon; *Man in Street:* John Pearce; *Maggie:* Car-
oline Reed; *Crocker:* Bob Shelton.

CREDITS

Director: Arthur Allan Seidelman; *Executive Producer:* Harvey Matofsky; *Producer:* Renée Valente;
Screenwriter: James Lee Barrett; *Cinematographer:*
Hanania Baer; *Art Director:* Ninkey Dalton; *Musical Score:* Billy Goldenberg; *Miss Taylor's Costumes:* Nolan Miller; *Other Costumes:* Ruby Manis;
Editor: Millie Moore; *Running Time:* 100 minutes.

THE FILM

Filmed in Old Tucson, Arizona, this lighthearted period Western was a vehicle TV-Taylored for Elizabeth, who plays a Boston Brahmin whose beautiful facade masks a tough professional gambler, the veteran champ of many a high-stakes poker game on the classier Mississippi Riverboats. But fate strands "Poker Alice" Moffett and her obsequious Cousin John (George Hamilton) in the dusty New Mexico Territory of 1876 where, in no time, she participates in a games that wins her both a sagebrush bordello and the love of a bounty hunter named Jeremy Collins (Tom Skerritt). Interviewed about her role in *Poker Alice*, Elizabeth Taylor said at the time: "I have been a gambler all my life. That's not surprising because I am rather compulsive about certain things. It's amazing, really, that I'm not a gambler."

CRITICS' CORNER

"While *Poker Alice* isn't *Masterpiece Theatre*, it is fun while it lasts. Taylor looks luscious and curvaceous—shoehorned into tightly cinched bodiced outfits—and has a hootin' hollerin' good time as poker-savvy Alice. The comedy-drama might not be four aces, but it still delivers a winning hand."

Miles Beller, THE HOLLYWOOD REPORTER

"Elizabeth Taylor may be *Poker Alice* tonight on CBS, but she doesn't have a poker face. In fact, it's her lovely candy-box features, slimmed down to perfection, that save the day for this lightweight costume Western, which co-stars her offscreen companion, George Hamilton, in his well-rehearsed role: keeping an eye on La Liz. This is a film designed for Taylor-watchers. If you like looking at Lady Elizabeth, you'll enjoy this all-too-familiar scenario. If not, there's not much to grab you. Her costumes are stunning, though, and so is she!"

Kay Gardella, DAILY NEWS

"Taylor's role here is no more demanding than her cameo in *North & South*, but it's a triumph nonetheless. As the star of *Poker Alice*, she forcefully reclaims her former status as a larger-than-life, hypnotically beautiful media personality. This is her show, and she approaches even the most familiar, tired scenes with obvious enthusiasm. And on the few occasions when she really has something to do, Taylor is charming."

David Bianculli, NEW YORK POST

As Alice Moffett.

With C. Thomas Howell.

Il Giovane Toscanini (Young Toscanini)

A Carthago Films/Canal Plus/FR3/La Sept/Italian
International Pictures/RAI-TV/Channel 1
Co-production/1988
In Technicolor

CAST
Arturo Toscanini: C. Thomas Howell; *Nadina Bulichoff:* Elizabeth Taylor; *Sister Margherita:* Sophie Ward; *Mother Allegri:* Pat Heywood; *Claudio Rossi:* John Rhys-Davies; *Dom Pedro II:* Philippe Noiret; *Claudio Toscanini:* Franco Nero; *Mantelli:* Irma Capece Minutolo; *And with* Nicholas Chagrin, Leon Lissek, Carlo Bergonzi, Giovanna Stella La Nocita, Simon Gregor and Elsa Agalbato.

CREDITS
Director: Franco Zeffirelli; *Producers:* Fulvio Lucisano and Tarak Ben Ammar; *Screenwriter:* William H. Stadiem; *Cinematographer:* Daniele Nannuzzi: *Art Directors:* Andrea Crisanti, Enrico Fiorentini and Angelo Santucci; *Costumes:* Tom Rand; *Editors:* Jim Clark, Brian Oats, Franca Silvi and Amadeo Giomini; *Associate Producer:* Giuseppe Pisciotto; *Singing Voice of Elizabeth Taylor:* Aprile Millo; *Running Time:* 120 minutes.

THE FILM

At press time, Franco Zeffirelli's controversial movie about the youthful Italian conducting genius, Arturo Toscanini (1867-1957), had yet to reach U.S. shores, either on the big screen or on video-cassette. Originally shown first to the public at 1988's Venice Film Festival in September, the $14-million-plus motion picture was met with uniformly negative response by the Italian press, partially occasioned by Zeffirelli's own sight-unseen condemnation of another Festival entry, Martin Scorsese's much-argued-about *The Last Temptation of Christ.*

For this loosely-factual biofilm, Zeffirelli used the Italian city of Bari to represent the story's Rio setting. Metropolitan Opera diva Aprile Millo was engaged to provide the singing voice of Elizabeth Taylor's character, a temperamental opera singer named Nadina Bulichoff, who's shown performing excerpts from Verdi's *Aida.* As Millo described it in *Opera News:* "They told me Taylor had worked on several *Aida* scenes but somehow seemed frightened, turned off—she didn't know the language or the character. 'Who is Aida?' she asked me. I wanted to help her explore this special world, so we had eight hours together and established a rapport. I told her to hunt for something spiritual in the music. She listened to me sing and actually cried. Other times I made her laugh, put her at ease. This great actress suddenly became like a little girl. She went nuts over *Aida.*" In her scenes from the opera, Taylor appears opposite the veteran Italian tenor Carlo Bergonzi.

CRITICS' CORNER

"Part of the hilarity arises from the film itself, a pompous comic rendition of the first bloomings of artistic genius amid costly overdressed sets, Liz in blackface singing *Aida,* and a Mother Cabrini nursing Brazilian slaves. Excess is the order of the day in *Young Toscanini,* and the film perversely won supporters for its very *kitsch.* Some of the pic's gems may be toned down by the director, who wants to trim 10 minutes from the version screened in Venice in the interest of subtlety. It would be a pity, as well as unavailing. For the charms of *Toscanini* lie exclusively in its brazen extravagance and anti-historical over-statement. Obviously directed at the kind of audience who used to get its kicks at the Colosseum, pic revels in its triteness and spares not even Taylor, who looks fabulous but does nothing to turn Nadina Bulichoff into a serious role. The high point, however, belongs to Liz, who steps forward in the middle of the opera, gripping the hands of two crawling black extras, and launches a plea for the abolition of slavery. This ludicrous scene—taken from history, yet—ends the film on the note it began, and occasions, for the third time, the line, 'There are things more important in life than music.'"

"Yung," VARIETY

As Nadina Bulichoff.

As Alexandra Del Lago.

Sweet Bird of Youth

An Atlantic/Kushner-Locke Production
for the NBC Television Network/1989
In color

CAST
Alexandra Del Lago/The Princess Kosmonopolis:
Elizabeth Taylor; *Chance Wayne:* Mark Harmon;
Boss Finley; Rip Torn; *Miss Lucy:* Valerie Perrine;
Heavenly Finley: Cheryl Paris; *Tom Junior:* Kevin
Geer; *Aunt Nonnie:* Ronnie Claire Edwards.

CREDITS
Director: Nicolas Roeg; *Executive Producers:* Donald Kushner, Peter Locke and Linda Yellen;
Screenwriter: Gavin Lambert; *Based on the Play
by:* Tennessee Williams; *Cinematographer:* Francis
Kenny; *Editor:* Pamela Malouf; *Miss Taylor's Costumes:* Nolan Miller.

At press time, full production information was not
yet available on this TV-movie adaptation of Tennessee Williams' play, which was scheduled to
premiere during the 1989-90 season. On Broadway,
the 1959 drama had proven an eloquent showcase for
the well-honed talents of Geraldine Page and Paul
Newman, who later re-created their roles for the
excellent—if somewhat watered-down—screen version that Richard Brooks wrote and directed for
MGM in 1962.

In the early 1980s, when Elizabeth Taylor was
involved in Broadway theatrical activities with producer Zev Bufman, there were rumors of their
reviving *Sweet Bird of Youth* as a vehicle for her. But
no such plans came to fruition. To date, the play's

With Mark Harmon.

only major New York City revival occurred in 1975, when Irene Worth made it a personal triumph, opposite Christopher Walken. Subsequently, Lauren Bacall starred in a London production and another in Los Angeles and Joanne Woodward appeared in a mid-'80s Williamstown Festival and Toronto production of the work.

But, despite the Brooks film—which built up its leading male role for Newman, at the expense of Page's role—this is a wonderful vehicle for middle-aged actresses. Alexandra Del Lago (aka: The Princess Kosmonopolis) offers a *tour de force* for any woman capable of portraying this substance-addicted, slightly-over-the-hill movie star who, convinced that her career is over, has fled Hollywood in the company of young, opportunistic Chance Wayne, her lover of the moment. Together, they have driven cross-country to the Florida Gulf Coast community from whence he originally hailed—and in which unspoken elements in his past (involving the daughter of the town's politically powerful Boss Finley) continue to make Chance *persona non grata*. Confined to a short time span, the story centers on the rocky relationship between the formidable Alexandra and Chance, who take a hotel suite, from which he attempts to resume with his former girlfriend. At the same time, his protectress learns—in a memorable phone call to Los Angeles—that her presumably failed attempt at a

motion-picture comeback is actually a trimphant success! Alexandra's universe now centers once again on herself and her film career, as she abandons her self-serving stud to battle the avenging forces of the Finley clan, while she heads back to Hollywood. In the stage play, Chance faces castration; the 1962 film merely left him with a severe beating. Also in this version is Rip Torn, this time as Boss Finley. In both the stage and screen versions, he played Junior.

Recalling the personal career highlights associated with her earlier Williams roles (*Cat on a Hot Tin Roof; Suddenly, Last Summer; Boom*), Elizabeth Taylor recently remarked, "I have always loved Tennessee Williams, so this is like a very happy reunion for me."

Among this *Sweet Bird*'s factors ruled controversial by the gossip columinists were (1) Taylor's continuing weight fluctuations, (2) her supposed refusal to perform topless for maverick British director Nicolas Roeg in a steamy love scene, and (3) an allegedly prickly on-the-set relationship with co-star Mark Harmon, who was reported impatient with filming delays caused by Elizabeth's back problems and her perfectionism. Her quoted comments to a friend: "Mark hasn't paid his dues yet. He has to earn them, like I have over the years. I want this movie to be a success, and I'm doing all I can to make it work."

ORDER NOW!
More Citadel Film Books

If you like this book, you'll love the other titles in the award-winning Citadel Film Series. From James Stewart to Moe Howard and The Three Stooges, Woody Allen to John Wayne, The Citadel Film Series is America's largest and oldest film book library.

With more than 150 titles--and more on the way!--Citadel Film Books make perfect gifts for a loved one, a friend, or best of all, yourself!

A complete listing of the Citadel Film Series appears below.
If you know what books you want, why not order now!
It's easy! Just call 1-800-447-BOOK and have your MasterCard or Visa ready.

STARS
Alan Ladd
Barbra Streisand: First Decade
Barbra Streisand: Second
 Decade
Bela Lugosi
Bette Davis
Boris Karloff
The Bowery Boys
Buster Keaton
Carole Lombard
Cary Grant
Charles Bronson
Charlie Chaplin
Clark Gable
Clint Eastwood
Curly
Dustin Hoffman
Edward G. Robinson
Elizabeth Taylor
Elvis Presley
Errol Flynn
Frank Sinatra
Gary Cooper
Gene Kelly
Gina Lollobrigida
Gloria Swanson
Gregory Peck
Greta Garbo
Henry Fonda
Humphrey Bogart
Ingrid Bergman
Jack Lemmon
Jack Nicholson
James Cagney
James Dean: Behind the Scene
Jane Fonda
Jeanette MacDonald & Nelson
 Eddy
Joan Crawford

John Wayne Films
John Wayne Reference Book
John Wayne Scrapbook
Judy Garland
Katharine Hepburn
Kirk Douglas
Laurel & Hardy
Lauren Bacall
Laurence Olivier
Mae West
Marilyn Monroe
Marlene Dietrich
Marlon Brando
Marx Brothers
Moe Howard & the Three
 Stooges
Norma Shearer
Olivia de Havilland
Orson Welles
Paul Newman
Peter Lorre
Rita Hayworth
Robert De Niro
Robert Redford
Sean Connery
Sexbomb: Jayne Mansfield
Shirley MacLaine
Shirley Temple
The Sinatra Scrapbook
Spencer Tracy
Steve McQueen
Three Stooges Scrapbook
Warren Beatty
W.C. Fields
William Holden
William Powell
A Wonderful Life: James Stewart
DIRECTORS
Alfred Hitchcock
Cecil B. DeMille

Federico Fellini
Frank Capra
John Ford
John Huston
Woody Allen
GENRE
Bad Guys
Black Hollywood
Black Hollywood: From 1970 to
 Today
Classics of the Gangster Film
Classics of the Horror Film
Divine Images: Jesus on Screen
Early Classics of Foreign Film
Great French Films
Great German Films
Great Romantic Films
Great Science Fiction Films
Harry Warren & the Hollywood
 Musical
Hispanic Hollywood: The Latins
 in Motion Pictures
The Hollywood Western
The Incredible World of 007
The Jewish Image in American
 Film
The Lavender Screen: The Gay
 and Lesbian Films
Martial Arts Movies
The Modern Horror Film
More Classics of the Horror Film
Movie Psychos & Madmen
Our Huckleberry Friend: Johnny
 Mercer
Second Feature: "B" Films
They Sang! They Danced! They
 Romanced!: Hollywood
 Musicals
Thrillers
The West That Never Was

Words and Shadows: Literature
 on the Screen
DECADE
Classics of the Silent Screen
Films of the Twenties
Films of the Thirties
More Films of the 30's
Films of the Forties
Films of the Fifties
Lost Films of the 50's
Films of the Sixties
Films of the Seventies
Films of the Eighties
SPECIAL INTEREST
America on the Rerun
Bugsy (Illustrated screenplay)
Comic Support
Dick Tracy
Favorite Families of TV
Film Flubs
Film Flubs: The Sequel
First Films
Forgotten Films to Remember
Hollywood Cheesecake
Hollywood's Hollywood
Howard Hughes in Hollywood
More Character People
The Nightmare Never Ends:
 Freddy Krueger & "A Night-
 mare on Elm Street"
The "Northern Exposure" Book
The "Quantum Leap" Book
Sex In the Movies
Sherlock Holmes
Son of Film Flubs
Those Glorious Glamour Years
Who Is That?: Familiar Faces and
 Forgotten Names
"You Ain't Heard Nothin' Yet!"

For a free full-color brochure describing the Citadel Film Series in depth, call 1-800-447-BOOK; or send your name and address to Citadel Film Books, Dept. 1151, 120 Enterprise Ave., Secaucus, NJ 07094.